E

The last chapter of this encyclopaedic book discusses our continent, Africa. Among other things, the author, Olusegun Aganga, says: 'African leaders must embrace and embark on major government reforms as most governments have remained vulnerable to "major malfunctions", very high cost of governance, weak political, economic and social institutions, weak economies, high levels of poverty, unemployment, insecurity, waste, predictable failures, flaws in the governance structure and so on. This requires and calls for authentic, values-based leadership. It requires courage, vision and commitment to improving the well-being of the people we serve.'

These frank and honest words apply as much to Africa in general as they do to virtually all its constituent member states, including the author's beloved Nigeria, which is the focus of this book. The author translates his broad conclusions into a studied and detailed panoply of specific diagnoses and remedies. It is very fortunate that our sage in this instance, Segun Aganga, is a highly competent practitioner in both the private and public spheres. As pan-Africanists we share his hopes that all Nigerians will listen to his highly educated plea that the country can and must position itself as the jewel of Africa by extricating itself from its many major malfunctions, and thus set Africa an invaluable example to emulate. What a great day it would be for all of us as Africans if the people of Nigeria were to use this work of love and deep thought, *Reclaiming the Jewel of Africa*, as a living manual for the renaissance of an eminent African country!

Thabo Mbeki
President of South Africa, 1999–2008

Reclaiming the Jewel of Africa speaks eloquently, discerningly and tastefully to Nigeria's widely acknowledged unparalleled human resources in Africa. It also articulates the country's inherent capacity, given the right leadership and structural conditions, to end its disappointing and odious history towards fostering immense human flourishing. In its extensive range, this book addresses urgent problems in a measured tone, dissects the obstacles to national possibilities, identifies the specific challenges and offers possible solutions. All those committed to the transformation of Nigeria from a 'crippled giant' to the *Jewel of Africa* should read this book by a man who has been at a vantage position in the vortex of governmental power.

Wale Adebanwi
Presidential Penn Compact Professor of Africana Studies
University of Pennsylvania, USA

RECLAIMING THE JEWEL OF AFRICA

A blueprint for taking Nigeria and Africa from potential to posterity

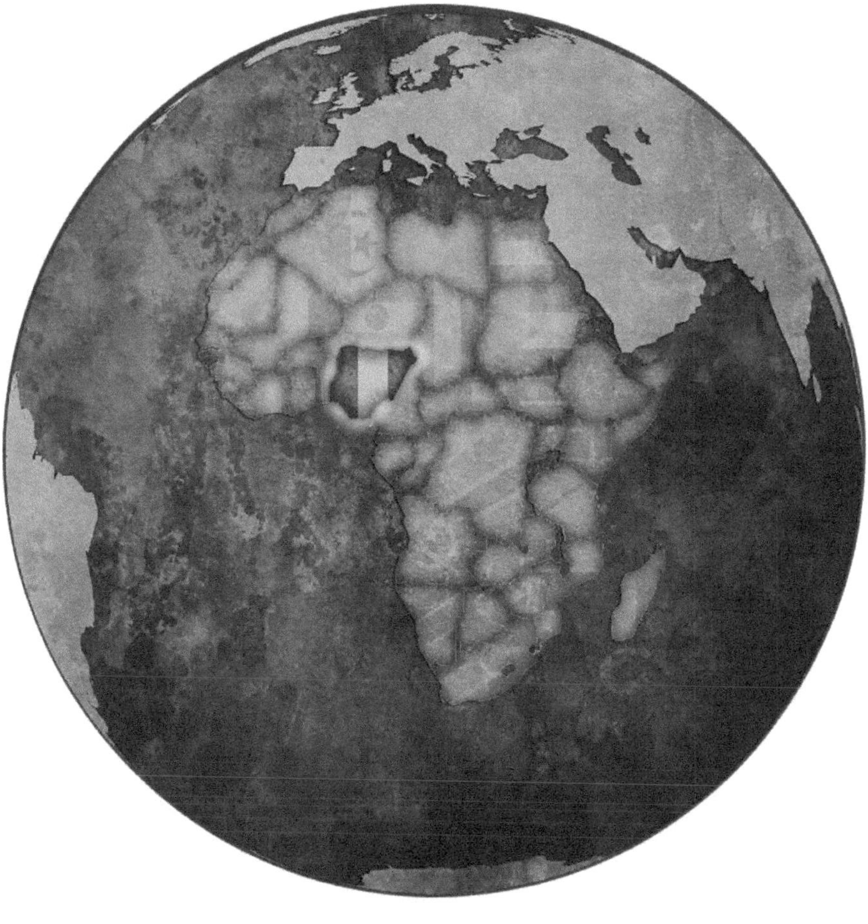

OLUSEGUN AGANGA

First published in Great Britain by Practical Inspiration Publishing, 2023

ISBN 9781788604499 (print)
9781788604512 (epub)
9781788604505 (mobi)

Want to bulk-buy copies of this book for your team and colleagues? We can customize the content and co-brand *Reclaiming the Jewel of Africa* to suit your business's needs.

Please email info@practicalinspiration.com for more details.

Practical Inspiration Publishing

MIX
Paper | Supporting responsible forestry
FSC www.fsc.org FSC® C013604

Table of contents

About the author

Olusegun Aganga was Nigeria's Minister of Finance and Chairman of the Economic Management Team from 2010 to 2011, and then its Minister of Industry, Trade & Investments from 2011 to 2015. Prior to this he was Managing Director at Goldman Sachs, and before that he was a senior director at Ernst & Young, London. He was also the chairman of the board of governors of the World Bank and International Monetary Fund (IMF) in 2010 and in 2011, and the chairman of the World Trade Organization's (WTO) Ministerial Conference. Currently, Olusegun is an advisor to companies and governments in the UK, US and Nigeria. He is the founder of the Nigeria Leadership Initiative, a board member of Technoserve in the US, an advisory board member of the Queen's Commonwealth Trust and a member of the investor advisory council of Time Partners in the UK.

Olusegun Aganga, Chairman of the board of governors of the World Bank and IMF addressing the Plenary in Washington, 2010.

President Obama and Olusegun Aganga during
President Jonathan's visit to the white house in 2010.

King Charles III and Olusegun Aganga at an event in London.

President Jonathan presenting a gift to President Kenyatta
of Kenya during the East meets West investment Forum in Abuja.

Foreword by Dr Christopher Kolade

One of the best things to happen to any human civilization is the documentation of experiences from which subsequent civilizations can learn and thus improve their living standards and accomplishments. This, of course, comes out better when the story is told by someone with a highly informed and reflective mind, like Segun Aganga, as he has spent most of his professional career in the private sector and served as a top government functionary, involved in the formulation of policies and also directly in the execution of the programmes and projects emanating from those policies.

The first notable aspect about this book is its wide-ranging coverage, which includes leadership, in which Africa and indeed Nigeria have a deficit, and then institutions, the civil service, the economy, resource management, people and multilateral institutions. Particularly interesting is the discourse on the economy, which looks at how it is at present (often what most analysts and commentators dwell on and end up painting is a dismal picture of Africa and Nigeria), and then a comprehensive list of recommendations that should bring the economy to what it should be (which is either short in supply or misplaced).

My shared passion with Segun is societal values, which is well represented in the book as well. Central to any society and its future are its values, and the author makes suggestions on how to revive the eroded values and restart the building of a new Nigeria where there will be sanctity of life, property, rule of law, contracts and access to basic necessities of life as a right.

A compelling read, this book carries a strong message and, unlike most books, provides practical solutions. The prose is accessible and the data deployed is as current as possible in the third decade of the 21st century. Such facts and figures, with narratives of an involved person, show that Nigeria indeed is the 'jewel' of Africa and could become very attractive for investments and be transformed to a first-world country with the commitment of all stakeholders. It is an essential read for leaders at the political, industry, community, educational and religious levels, giving hope that Nigeria and indeed Africa can be reclaimed.

I strongly recommend this book to African and Nigerian political leaders, students and to all lovers of Africa. With a population of 1.4 billion and the largest concentration of youth, compared to other geopolitical regions of the world, Africa, and indeed Nigeria, is the hope of this century and the next.

Nigeria and Africa continue to grow in importance in global affairs. From energy to minerals, from personnel to intellectual property, the range and relevance of the African angle to global affairs can no longer be understated. The unique quality of the book in your hands is that it is written by an African who has engaged Africa and the world from the position of knowledge. Keen observation, as well as candid, pragmatic perspectives make this book a singular contribution in the discourse of 21st-century Africa.

Dr Christopher Kolade
Former Nigerian High Commissioner to the UK

Preface

It is always a privilege and honour to serve one's country and fellow countrymen and women. In that privileged position, one sees and experiences many things that most people are not privileged to see and know. One also sees the gaps and develops some thoughts on how those gaps can be filled.

This is what I have tried to capture in this book – what I saw, did and why. And what still needs to be done – and much remains to be done. This is not a book that seeks to cast any aspersions on anyone or make public the occasional private disagreements that come with the territory. No. It is not about that. It is about reclaiming the greatness of the Jewel of Africa.

Nigeria is that Jewel of Africa, and my lifelong goal for Nigeria is to achieve its true potential and be one of the world's greatest and most prosperous countries. I have no doubt whatsoever that Nigeria has the potential to be really great. I am also persuaded that Africa as a whole is on the path to greatness. This book is my little contribution towards that goal. I hope the readers, policymakers and all those who aspire to lead our nations, and indeed Nigerians, will find it useful.

Olusegun Aganga (CON)

Acknowledgements

I have always said that I am what I am today because of the quality of my parental upbringing and the school I went to. For that reason, I acknowledge and express my profound gratitude to my parents, Humphrey Aiyesoro and Eunice Omolola Aganga. They are both deceased but they and the values they inculcated in us live in us.

We say in Africa that it takes a village to raise a child. I acknowledge, with gratitude, Justice Adebayo Adeniji, a former High Court judge in Lagos and Chief (Mrs) Folasade Adeniji, the Iyalaje of Ikorodu and the first Iya-oge of Ipakodo – Ikorodu, both of whom became my parents and played a major role in guiding my future. As the last child of our parents, my older brothers and sisters, were my role models. Thank you for giving me the space and support to focus on the Jewel.

I owe a debt of gratitude to President Goodluck Jonathan, who gave me the opportunity to discover more of the Jewel of Africa when I served the country in two critical economic ministries. Further, to President Obasanjo, who not only nominated me but persuaded me to go in to public service and was always available for guidance throughout my time in government. Moreover, to Dr Christopher Kolade, Dr Oby Ezekwesili and Oye Hassan-Odukale, who all played key roles in my decision to transition from the private sector to public service.

A very big thank you to the former President of South Africa, Thabo Mbeki, and Professor Wale Adebanwi for taking the time to read the manuscript and endorsing the book. And, of course, to Dr Christopher Kolade, the epitome of integrity and a rare gem in Africa for writing the Foreword to this book.

It was never my plan to write a book, either during or immediately after I left government. However, every time I responded to questions about Nigeria, Africa or, more importantly, my time in government, the discussions always ended with a strong advice that I must write a book. Some, such as my in-law Bashorun JK Randle, Robin Aitchison and Jimi Morgan, were persistent about it, while others, such as Dr Waheed Olagunju, went further to put a team together to start and support the project. It is difficult to mention everyone, but you know yourselves. To you all, I am most grateful.

I want to thank my former colleagues in the Ministry of Finance, Ministry of Industry, Trade and Investment and the agencies under the ministries, and my former colleagues in the Federal Executive Council. We went through most of the experiences narrated in this book together, and many times you provided the motivation and inspiration for me to continue and to focus on our shared vision for the country. Thank you for believing in a brighter future for our country and for working towards that brighter future. You have played your role. I also thank those who wrote to me and allowed me to share excerpts in this book. Unfortunately, it was not possible to include all your contributions in the final manuscript.

None of this would have happened without a strong team of researchers, contributors, proofreaders and editors led by Dr Biodun Adedipe and his team at BAA Consulting and the award-winning Tade Ipadeola. They were with me from conception to completion. To my friend, Alec Erwin; former South Africa Trade and Industry Minister, Dr Abraham Nwankwo; the cerebral and ever dependable former Chief Executive of the Debt Management Office, Amb Oke; plus Segun Awolowo, Ngozi Ikpechukwu, Uju Baba-Hassan, Nima Salmanmann, Jalal Aminu, Dr Latif Busari, Lola Mabogunje and Amb Musa Abdulkadir, who all made vital contributions – I am deeply grateful to you all.

Thank you to the core staff in the Minister's office: Georgina Muruako, Akeem Oyapidan, Mayowa Oyekanmi, Busari Adeeyo for making my time in Government so memorable. I cherish your support, diligence and professionalism.

Alison Jones and her team at Practical Inspiration Publishing offered guidance and rigorous, intelligent and incredible feedback throughout the process. They also brought professionalism, creativity and insight to bear in all the aspects of editing, production, marketing and publicity. The staff at Newgen Publishing were always polite and supportive as they worked on the design, copy-editing, proofreading and managed the project. The editor, Ivan Butler, the project manager, Mary McCormick, and Michelle Charman were particularly professional and helpful. It is impossible to mention all the names. I am grateful to you all. I feel very fortunate that my book ended up in their capable hands.

Finally, I want to thank my wife, Abiodun, for encouraging me throughout the process and creating a conducive environment that allowed me to focus on writing the book. Thank you to my in-laws,

Kolapo and Yinka Lawson, for their encouragement. I cannot thank the children enough – Toyosi and her husband Kanmi, Fiifelo, Olupitan and Ibukun – for their support and review of some of the chapters. And to our grandchildren, Tirenimi and Tamilore, who allowed granddad the space to reflect and write so that your tomorrow may be better than our today – I thank you too.

Undoubtedly, I would not have met all the publisher's deadlines without the organization, diligence and assistance of Ibukun, who worked very closely with me to proofread, update and revise the manuscript. She also liaised with the publisher and provided several suggestions that improved the book. A special thanks to you IBK.

From the conception to the writing of this book, the unborn Africans were in my thoughts. May they inherit and inhabit a greater continent. This book is for them too.

List of abbreviations and acronyms

AfCFTA	African Continental Free Trade Area
AfDB	African Development Bank
BOI	Bank of Industry
BPSR	Bureau of Public Service Reforms
BRIC	Brazil, Russia, India, China
CBN	Central Bank of Nigeria
DMO	Debt Management Office
ECOWAS	Economic Community of West African States
EFCC	Economic and Financial Crimes Commission
EPA	Economic Partnership Agreement
EU	European Union
FAAC	Federation Account Allocation Committee
FCT	Federal Capital Territory
FEC	Federal Executive Council
FIIRO	Federal Institute of Industrial Research Oshodi
FRC	Financial Reporting Council
FX	Foreign Exchange (market)
GDP	Gross Domestic Product
GIFMIS	Government Integrated Financial Management Information System
HIIC	Honorary International Investors Council
ICM	International Capital Market
ICPC	Independent Corrupt Practices Commission
IGR	Internally Generated Revenue
IIT	Indian Institute of Technology
IMF	International Monetary Fund
INEC	Independent National Electoral Commission
IPPIS	Integrated Personnel and Payroll Information System
ITF	Industrial Training Fund
KPI	Key Performance Indicators

MDA	Ministries, Departments and Agencies
MITI	Ministry of Industry, Trade and Investment
MP	Members of Parliament
MPR	Monetary Policy Rate
MSME	Micro, Small and Medium Enterprises
NBS	National Bureau of Statistics
NCC	National Competitiveness Council
NCCG	Nigeria Corporate Code of Governance
NEC	National Economic Council
NEDEP	National Enterprise Development Programme
NEPC	Nigerian Export Promotion Council
NEPZA	Nigerian Export Processing Zone Authority
NGO	Non-Governmental Organization
NHS	National Health Service (in the UK)
NIPC	Nigeria Investment Promotion Corporation
NIRP	Nigeria Industrial Revolution Plan
NLI	Nigeria Leadership Initiative
NLNG	Nigerian Liquified Natural Gas
NSDC	National Sugar Development Council
NSIA	Nigeria Sovereign Investment Authority
NSMP	Nigeria Sugar Master Plan
NSWF	Nigerian Sovereign Wealth Fund
NYSC	National Youth Service Corps
OECD	Organisation for Economic Co-operation and Development
OEM	Original Equipment Manufacturer
OPEC	Organization of the Petroleum Exporting Countries
PFI	Private Finance Initiative
PHDC	Presidential Honorary Diaspora Council
PPP	Purchasing Power Parity
SABIC	Saudi Basic Industries Corporation
SME	Small and Medium-sized Enterprises
SMEDAN	Small and Medium Enterprises Development Agency of Nigeria

SOE	State-Owned Enterprise
SWF	Sovereign Wealth Fund
TCF	Trillion cubic feet
TSA	Treasury Single Account
UNCTAD	United Nations Conference on Trade and Development
UNIDO	United Nations Industrial Development Organization
WTO	World Trade Organization

Reclaiming the Jewel: an introduction

'The world will not respect Africa until Nigeria earns that respect. The black people of the world need Nigeria to be great as a source of pride and confidence.'

Nelson Rolihlahla Mandela, 2007

Africa has made significant progress in the last five decades, but a few areas still hold it back from fulfilling its full potential as the last 'frontier'. From being the acknowledged cradle of mankind, the continent has witnessed the migration of *Homo sapiens,* first to the Middle East, Europe, Asia, Australia and the Americas. For centuries at a stretch, the continent hosted markets to trade goods from across the world, even as its knowledge centres stimulated thought in subjects as varied as mathematics, medicine, literature, law and religion. The libraries at Alexandria were for centuries the largest of such facilities known to mankind; in more recent times, the University of Timbuktu has become a centre of learning in the Islamic world. There are more pyramids in Sudan than in Egypt or anywhere else on Earth. The Ashmolean Museum in Oxford today holds hundreds of manufactured items and manuscripts from Meroë and its civilization, which are yet to be fully understood or translated into any modern language. This is another way of saying that the 'last frontier' was also the 'first field'.

Past centuries have witnessed a steep decline on the continent in many domains. With an end to slavery followed by independence for many countries, and its doors open to modern thought and processes once again, Africa has rallied quite remarkably against the odds and has provided exemplars in various fields.

This book examines the progress made to date on the continent; it identifies the missing links and proffers practical solutions using the largest economy in Africa, Nigeria, as a case study. Nigeria is a country with so much promise, blessed with abundant human and natural resources: a country with about 91 million hectares of land where almost everything can be grown, a nation with more than 44 solid minerals in commercial quantities, a top-fifteen oil and gas producer, a country that has a demography that is the envy of the world and more. Nigerians in the diaspora are highly successful and have imbibed the values and culture of those countries where they thrive.

This book is intended as the beginning of many conversations and discourses, which are necessary and even urgent. It is not and was not conceived to be a one-stop shop of solutions that drives progress in Nigeria or on the continent. What it offers is a view from inside the cockpit of a continental flight. The 'stopovers' are the chapters and the ultimate destination is that reclaimed Africa that is every day gathering substance and transforming into something much more than a mere dream. The world keeps changing and those bold enough to find their bearings in the midst of the constant changes shape the world.

War has broken out between Russia and Ukraine, changing many things from food supplies to energy prices. Nigeria and Africa are not isolated from the effects of the war in Europe. Just as the manuscript for this book was nearing completion, the world stood still to honour the life and legacy of Queen Elizabeth II, whose reign spanned all of 70 years and witnessed the birth of modern Nigeria, and the decolonization of the British Empire. King Charles III, her successor, is going to relate with a very different Nigeria, a very different Africa, indeed a very different time. Political, economic and religious leaders from various parts of the world acknowledge the birthing of a new global order. These profound and unexpected developments compel all – Nigerians, Africans and non-Africans – to examine critically and hopefully realistically the enormous promise of Nigeria and Africa, its place in the world and the increasing roles to be played by the now geopolitically understanding and strategically aware Africans, going forward.

Chapter 1

Leadership: political and governance structure

'How can we so organize political institutions that bad or incompetent rulers can be prevented from doing too much damage?'

Karl Popper, 'The Paradoxes of Sovereignty'

My generation was born to witness the rise of Africa. Our destiny was to be a significant part of a post-colonial beginning, our work was cut out for us and we were going to be active in the African renaissance. When I was born, most of Africa was under colonial rule. Today, of 54 African countries (excluding two disputed territories: Western Sahara and Somaliland), 25 are democracies.

At the stroke of midnight on 1 October 1960, in what was then the more open and more modest grounds of the Lagos Race Course, the Union Flag of Great Britain was lowered, and the Nigerian flag of vertical green, white and green flew for the first time in an independent Nigeria. The day before had witnessed a lot of activities, which Sir James Robertson and Princess Alexandra, both emissaries of the UK, superintended.

Taking the leadership baton

Between 1960 and today a lot has changed in Nigeria's political, economic, demographic and social structure. I have observed the outstanding successes of Nigerians both in the diaspora and inside the country. In April 2006 I founded the Nigeria Leadership Initiative (NLI) working with the Aspen Institute in Colorado. The initiative was launched to raise the bar for leaders by sharpening their values-based leadership skills and providing them with a platform to play a transformative role in Nigeria. The World Bank sponsored the NLI to run a similar seminar in Rwanda many years ago. The NLI has since worked with some 400 Nigerian leaders from various fields, many of whom hold very high offices today in the public and private spheres. I understood that when Nigerians did well at home and on the world stage, we all stood that much taller.

Eventually, I was invited to come and play my part in two distinct ministerial positions in the country's development. My first assignment was as Minister for Finance and Chairman of the Economic Management Team. The second role was as pioneer Minister for the Ministry of Industry, Trade and Investment (MITI). Coming to serve in the executive arm of government has affirmed to me the unique position of Nigeria as the crown jewel of Africa, even as I gained first-hand experience of how the country works and what needs improving. Nigeria is first among equals. I do not say this simply because I am Nigerian and therefore inexorably biased towards my country. In spite of all its challenges, I am of the conviction that purposefully overcoming the odds will transform the country into what it always had the potential to be.

Nigeria today operates the presidential system of government. Before now we had military rule and before that we ran a parliamentary democracy. The political and governance structures we have are, by general assessment, costly, far removed from the citizens and skewed in favour of political considerations over economic growth. Any random poll of Nigeria's problems throws up one factor consistently: poor leadership. The diagnosis of the dearth of quality leadership in the public space is true of most African countries regardless of what system of government exists there. This much I understood long before coming to serve in government and was the *raison d'ȇtre* for the NLI, which was conceived as an accelerator for qualitative leadership in both public and private spheres.

Dr Christopher Kolade, an eminent statesman and outstanding leader, agreed to be the patron of the NLI. The NLI board designed and executed a rigorous selection process under which only highly credible and accomplished individuals made the grade. Since its inception, the initiative has had prominent world-class leaders participate in it. NLI alumni boast a range and diversity of leaders of the calibre of Dr Titi Banjoko, Bayo Ogunlesi, Jide Zeitlin, Professor Lawal Marafa, Professor Oba Nsugbe QC, Dr Lola Oni (MBE), Dr Seyi Solebo, Professor Jacob Olupona (Havard), Professor Akintunde Akinwande (MIT), Professor Femi Oyebode, Professors Olu Obaro, Dele Olojede, and the late Professor Raufu Mustapha (Oxford), Dr. Muhammad Ali Pate from the diaspora (Europe, US, Asia and South Africa), and Professor Yemi

Osinbajo (Nigerian's vice-president), Asue Ighodalo, Tony Elumelu, Jim Ovia, John Momoh, Maryam Uwais, Nuhu Ribadu, Bishop Hassan Kukah, Oye Hassan-Odukale, Moyo Ajekigbe, Dr Efunbo Dosekun, Jimi Morgan, Professor Chidi Odinkalu, Bridget Itsueli, Udo Udoma, Ibrahim Bashiru, Nasir El-Rufai, Gbenga Oyebode, Dr Rueben Abati and Dr Sarah Alade from Nigeria, among so many other highly credible and accomplished Nigerians who are fellows and associates of NLI. Two of the Fellows: Fela Durotoye and Chukwuka Monye have ran for elections to become the President of the country. An exhaustive list of senior fellows, fellows and associates can be found on the NLI website.

Despite daunting obstacles, Nigeria produces world-class players in different fields. In the professions, in militaries, in academia all over the world, in entertainment and media, in sports and the arts, Nigeria has shown that it has what it takes to shine. Could we, as a people, identify our areas of strength while isolating and containing the causes of weakness that have held us back for so long? I am persuaded that we can and these reflections are part of my contribution to the reinvention of individual lives of value as well as sterling public life and service.

A bird's-eye view of the issues

A brief word about the Democracy Index, which is compiled annually by the Economist Intelligence Unit of the Economist Group. It measures the state of democracy in 167 countries, of which 166 are sovereign states and 164 are UN member states. The index is as strong an indicator of where the countries are as can be measured and is based on 60 indicators grouped into five different categories:

- Electoral process and pluralism
- Functioning of government
- Political participation
- Civil liberty
- Political culture

Nigeria is categorized in the most recent survey as a country with a hybrid democracy. Nigeria's overall democracy scored 4.11 points as of 2021, which is extremely near to being classified as an authoritarian regime (four points or less). Its score was about half of that of the top five countries in Africa: Mauritius, Cabo Verde, Botswana, South Africa and Namibia. Electoral process and pluralism scored 5.17 points; however, Nigeria's political participation, civil liberty and political culture rankings were extremely low, scoring below four points.

Figure 1.1: Nigeria's democracy index points, 2021

Category	Democracy index points (10 = full democracy)
Electoral process and pluralism	5.17
Functioning of government	3.93
Political participation	3.89
Civil liberty	3.82
Political culture	3.75
Overall score	4.11

According to the Economist Intelligence Unit, despite the improvements in democracy in Nigeria over the past two decades, particularly between 2014 and 2015, when the index increased by almost one percentage point, Nigeria has remained a hybrid democracy since 1999. Nigeria has not even made it to the next rank of flawed democracy in 23 years!

Figure 1.2: Nigeria's democracy regimes, 1960–2021

Period	Regime	Remark
1960–1966	Flawed Democracy	Poor political culture; constrained civil liberties
1966–1979	Authoritarian	Totalitarian military rule
1979–1983	Flawed Democracy	Weak functioning of government; limited political participation
1983–1999	Authoritarian	Totalitarian military rule
1999–2021	Hybrid	Low level of trust in political institutions and election results, regular electoral frauds, widespread corruption around elections, anaemic rule of law, pressure on media, judiciary

Source: The Economist Intelligence Unit

Hybrid regimes combine autocratic features with democratic ones and can simultaneously hold political repressions and regular elections. The attributes of democracy, such as having regular elections, a multi-party system and legal opposition, are all present in hybrid democracies or regimes but they also have a low degree of representation of the interests of citizens in the process of political decision-making, a low level of political participation by the people, particularly in voting at elections, and very low level of trust in political institutions and election results. They are nations with regular electoral frauds, preventing them from being fair and free democracies. These nations commonly have governments that apply pressure on political opposition, non-independent judiciaries, widespread corruption, harassment of and pressure placed on the media, anaemic rule of law, underdeveloped political culture and issues in the functioning of government.

For Nigeria to claim its rightful place in the world and as a leader in Africa, it must address these issues once and for all and make a determined effort to move up the rankings. I will expand more on these issues and share some thoughts on what can be done later in this chapter.

There are numerous studies by reputable social/political scientists about what ails Nigeria and Africa as a whole. If we took a poll in Nigeria today, the broad issues that need our most urgent attention would emerge as very much the same as those that studies have affirmed in the course of public life since the oil boom of the early '70s and can be summarized or grouped into the areas outlined below.

Poor leadership

The shortage of quality political leadership with the national interest at heart at every level of public life is a problem in our plural society. Obviously, the leadership potential is present, but the political system does not attract the best talents. Why does the system not attract the best talents? The short answer is that the political party apparatus is composed so that the best talents are unable to emerge from the existing party structures, which are primarily driven by money and are self-serving. It is a catch-22 situation. A candidate for any office who has expended a fortune to be a candidate and to be elected, whether at the local, state or federal level, will become essentially a soldier of fortune, feathering his or her own nest first. However, Nigerians have historically preferred visionary leadership based on strong values. The late Aminu Kano, Obafemi Awolowo and Nnamdi Azikiwe were such leaders – energetic and vibrant, inspirational, intellectually robust, exposed and demonstrating the ability to understand and effectively manage the affairs of a diverse nation. More than at any time before, we now need leaders who are able to build strong teams to deliver on a progressive vision for society, men and women who have a reputation for defending the citizens and who are accountable to the people. While it is understood that not every African leader can be a Nelson Mandela, with the right mindset, every mindful person can develop the right leadership skillsets and be a role model. Kwame Nkrumah, Seretse Khama and Thomas Sankara are great examples.

Leadership must be inculcated in the educational system's curriculum, starting from the primary school. For example, in the 1960s, civic education was taught at the primary school level, followed by general studies in secondary schools. The arguments that informed these actions have remained hazy and myopic. Little wonder that products of the educational system are no longer ingrained in the core principles of leadership and its demands. Without a proper grounding in civic responsibilities and leadership, it is short-sighted to expect the products of our educational system to espouse values that they have not been exposed to or taught.

Inchoate democracy and weak electoral framework

Democracy, from the Greek *dēmokratia* (*dēmos* 'the people' plus *kratia* 'power'), is the holy grail of governance as practised by humankind on Earth. The late Kofi Annan, former Secretary-General of the United Nations, asserted that 'good governance is perhaps the single most important factor in eradicating poverty and promoting development'. Governance systems on the African continent can be categorized into:

- Full democracies
- Flawed democracies
- Hybrid regimes
- Authoritarian regimes

Flawed democracies are characterized by regular elections, which are somewhat free but lead to governance structures in which basic civil liberties are present, although with apparent issues such as repression of freedom of expression and the propping of state media over a free press. These nations have significant faults in other democratic aspects, including underdeveloped political culture, low levels of participation in politics and issues in the functioning of governance. The hybrid system of governance integrates both democratic and autocratic systems. It is somehow prevalent in Africa due to long periods of military regimes that are patently autocratic. When these transit to democracy, they tend not to be functioning democracies. This military intrusion into the democratic system undermines the critical elements of the democratic culture, such as fundamental human rights, equality before the law, justice, free and fair elections, among others. The autocratic regime is authoritarian by nature, promoting dictatorship and discouraging the participation of the people in the choice of who leads them.

While the aspirational goal in Nigeria and most of Africa remains a democracy in the true sense of the word – government of the people, by the people, for the people – Nigeria has remained in the hybrid state for a long time and must now transform into true democracy. It is more a government by the political class, of the political class, for the political class. This book is conceived, in part, as source material for a redress of these lapses.

Inefficient and ineffective structure of the country

It is said that all politics is local. Democracy should build from the ground up. The poor implementation of our presidential system in Nigeria has meant that there is more focus on the centre than on the federating units. Very few states are viable on a standalone basis and yet they run a costly system with a high ratio of recurrent expenditure to revenue. States rarely run transparent elections into local government offices, with the net effect that almost all the states have local government officials from the same political party as the governor of that state. The Nigerian constitution has more items on the exclusive (federal) list than any other federal constitution, thus the concentration of power at the centre. This over-concentration of power at the centre does not promote national cohesion. My firm belief is that Nigeria must restructure to develop, expand and diversify the economy to achieve its potential. I have been in the centre, and I know it is sub-optimal. Restructuring is not about if but when and how.

Political system

Mushrooming political parties in Nigeria engage in a theatre of sorts in which several are registered and many of these are deregistered in four-year election cycles. The legitimacy of the results of these expensive exercises is called into question when you realize that many voters do not even know who their representatives are and therefore cannot engage with them to any meaningful or positive end. The Representatives do not have functional constituency offices or contact phone numbers or addresses.

Once elected into office, it is difficult for voters to hold their representatives responsible for how they vote. Even though the National Assembly and many state legislatures have facilities for electronic voting, the voice 'yea/nay' method preferred by these legislative houses does not allow the constituents to hold their representatives to account without any records. Constituents are never consulted on any important National matter and therefore do not have any say on how their Representatives vote.

Poor management of conflicts

There are many areas of conflict in the present structure. These areas need to be identified and addressed through stipulated measures. For example, our legislators are currently tasked with fixing their own salaries and allowances. The result is that they are indirectly put in a situation where they are exposed to a serious conflict of interest regarding how much they vote for their own remuneration and how much is voted for the nation's development. There must also be a more effective and efficient process for effecting citizen-led demands including the review of the constitution and restructuring of the country.

The current political system is like a minefield of developing or fully manifesting conflicts, which only a proper review of the constitution by the people can resolve. States are in a constant power tussle with the centre and the local government system, on the one hand, while the judiciary is caught in struggles for autonomy between the executive and the legislature on the other. One way to address this challenge is to have the country constitute a group of eminent persons, statesmen and women, civil society leaders, respected religious leaders and business leaders to address these challenges in order to free up the energies of our legislators in addressing pressing national security matters, and economic and development challenges.

Another way is to incorporate the Swiss model of challenging the law made by the legislature and the executive. The Swiss have a mechanism for challenging any legislation by a referendum of the citizens, who invoke their right to referendum by gathering a minimum of 50,000 petitions. Switzerland has utilized this provision in its constitution up to 321 times since it came into effect in the 18th century. The UK has a similar approach to challenging legislation or escalating issues to be debated by its parliament.

For us in Nigeria and Africa, the point is to evolve a pattern of review that works for us just as the Swiss and the British have done. It requires a deliberate and focused approach, but it can be done. Building a more transparent and less fraught governance structure is urgent and essential.

Strong individual vs strong system

Africa, and, indeed, Nigeria, have always relied on personalities and individuals and have paid very little attention to building a strong system. This raises questions about Nigeria's governance system. Does Nigeria have a credible and robust system that will always ensure that the most competent person emerges in an election? Is the system so strong that if for any reason a bad leader emerges, they can be prevented from doing too much damage? Some would reply yes to those questions and argue that a president or governor can always be impeached by the national or state assemblies but, in reality, is this possible where and when you have a rubber-stamp assembly controlled by the same party, in assemblies that are not accountable to the voters or where values-based leaders are in short supply?

The philosopher Plato, in *The Republic*, observed that 'man and city are alike'. He postulated that humans without souls are hollow. Cities without virtue are likewise rotten. In modern times, a lot of emphasis is laid on the quality and quantity of infrastructure undergirding a country. However, as important, if not more so, is the quality of humans in the country for whom the infrastructure is built. Those entrusted with keeping the country on course must be people of capacity if the task is to be accomplished. Plato was concerned about the very pertinent question of who should rule. It was his conviction that those who should rule must be virtuous.

Karl Popper, perhaps the greatest of the political thinkers of the 20th century, followed the arc of moral and political thought preceding the modern age. In his own submission, the most pertinent question is not who should rule or how much education leaders should possess but: 'How can we so organize political institutions that bad or incompetent rulers can be prevented from doing too much damage?'

In Nigeria today, the urgent questions and considerations are as Plato and Popper posed them. We must think through the organization of our society and institutions so that the best people occupy public office and society does not sustain lasting damage regardless of who is in office.

Experience from around the world shows that this task is not as simple as it appears and certainly requires our best efforts. The American presidential election of 2020 shows most clearly that even the most advanced democracies need to pay careful attention to these considerations if a bad political actor is not to compromise the system's operation.

Redefining public service

Corruption: limitation to good governance

Corruption is a key challenge limiting the development of Africa, as resources for development are captured for private use rather than for the common good. Using the 2020 survey of 180 countries and territories by Transparency International, the global top-ten least corrupt countries and African top-ten are referenced here. Most of these countries enjoy a high rate of economic growth/development and also rank highly in the human development index, suggesting a strong correlation between good governance and prosperity.

Figure 1.3: Corruption Perception Index: global top-ten and top-ten Africa

S/ No.	Global Leaders	Rank	Score	S/ No.	African Leaders	Rank	Score
1.	New Zealand	1	88	1.	Seychelles	27	66
2.	Denmark	1	88	2.	Botswana	35	60
3.	Finland	3	85	3.	Cabo Verde	41	58
4.	Switzerland	3	85	4.	Rwanda	49	54
5.	Singapore	3	85	5.	Mauritius	52	53
6.	Sweden	3	85	6.	Namibia	57	51
7.	Norway	7	84	7.	São Tomé and Príncipe	63	47
8.	Netherlands	8	82	8.	Senegal	67	45
9.	Luxembourg	9	80	9.	South Africa	69	44
10.	Germany	9	80	10.	Ghana	75	43

Source: Transparency International

Corruption is manifested in many ways across the entire ecosystem. On the leadership and political structure, vote buying during primaries and general elections or any form of inducement by any party with regards to elections are all corrupt practices, and the police, the Independent National Electoral Commission (INEC), Economic and Financial Crimes Commission (EFCC) and the Independent Corrupt Practices Commission (ICPC) must work together to stamp these out.

As a country, we need to reinvent our understanding of both leadership and public service. Public service is seen by most as just another career path. This may have sufficed in the past. Today, the understanding of what public service is needs to evolve, especially for the African, and this can be realized through vigorous education and campaign. Public service is not a money-making path or a wealth-generating venture. Those who are interested in money and wealth should pursue private enterprise. Public service is 'service to life'. It is a calling and an opportunity to serve humanity generally and fellow citizens in particular. To serve effectively and successfully, political leaders and other public servants must not only have competence and vision, but they must also live the values of integrity, compassion and justice. They must have empathy, which can be described as loving your neighbour as yourself in religious terms. This is what Nelson Mandela meant when he said. 'A good head and a good heart are always a formidable combination.' Like teachers, doctors and other vocations, the satisfaction comes from the difference that the individual and their work have been able to make in the lives of others. Serving your country should be like being called upon to represent your country at the Olympics. It should be the greatest honour and privilege to serve and not an opportunity to make money. If money is the motivation, then public service is not the way to go; the private sector will be a much better option.

A federal minister must understand that public service is not service to his or her village, town or city. Public service is service to the country as a whole. A state commissioner should know that they bear responsibility towards everyone in the state and not just the ward they come from. The latitude, scope and understanding of the African public servant, therefore, have to transcend ethnic lines. This is a challenge in Nigeria where the first set of congratulatory messages are usually from one's townsmen and women! It is all well and good and natural for peers and relatives to acknowledge one's accomplishments, but education of the general populace must drive the understanding that public service is an objective task.

The logic of successful societies dictates that these values are inculcated into and are embraced by the majority of citizens from whom leaders emerge. All of us, therefore – individuals, corporates, the executive, the National Assembly, the judiciary, media, religious organizations, traditional institutions, the organized private sector, civil society, schools and socio-political institutions – have a role to play.

Some success factors

Values are sacred

History has shown that successful countries and companies are built on a set of core values and the values of the leaders determine how they execute leadership.

To give an accurate assessment of governance from afar is near impossible anywhere in the world and especially so in Nigeria. This was brought home to me in numerous events that have remained indelibly stamped in my consciousness. I will recount a few of these in this book to illustrate the dynamics of governance in the Nigerian context. As Minister of Finance, I met with the president fairly regularly to iron out matters of state as they pertain to fiscal and other measures. Some of those meetings unavoidably ran late into the evenings or the early hours of the next day. There was never enough money to do all we wanted to do as a government, and this meant prioritizing. On one particular occasion the meeting took much longer than anticipated and, at about 1am, the president asked me to excuse him so he could catch some sleep. I was to come back at 8am as he had some files to look at for matters coming up later that day. When I went back at 8am, the president was at his home office, but still in his clothes from the day before and he explained that he had not slept because there were some pressing matters which came up after I left at 1am. He then asked me to come back later in the evening in order to conclude our prior meeting. It was just one example of how the office of the president imposes demands on the occupier of that office. It is extraordinarily taxing and unpredictable. When the leadership of the country takes diligence as a core value, however, it sets the tone for the whole country. With the benefit of hindsight, Nigerians now know that President Jonathan gave his all to the work set before him. It was a joy working for President Jonathan, and the reasons are simple. He was knowledgeable, accessible, hard-working, and you could always appeal to his reasoning because he always had one interest – the best outcome for the country.

I recall listening to the former Norwegian prime minister Dr Gro Harlem Brundtland at a dinner. She was the first female prime minister of Norway and, at 41, the youngest person ever to be appointed to that position in her country. At the end of her speech, someone asked her what the secret of her success was. In her response, she said her success was down to two things:

1. She was always guided by her core values whether she was leading or following.
2. She was always prepared to leave and return to her profession if at any time she found herself in a position where she had to compromise her core values.

I also recall another episode much closer to home of the exercise of core values in the proximity of power. After winning the 2011 election, President Jonathan remarked that the Nigerian president was vested with so much power that it was best to check oneself in the exercise of those powers. He confided in those closest to him to remind him of his decision to observe boundaries in using presidential power. This he did consistently throughout his tenure even when others thought it was a sign of weakness. He was determined not to use the power in a detrimental way. The experience has remained with me.

Good behaviour cannot be legislated. The law can only punish bad behaviour. In order to drive the change we need as a society, positive core values are critical. We must develop values-based leaders with a clear understanding of their civic responsibilities right from school. Historically, traditional societies placed a premium on such values as integrity, diligence and hard work. The older school curricula taught subjects such as civics. One of the NLI's aims was to sharpen leaders in their value consciousness. The point is to keep reinforcing these positive values, their importance and their inculcation. This is why, while envisioning the NLI, I tried to put it on record that:

> Great leaders are vision-driven authentic leaders who are not motivated by wealth or power but by the opportunity to serve. They already have the greatest wealth, which is contentment. People of the highest integrity who are competent and committed to building a prosperous nation. Leaders who have a deep sense of purpose are true to their core values and recognize the importance of their selfless service to the society.

Values-based leaders are more interested in empowering the people they lead to make a difference than they are in money, power or prestige for themselves. They are guided by qualities of the heart, by passion and compassion, as much as they are by qualities of the mind. They also recognize their shortcomings, work hard to overcome them and will not put themselves forward for leadership positions until they are ready. Building a team of competent and values-based leaders is normally a priority of a successful leader.

Meritocracy is key: escaping the political Bermuda Triangle

Pre-Covid, events such as Christmas, Mother's Day, Father's Day and Valentine's Day were played up to promote consumer spending and support the economy. In Africa, and indeed Nigeria, election periods are like Christmas season. There is increased liquidity and economic activities in the local system. Even the Central Bank and some businesses plan around it. The reasons for these are simply:

African and Nigerian politics and systems are still very dependent on three factors – tribe, religion and money – which I call the 'political Bermuda Triangle'. When you get trapped in this triangle, there is no progress, no prosperity and the people and the country are like cows milked daily by the pretend democrats and progressives for their own personal interest. This triangle is prevalent in countries where the level of poverty, unemployment and the number of the uneducated electorates are high. These group of voters are only influenced by tribe, religion and money. That explains why the voting pattern of the electorates in the cities like Lagos is always different from the other parts of the country where you have most of the voters. It is impossible to address this issue without addressing the issue of poverty, political education, unemployment and if necessary changing the voting system.

Nigeria, and indeed the real democrats and progressives, must do everything they can to escape from this triangle to a new paradigm based on the three pillars of competence, vision and values, built on a foundation that is composed of strong institutions, meritocracy, inclusiveness, continuity and a just, fair and equitable society. These are the critical pillars and foundations upon which we can build a prosperous, indivisible and strong nation. Our political system, electoral actions and constitution must reflect these pillars and foundations for Nigeria to realize its true potential.

Merit and federal character are not mutually exclusive. No one would submit to surgery to be performed by a pilot or lawyer. The reason is simple: they lack the skills necessary to execute the procedure. It is important that citizens realize that qualified technocrats handle certain aspects of public life better. Merit and equity are not opposing criteria, because there are competent people in every corner of the country. The challenge is finding them, developing them and putting their talents to work for the greater good. Political patronage and influence are a part of the political life of every society, but there should be limits. We all thrive when we put the right men and women in the right seats.

In my stewardship, I helped the country institute the Sovereign Wealth Fund (SWF). It remains a beacon of meritocracy today. Studying worldwide developments on how countries far richer in hydrocarbons than Nigeria have diversified helped in no small measure to actualize this. Today, the country as a whole is reaping benefits from the idea and execution of the SWF.

There is no need to reinvent the wheel for integrating merit into the national ethos. Many countries have addressed these issues and the question should be more about what we can learn from them.

Performance-based governance

A powerful dynamic in governance is the link between meritocracy and performance. Where a matrix successfully couples merit and metrics for measuring outcomes, the task of leading society along charted paths is easier. The performance gap in government agencies is largely due to a lack of performance-based metrics on the goals and objectives of the agencies. For instance, the Chilean government designed performance indicators for its ministries, departments and agencies, and the results are publicized. Even though the Chilean political system is autocratic, the government was able to reduce the implementation gaps among political office holders, the bureaucracy and citizens.

Improving accountability

Nigeria can take deliberate action to encourage accountability. For example, it can be made mandatory for local council chairmen to have town hall meetings quarterly or half-yearly. These should be attended by the state and federal House of Representatives and senators. Another tool for political accountability is a quarterly or half-yearly presidential and governors' question time, which will involve the main opposition parties and should be attended by all stakeholders. This should also include a state of the nation or state address at least once a year. There should be a penalty for any deliberate effort to mislead the electorate. Legislators should have constituency offices and clinics where constituents can meet with them, on appointment, to discuss issues and the assistance they require.

Citizenship, people and the power of the ballot

Nigeria remains a special case when it comes to the population of highly credible, talented and successful citizens in the diaspora. Next to India, perhaps, and without doubt being the African country with the most skilled citizens outside the shores of the country, it is important to think in a structured manner about the linkages between

Nigerians resident in Nigeria and the Nigerian diaspora. It was for this reason that every NLI class had equal numbers of Nigerians in the diaspora and from within Nigeria, and this showed in the quality of our discussions. I have expanded on this idea in Chapter 7.

Beyond the well-known fact that diaspora remittances have been a vital part of the Nigerian economy, the diaspora population has been critical in skills and technology transfer back to the home country. Nigerians abroad want to contribute to the home country and are just looking for the right platform to do this effectively. It is time to engage this pool of talent positively. Nigeria could use a 'presidential diaspora council'. The reasons are many, but the chief one is the huge diaspora with skills that Nigeria is not utilizing optimally at the moment.

Nigeria needs to have a mechanism for giving full franchise and citizenship rights to all Nigerians in the diaspora as well as at home. The nexus between citizens, home and abroad, is yet another way to safeguard and protect the ballot. This is absolutely necessary so that citizens can more ably resist the purchase of their votes, on the one hand, and participate meaningfully in civic life on the other.

This is not mere egalitarianism. The National Assembly missed an opportunity to include the diaspora in the electoral process when it voted against the right of Nigerians in the diaspora to vote in elections, effectively denying millions of Nigerians their franchise. Some consider this as another area where there is conflict of interest, particularly from those who benefit from the current system, which prevents Nigerians in the diaspora from voting, people who are not only highly educated but know the power of their votes. It is vital to realize that the diaspora is not only useful for remittances alone. For far too long Nigeria has deferred the enactment of modern electoral reform laws, which secures this bedrock of industrial democracies. To ensure we have a democracy that is participatory and beneficial, Nigerians must have real power to express their wishes in the voting process.

A little-known event in our political history illustrates how President Jonathan walked the talk in this regard. He wanted Nigerian democracy to be as robust and as respectable as any in the world. I was with him at the meeting with President Barack Obama, where, when asked his priorities, without blinking President Jonathan said free and fair election, and electricity. He thought that the electoral process, being one aspect of the practice of democracy that most individuals readily recognize and engage with, would be a great starting point. President Jonathan insisted that he would rather be the man that organized a free and fair election and lost than the man who failed to do anything about electoral reform and 'won'.

Professor Attahiru Jega, who became the chairman of the INEC, came highly recommended and he scaled through the hurdles of various screening exercises for a person that will occupy such a sensitive office as the electoral umpire in the country. In 2011, at a meeting of a select group of National Assembly members and two ministers the president broached the issue by asking Professor Jega how he would score the credibility of Nigerian elections out of 100 points. I recollect that Professor Jega scored the process at about 40% or less. This was obviously a damning verdict, so President Jonathan asked what it would take to have the electoral process score 90% on the credibility scale. The INEC chair said ₦90 billion (approximately $562 million at the exchange rate of the time). This was a major sum at that time and almost everyone present exclaimed that this was too much to pump into the reformation of the electoral process, even for 90% credibility. Some said that 60% credibility at the polls would be a significant gain and something everyone would be happy with – or they should be.

The next day President Jonathan called me to his office and asked me to look into ways and means of finding the funds to make the INEC request a reality. He then summoned a meeting at which he, Professor Jega and I were the only participants. He asked Professor Jega to justify the figures, which he did in detail and in a thoughtful manner. If the country could execute the reform plan, everyone would benefit in the immediate and long term. At the end of the day, the INEC chairman was able to secure ₦87 billion from the government after convincing the National Assembly. The positive results were reflected in the 2011 and 2015 elections as attested to by national and international observers as well as the Democracy Index. Sadly, there has been a tapering-off in the outcomes since 2015, which is also reflected in the Democracy Index.

Some people have speculated that President Jonathan could not have done otherwise than he did leading up to the 2015 round of elections, which he lost to President Muhammadu Buhari. Nothing could be further from the truth. President Jonathan was fully aware of the possible outcomes of the electoral reform he set in motion as soon as he became president. He could have made different choices that could have influenced the outcome at the polls but he would rather have a credible system decide the outcome. As proof of his bona fides, he congratulated the president-elect as soon as the margin of the ballot revealed that it was going to be mathematically impossible for him to win.

Consider the very different scenario in the US leading to the emergence of President Joe Biden. All manner of obstacles were placed in his path by the incumbent who correctly assessed the probability of losing to Joe Biden much earlier than most. The incumbent and his supporters tested the political institutions of the US in ways that tested the resilience of that great country. At the conclusion of the election, and quite contrary to the tradition in the US, Donald Trump did not congratulate the president-elect, Joe Biden. He refused to concede defeat and whipped up his base support in a way that most political watchers and analysts believe contributed or led to the invasion of the Capitol.

When Nigeria is compared with the top-five democracies in Sub-Saharan Africa, the pattern shows that a lot needs to be refined in Nigeria's democratic institutions and political system. The Nigerian presidential constitution vests so much power in the president that only conscious and conscionable exercise of these powers can save the holder of the exalted office from themself. In many parts of Africa the incumbent has used executive powers to effectively organize constitutional amendments to remove term limits. Some incumbents have superintended elections, which they claim to have won, sometimes with more than a 90% margin! In no other plural society are the African margins ever recorded and it is a shame on Africa. The obvious challenge is to identify how and what steps are necessary to prevent abuse of power and conflicts of interest.

So far the measures in place have not stopped politicians from using proxies to thwart transparency in governance or to use insider information to compromise institutions that have to do with their stay in office. A new code of conduct is needed for all public officers that ensures that from the very onset a public official discloses any conflicts of interest in order to allow a dispassionate appraisal.

Party and election financing

Party and election financing is a very important and difficult area in all democracies. If not well managed it can undermine democracy completely. That is why in most countries there are specific laws around it, which are reviewed regularly to block any loopholes. For example, in the UK and the US, there are rules on who can make a contribution or donation to a political party or candidate. Generally, foreign donors are not allowed, there are limits on the amount that can be donated, there are monitoring and reporting requirements, cases are reported by the electoral commission to the police for investigation and there are stiff penalties. In Nigeria there are laws too but enforcement is weak. In some cases the laws are outdated or require significant improvements.

In Nigeria there are other financing considerations across the whole ecosystem, from how the day-to-day party activities are funded to payment for expression of interest and nomination forms to contest an election, campaign financing, incentives to delegates during the primaries of the different political parties and cash for votes during elections. Vote buying days before the primary and general elections and on the day of the elections is rampant and yet no one has been reprimanded or charged for these offences. Members of political parties do not pay subscriptions or fees but they expect to benefit from the party and most parties are funded mainly by individuals who want to contest elections and who therefore see their contributions as an investment that will generate financial returns when elected.

Political appointees, members of the National Assembly and state governors are also primary sources of funding for political parties. This does not only undermine democracy but it is one of the root causes of corruption. In effect, the funders become investors and the parties become investment companies through which they invest. That is how politics, which should have been a call to provide selfless service to the nation, becomes the most viable and financially rewarding business. No country can progress if its politics is more profitable than industry, as explained in Chapter 4. Unless these are properly addressed, corruption and poor governance will remain a major problem in Africa and in particular Nigeria.

The cost of obtaining expression of interest and nomination forms can be outrageous. For example, the cost (₦ million) for the expression of interest and nomination forms for the two major political parties, the APC and PDP, for the 2023 elections are as stated in Figure 1.4 for the main elective offices.

Figure 1.4: Costs of expression of interest and nomination forms 2023

Office	APC (₦ million)	PDP (₦ million)
President	100.0	40.0
Governor	50.0	21.0
Senator	20.0	3.5
House of Representatives	10.0	2.5
House of Assembly	2.0	0.6

The APC forms are free for female aspirants and people living with disability, while those between the ages of 25 and 40 have a discount of 50%. PDP also offered 50% discount to those between the ages of 25 and 30. For the political parties, the cost of obtaining forms for expression of interest and nomination is an effective and efficient way of raising funds for the party. In total, more than ₦30 billion was raised by one of the political parties from this exercise alone. However, the cost of obtaining forms for expression of interest and nomination is just the beginning of a long process for aspirants, as explained above. There are more funds required for consultations, primaries, the general election, campaigning, etc.

There are several issues here, beginning with the amount. The forms are expensive, especially when compared to the US, from where Nigeria has copied its presidential system. The highest sum ever paid for nomination and declaration of interest in US elections is around $40,000, which translates to ₦22 million at the current exchange rate. It does not reflect the state of the economy, high level of poverty and unemployment. The amount paid to obtain an expression of interest and nomination for most of the offices is almost double the annual salary for those offices. And remember, this is only the beginning of the process! It also means that only candidates with deep pockets can contest an election or put themselves forward to serve. The options presented to electorates are limited to those who have acquired wealth, regardless of the source of the wealth.

The new Electoral Act 2022 seeks to address campaign finance abuse by imposing ceilings and penalties for violation. There are campaign finance thresholds for parties and candidates. Section 88 of the Act limits election expenses on candidates as follows:

Figure 1.5: Election expenses limits

Office	Maximum Limit (₦ million)	
	Old	New
President	1,000	5,000
Governorship	200	1,000
Senatorial	40	100
House of Representatives	20	70
State Assembly	10	30

The maximum amount that an individual or entity can donate to a candidate was increased from ₦1 million to ₦50 million. Breach of these limits is punishable under S. 88 (9) & (10) by a fine of 1% of the limit allowed or imprisonment of up to 12 months, or both. Section 95 (2) of the Act also asserts that state apparatus such as vehicles, aircraft, personnel, money, public buildings, etc. must not be employed to the advantage or disadvantage of any political party or candidate at any election.

Overall, the Electoral Act 2022 is a step in the right direction but there is scope for improvement if Nigeria is to strengthen its democracy and quality of leadership. First is the issue of enforcement, which is very poor. Nigeria had limits before but it is public knowledge that they were breached and there were no consequences. There were cases when someone would say they and their friends had donated ₦100 million, when the limit for individual donations was ₦1 million, but no one followed up to obtain a list of the other 99 'donors' to confirm that they actually made those donations. It is one thing to have laws, but it is another to enforce the law, and this is where Nigeria has to take appropriate steps to improve accountability, enforcement and to clearly spell out the role of the INEC, the police and the other relevant agencies. Electronic transmission of results from polling booths is also a major improvement if the guidelines are adhered to very strictly. The federal government, as a matter of urgency, must prioritize the establishment of an electoral offences commission to deal with electoral offenders.

There is a potential conflict of interest, which has either not been identified or properly managed. You cannot ask politicians to make laws on party and election financing. It is like asking them to determine their own salaries and allowances. As lawmakers they should be involved in the process but there is a need for an independent body to determine, review and approve. Given the nature of elections and the need to improve after every election, there is a need for a more regular review of the Act so that new issues identified are addressed promptly. For example, vote buying and underage voting should be made a criminal offence, reportable to a special election court/tribunal. The thinker, Arthur M. Okun, in his book of essays, *Equality and Efficiency: The Big Trade Off*, said, 'The rights and powers that money should not buy (like votes) must be protected with detailed regulations and sanctions.' I agree.

And finally, the penalties for election offences are very light and are unlikely to act as a deterrent. In the US, for example, a Republican from Nebraska, who lied to the FBI about taking illegal donations, could be sentenced to about 15 years in prison. Both Republicans and Democrats have called on him to resign or be expelled. The rationale is that lawmakers are supposed to set the right example by following the law. In the UK it is common for the police to launch an investigation into party financing, including complaints by donors into crowdfunding on how the money raised was used.

The reporting requirements set out in the new electoral law can be considered to be minimal when compared with other countries with stronger democracies. For example, in the UK the register of Members of Parliament (MP) interests, which includes other interests, employment and gifts, is required to be updated by MPs within a specified period. This is monitored regularly and MPs who fail to make the correct declarations are sanctioned. Parties themselves must report donations and loans of more than £7,500 to the Electoral Commission. Again, there are stringent sanctions if political parties break the rule and serious offences are reported to the police. It is important that the necessary amendments are made to the Electoral Act 2022 to enhance and protect the integrity of Nigeria's democracy.

The fourth estate of the realm

The press is critical to democracy. Following examples from older democracies, some of which have instituted press freedom and power for over 300 years, the Nigerian press can and should be strengthened through legislation and fiscal support to deliver premium service to the citizens.

Some societies are not as welcoming of press freedom, but Nigeria cannot afford to be one of those. The press is a powerful check on the excesses of government. The press is a moulder of public opinion. It is the mirror for investors seeking to understand the society. It is a powerful forum for the exchange of ideas. If properly harnessed, the press can be instrumental in transforming the image of Nigeria. However, any attempt to constrain the media, as is currently being contemplated through amendments to the Nigerian Press Council and National Broadcasting Commission Acts, will be a retrograde step that will imperil democratic practice. The stakeholders in the media must sanitize the sector and embrace best global practices, including introducing a self-regulatory regime.

Innovating forward: a case for regulated lobbying in Nigeria

Our reputation as a country could be improved tremendously if we took the time and trouble to legalize and regulate lobbying. Lobbying is a global practice that exists even in supposedly rigid political environments. In Nigeria, failing to be proactive and to legitimize the process by which interest groups seek to influence legislators to make laws is a missed opportunity. Regulating lobbying has many advantages. It removes the shroud of secrecy around what is to be tabled by interested legislators. The required statutory disclosures greatly assist the state in projecting and assessing revenue. This is a low-hanging fruit that the country can address almost immediately.

Revisiting the governance system

The interesting point about the chart of good governance is that the top 15 countries all have a parliamentary system of governance and a few home-grown systems by countries that have adapted the parliamentary system to suit their own local peculiarities and economy. Switzerland, the top country on the chart, has its own system of governance, and the US, which is the epitome of the presidential system, is way down the ladder. If there is one fundamental constitutional change that data suggests we should consider in Nigeria, it is the merits of parliamentary democracy, and the possibility of developing our own hybrid parliamentary or presidential system. Not merely an administrative change but a holistic reform of the entire system that would guarantee a more active political engagement across the board and address the mix of the electorates and our diversity. Comparative data from across the world suggests that Switzerland is an excellent place to look for ideas.

Figure 1.6: Changes in confidence in national governance 2007 to 2014

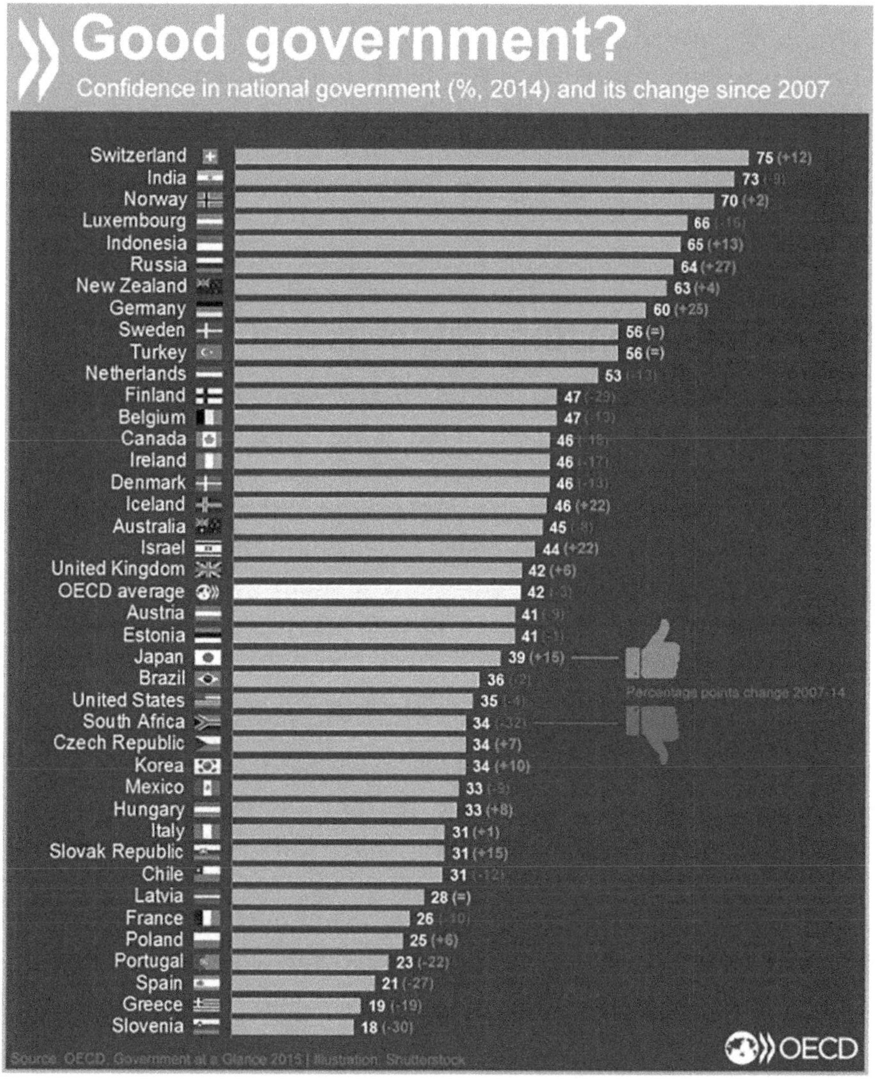

Like Nigeria, Switzerland is a federation. Unlike Nigeria, however, Switzerland is a parliamentary democracy with a Federal Assembly characterized by a low level of conflict, fragmented party groups and the inclusion of all major party groups in the government. It is a home-grown system. The Swiss Federal Council, the federal government, consists of seven members who are elected by the parliament. The presidency is rotated. The bicameral parliament of 246 members are elected by some five million voters who aggregate in some 15 political parties. Despite the apparent plurality of the parliament, there are known patterns of the parliamentary opposition, depending on the strength of partisanship and on the levels of the topicality of issues. The Swiss Assembly plays a major role when partisanship and salience of topics are high. Issues on which there are deep cleavages in society are the issues over which the Assembly plays its most important roles. If Switzerland can fashion a system that works for its citizens, certainly Nigeria can.

The national honours system as tool

Cultural capital is a great part of life in Africa generally. It affirms the contributions of individuals to the life of the community.

The national honours system should recognize and promote role models who contribute to national development and live the values of the nation. There should also be delisting criteria and removal of undeserving people from the list. The awards should come with some privileges; for example, recipients are placed on the federal government's guest list to some events. The integrity and credibility of the awards should be strengthened by assigning supervision of the process to carefully selected eminent and reputable Nigerians.

There is a need to more consciously utilize the national honours system to shore up national values. Beyond the undeniable prestige associated with national honours, there is a higher end that the system as it exists today can serve. Nigerians should be encouraged to see the system as aspirational by awarding national honours only to those who deserve them and no one else. Infamous conduct should promptly lead to stripping a recipient of the national award.

Vision, values, competence and continuity: some prescriptions

Based on substantial studies, I propose to highlight four main indicators – vision, values, competence and continuity (2Vs and 2Cs) – to assist leaders and stakeholders make concrete, granular progress in moving the country forward. So, how do the 2Vs and 2Cs work in real terms? Essentially, their presence or absence helps to make critical decisions about the quality of leadership on offer.

- **Vision**. A leader must have a clear vision of where he or she wants to take the country. In addition, a leader should have the ability to properly articulate this vision and how they want to achieve it. Finally, the leader must be able to get his or her team and the country to buy into this vision. Lee Kuan Yew, the founding and first prime minister of Singapore, who served from 1959 to 1990, is a good example of a visionary leader. Singapore was a small island lacking natural resources and having only a natural deep harbour. The exceptional leadership by Lee Kuan Yew transformed the nation from an underdeveloped third-world one to a developed high-income one and a regional economic hub, by matching the vision with appropriate actions and policies. From a population of about 1.59 million and per capita gross domestic product (GDP) less than $400 in 1959, Singapore grew to a population of 5.7 million and $107,604 per capita in 2020 (purchasing power parity, or PPP). Some of the specific actions taken were:
  - Enabling an environment for high-tech firms to operate and become a manufacturing hub for the South-East Asia market.
  - Strong alliance with the US and China to explore growth opportunities.
  - Worked with a team of technocrats that trained in developed countries and arranged a skills transfer programme that encouraged the youth to return to invest in Singapore.
  - Carried out massive infrastructure investments to attract foreign firms that made Singapore their base.
- **Values**. A leader should be a person of integrity whose decisions are driven by some core values. In life, when your decisions are

driven by core values, you make the right decisions most of the time, and when you make the wrong decisions it is a lot easier to admit them and reverse those decisions. Value-driven leaders have love for their people. They serve fellow citizens with compassion. They are patriotic. They put the nation first and not their personal or party interest. Values-driven leaders rise above ethnic and religious divides.

  - Values are critical to vision setting. Values of the leaders are often developed through social agents such as family, school, religion and society, largely influencing the social well-being of the leaders.
  - The bedrock of a prosperous nation and future leaders is the value system of society. This underpins the workings of the society, shapes the attitude and character of its people and defines its leadership and what is acceptable or not in that society, the attitude to work and the choices that the leaders make.

- **Competence**. This quality is about the capacity and ability to lead and to serve. Intellectual robustness helps but it is not essential. Ability to read, understand, communicate effectively, reason, address issues and deliver on the vision.
- **Continuity**. This quality is essential for success and sustainability. The system/structure must provide for or allow for continuity in implementing the plans, programmes and policies of government across all levels. Across Nigeria, thousands of abandoned projects initiated by federal, state and local governments have effectively tied down billions of naira in value. This is sad in a country that badly needs to see results from resources. Nigeria should adopt a model where the political party is stronger than the candidate. Lagos State is not too far from achieving this but needs a strong economic structure to complement the relatively strong political structure that has provided some level of continuity. There is no point in spending so heavily on any political structures or machines where the economy is not gaining as well as the politics.

A new code of conduct for public officers and guidelines for elections

Developed democracies place a premium on a code of conduct for public officers. This is for good reason, as vigilance is the eternal price of freedom. In my experience, a high government official or politician in Nigeria is required to declare his or her assets at the beginning of a term of office and at the end. For a great number of public officers and civil servants, this is about the full extent of their engagement. In this day and age we need to adopt best practices from other places and get basic laws and records in place to make this aspect of public life a working reality. Countries such as Canada, Switzerland, Germany and the US already operate these standards in public conduct.

- There needs to be a registry of gifts given to occupiers of public office. The register must include the identity of the giver, the value of the gift and the identity of the recipient.
- There needs to be a limit to the value of gifts to public officials. A belt or a bag may be acceptable but a private jet is not. Some countries have a store into which these gifts go and only release the gifts to the intended recipient after their term of office.
- Independence for staff of the body charged with enforcing these standards should be enshrined in the law. In the past, political interference has reduced public confidence in the process of ensuring compliance. There must be provision for putting indictment for public officers protected by immunity clauses under seal until the term of such officials has expired.
- Although there are provisions for funding of political parties and candidates in Nigeria's new Electoral Act 2022, there are lessons still for Nigeria to draw from other nations to address the observed anomalies:
  - Make the funding model transparent and parties/candidates accountable. Have a mechanism in place to enforce the new electoral law.
  - Political parties should submit their spending reports to the INEC, which should publicize them.
  - Parties should explore the diverse financing options and reduce their reliance on party members elected or

appointed to government offices and 'investors' who see politics as a business and expect to receive some funds or favours as a return on their investment.

- Non-governmental organizations (NGOs) and media should actively engage public awareness and hold political parties and their candidates to account.

The case for voter education in local languages and electronic voting

Credible and non-partisan NGOs should actively participate in nationwide voter education, aimed at reducing electoral fraud and increasing citizens' participation in the electoral process. It is important that education materials are in local languages and are simple to understand, given the level of illiteracy in the country.

Electronic voting, particularly for the diaspora, should become a national priority. In the course of the last 60 years, Nigeria has come to have over 12 million citizens in the diaspora. This population has some of the best-trained Nigerians and therefore constitutes an invaluable resource to the country. According to data published by the World Bank and which was echoed by credible newspapers in Nigeria, including *The Punch*, the Nigerian diaspora remitted over $65 billion to Nigeria between 2018 and 2020.[1]

Going forward, Nigerians in the diaspora must be given the option of electronic voting using a central server. The advances in technology of today are such that no excuse is tenable for not allowing Nigerians in the diaspora to exercise their franchise. It is a matter of both political and moral justice to ensure that the voices of these Nigerians are heard, and it will be a landmark development when Nigerians can cast their votes wherever they are in the world.

The age of proportional representation?

All over the world the electoral systems as we know them are undergoing reforms and every democratic system is aiming for a

---

[1] https://punchng.com/nigerians-in-diaspora-remit-65-34bn-in-three-years/

greater measure of efficiency. In Europe, for example, proportional representation has been introduced to alleviate some deficiencies in democracy.

What is proportional representation? Basically, it is a system that ensures that every voter, every vote and every demographic counts. Proportional representation is not designed to be mathematically exact in the representation of political opinion but it works towards the ideal of proportional representation. The current system we operate, which often rewards the winner by bare majority, encourages a winner-takes-all approach.

The idea can work in a variety of ways but a good starting point might be in how representatives are elected into the various legislative houses. Thus, if Party A won at the polls with a majority of about 52% of total votes cast, there would still be room for about 48% of the other parties in the running of the assembly and therefore of the society.

Another pragmatic approach to proportional representation may be to reserve, say, 10% of the seats in an assembly for highly skilled technocrats who are not necessarily aligned with existing political parties and who may in fact be running as independent candidates. This would solve the current problem where party leaders reward candidates with deep pockets rather than candidates with requisite skills for building the society or the economy.

The executive arm of government can also utilize proportional representation by ensuring that vital portfolios are always reserved for technocrats rather than handed to party stalwarts as a reward for party loyalty. The point is that proportional representation ensures that all shades of electoral choices are reflected in policies, programmes and developments, and not just the choices of the ruling parties or godfathers.

Overhauling the political system: time for the home-grown model

In developing countries, including Nigeria, holding public officers and politicians accountable has not been an easy or successful exercise due to a combination of factors: the governance system, level of education, level of poverty, a press that is not independent and which relies mainly on advertisements from government or government-controlled companies, sponsored NGOs and the possibility of being targeted or victimized by government or government agencies. Businessmen whose companies rely on government policies or patronage have seen their companies targeted and some newspapers have had close down because adverts were withdrawn or cancelled when they tried to hold public figures accountable. And yet the ability to hold public figures accountable is one of the pillars on which democracy is built.

It is therefore important that systems are built into the governance structure, backed by law, to ensure some level of accountability. One such system is for the main opposition to have a shadow cabinet as well as a weekly forum (question time) where questions are asked and government is held accountable. A shadow cabinet has an added benefit in the sense that it significantly reduces or eliminates the one-year learning period for a new cabinet. At the moment, most administrations are only productive for two years in a four-year term. This is because the first year is spent learning and understanding the ministry, government, the staff and agencies, while the fourth year is spent preparing and planning for the next election.

In the same vein, the consensus is that the American-style presidential system has proven too expensive for Nigeria. Can we learn from Italy and reduce the number of legislators we have in parliament? Can we insist on a limit to the number of executive aides that attend to the president, governors and local government chairmen?

The country has several bad laws on the books – some inherited from the colonizer and some legislated locally by Nigerians themselves. It is time to have a system in place, like the Swiss, for citizens to be able to challenge any legislation within a stipulated period of passing through parliament and before executive assent.

It is time for us in Nigeria, like Singapore, to have a policy in place, for women especially, to have access to free and compulsory education and for those appointed to the cabinet to have a track record of excellent performance. Women's participation and representation in local, state and national political arrangements should be backed by policy.

No earthly condition is permanent. Our leaders and stakeholders must respond to the youth bulge in our demographics with a more inclusive approach so that young voices are heard and heeded in the reckoning of our political future. Our system must now prioritize bringing every hand to deck and harnessing the energy and vibrancy of the youth to national growth and development. A great society is one that hears out every segment of the population. We now have, for the first time, the ability and technology to make this happen.

Rising to the occasion: a time to act

While a poll would identify leadership as one of the main issues affecting or delaying Africa's and indeed Nigeria's development, I would argue that, from my experience at the NLI, in the diaspora and in the government, Nigeria is not short of competent leaders. We have leaders in abundance in Nigeria and the diaspora. What we lack is political leadership. The question we then must address is: why does a nation that has abundant, credible and intellectually robust leaders who excel in the diaspora have poor political leadership at home? This should be addressed as a pressing and current challenge.

Nigeria today is a country where visionary leadership and values-driven governance need to happen together. Leadership that positively inspires the population, leadership that rises to the moment and that makes the dream of strength in its diversity come true.

I have tried to show in this chapter what the benchmarks are in governance and leadership from all across the world. If we are mostly in agreement that the status quo is not delivering the dividends of democracy or optimizing our economic potential as a country, then we have some serious questions to ask ourselves and very definite steps to take.

Do we retain the presidential system currently in operation with changes to address the issues of our time? Do we effect wholesale change and adopt the parliamentary system of government where the opposition is more active and ready to govern immediately after any election? Do we, after serious deliberations, come up with our own mixed presidential/parliamentary system that brings out the best in both together in a unique Nigerian way?

We may decide to continue running the presidential system with modifications or the parliamentary system with adaptations. We may have a hybrid of the two systems. What matters is that the energies of our population at home and in the diaspora come together for the much-awaited transformation of our country. If China did it in three decades, we most definitely can achieve it over a shorter period. But the journey of a thousand miles begins with the first step.

Chapter 2

The fundamentals: political, economic and social institutions

> *'There is a strong synergy between economic and political institutions. Nations fail when they have extractive (weak) economic institutions, supported by extractive political institutions that impede and even block economic growth.'*
>
> **Daron Acemoglu and James Robinson, in *Why Nations Fail***

Once, after the Second World War had just ended, an American tourist in rural England had an encounter with wry English humour. When the tourist asked his local guide whether any great men were born there, the old guide paused in his stride, turned to the American slowly and said, very thoughtfully, 'No. Only babies.'

There is a profound lesson in this seemingly ordinary exchange. The natural tendency is to admire great results, outstanding talent and effective methods even as we overlook necessary processes. But just as great men were once infants, nurtured and trained into mature and productive adults, institutions generally start weak and only become firm with nurture and discipline. Globally, it has been proven that solid and functioning institutions promote growth and reduce poverty. This is true of all countries and particularly true in developing countries. Strong institutions enable societal transformation by providing a conducive environment for policy implementation and sustainable development programmes.

We will be considering the three central institutions leading Nigeria and the opportunities that these have in actualizing the nation's potential. The leading institutions are political, economic and social. When these are robust, they provide stability, sustain values, promote peaceful conduct in the nation and lead to prosperity. Most social institutions are established as mechanisms to control social behaviour and produce talent for the political and economic institutions. Economic institutions control and regulate the material necessities of people; political institutions control the basic functioning of society through formal agents such as the judiciary, the executive and the legislature. In this chapter we will also consider the increasing importance of NGOs and their institutional contributions.

All institutions are essential, but some are so systemically critical that they cannot be allowed to fail. These systemically vital institutions will differ from country to country and from time to time. Still, they must be identified and given the special attention they deserve for the good of society. For example, there is a need to prioritize and build the political institutions that support and enhance the democratic system and ensure the adherence to the rule of law, and economic institutions that drive economic growth, investment and regulate the economic and trade environment so that efficiency, transparency and fairness are the norms in society. Social institutions such as education, health and family are also generally regarded as systemically critical institutions.

We need to make political offices unattractive for private material gain but ennobling as largely selfless service to society. Across the board we need to adopt and enforce the Financial Reporting Council's (FRC's) Nigeria Corporate Code of Governance (NCCG) for the public sector. Why must critical appointments such as ambassadors, heads of parastatals, board members, etc. go to party members as 'dividends of democracy'? That is not the dividend of democracy. The reward of democracy should be *good governance*, which benefits all, not just a small group of politicians. Society needs to institutionalize the appointment of experienced technocrats to key ministries (Finance, MITI, Petroleum, Agriculture, Justice and Foreign Affairs). The Obasanjo administration started this process, which was continued and expanded by the Goodluck Jonathan administration, but unfortunately jettisoned by other administrations. A president is only as good as his or her team. Therefore, systemically critical institutions must be reinforced and protected.

There is an urgent need to change our understanding of public service through education and campaign. It is a calling and an opportunity to serve humanity, particularly fellow Nigerians – a call to serve life effectively and successfully.

Countries differ in their economic success because of their different institutions, the rules influencing how the economy works and the incentives that motivate them. North and South Korea are examples. Institutions also have an essential redistributive role to play in the economy – they ensure that resources are appropriately allocated and that the poor or those with fewer economic resources are protected. They also encourage trust by providing policing and justice systems that adhere to ordinary laws.

In developing countries, institutions strongly affect economic development in society at all levels. They determine the volume of interactions available, the benefits from trade and the form they can take. Our economy, development, quality of life and life expectancy depend upon the quality of our institutions. The performance-monitoring unit within the presidency (or the governor's office) may also have a risk management team. Part of the team's job should include identifying systemically important institutions, what can go wrong, the risks and mitigants and generally managing the identified risks.

According to the United Nations, good governance has eight major characteristics. It is participatory, follows rule of law, is transparent, responsive, consensus-oriented, equitable and inclusive, as well as effective, efficient and accountable. This means being responsive to the present and future needs of society; corruption is minimised; and the voices of minorities, the most vulnerable and poor people in the society are heard and acted upon by the decision-makers. Institutions are assigned these roles in society, and their strength or effectiveness determines whether or not the society is well governed.

Some challenges

There is enough evidence to show that, whereas institutions have played a more significant role in the economic development of several East Asian countries, in Africa they are weaker and ineffective because of poor law enforcement, incompetent leadership, heavy political interference in the appointment of leaders of the institutions, mismanagement, absence of strong civil society and weak press. Even where a competent leader is appointed, they may not be able to deliver if the environment is not conducive. An atmosphere may not be conducive when the person leading the institution does not have the resources to perform, the full support and protection of the political leaders and where there is no reward for performance or integrity.

History and research have shown that countries fail because they have been ruled by a narrow elite, mainly the political class that has organized the society and institutions for their benefit at the expense of the vast mass of their people. In such environments there are no incentives for those few who control such political power to build vital institutions. The result is that a few get more prosperous and the majority and country become poorer and poorer. This is not a sustainable model and there are examples in Zimbabwe, North Korea, Egypt, Sierra Leone and the Central African Republic. The challenge is for Nigeria to clearly prove through its performance and existential conditions that it does not belong to such a category.

The process of strengthening institutions can be difficult and requires sacrifice for the greater good of the society. Countries such as the UK and the US became rich because their citizens overthrew the elites who controlled power and thus compromised and weakened their institutions, and they created a society where political rights were much more broadly distributed, where the government was accountable and responsive to citizens, and where the great mass of the people could take advantage of economic opportunities. Although Magna Carta had been in existence as English Law since 1215, it was Britain's revolution of 1688 that transformed the politics and the economy of the nation.

Democracy relies on the support of strong, transparently independent and effective institutions. A democracy will remain weak and unable to deliver good governance if the institutions supporting it are inadequate and compromised by the political class – a situation many developing nations have found themselves in.

Political institutions

Political institutions determine the power and influence the citizens have over the political process and ensure that leaders do not deviate too far from public interest. Strong and effective political institutions prevent political leaders from organizing the economy for their private interest. Research has shown that some politicians and rulers who have the power to strengthen economic institutions do not find it in their interest to empower the citizens financially and make them financially independent. Most will *always* prioritize their personal interest over public or national interest, especially in developing economies.

We need political institutions that stamp out practices such as vote buying at general elections and the primaries, and underage voting, and that bring order and discipline to our political parties. We need political institutions that will attract the best brains in our society into politics. A society that has weak political institutions, which allow those who have no integrity and have entered politics to get rich to dominate the political space is bound to fail. It is a path of perpetual underdevelopment, poverty, corruption and insecurity.

Political party reform and local government

Our political parties have no ideology, weak internal democracy and are primarily platforms for contesting elections. As a result, there is no allegiance to the party, since you can easily move from one party to another and back again. They do not attract or retain the most credible and accomplished leaders. Most are reliant on the 'big players', such as governors or 'political investors' to finance the party. There is a lot of work to get the political parties as political institutions to deliver on the electorate's needs.

Turnout for elections is low; in the November 2021 Anambra State Gubernatorial election only 10.3% of the registered voters showed up. This was partly because most electorates believe they have been presented with bad options and therefore opted not to vote for any candidate. Political party reform is urgently required if the larger goals of political restructuring, local government autonomy and fiscal federalism are to be realized.

Local governments are part of political institutions. There are 774 local government areas in Nigeria, all listed in the Nigerian Constitution. The Constitutions of Nigeria from 1960 to 1999 (with amendments) provide for three legislative lists, which regulate the three tiers of government – federal, state and local government. The Exclusive list contains items that only the federal government can legislate upon, such as the Nigerian military and police, the ports and railways, and the Nigerian currency. The Concurrent list contains items over which the federal and state governments can legislate, such as taxes, roads, education and health. Where there is a conflict between the federal and the state governments on a matter on the Concurrent list, the federal government prevails.

As amended, Schedule IV of the 1999 Constitution contains the responsibilities of a local government council. The responsibilities include:

> 'The construction and maintenance of roads, streets, street lightings, drains and other public highways, parks, gardens, open spaces... assessment of privately owned houses or tenements to levy such rates as may be prescribed by the House of Assembly... the provision and maintenance of primary, adult and vocational education... development of agriculture and natural resources [and] the provision and maintenance of health services.'

The items listed in Schedule IV are known as the Residuary list. Unfortunately, even these are constantly intruded upon by federal and state governments to raise revenue. The net effect is that local government authorities do not have the financial resources to provide services necessary in every community.

Furthermore, the states conduct elections for the local governments, but it is often a selection rather than a free and fair election. Positions are 'shared' with party 'faithfuls' and those loyal to political leaders or state governors. Many are incompetent and illiterate. The norm is for the party controlling the state to 'win' all the positions contested at the local government level.

Added to the above is the poor funding of local government authorities. Monthly allocations are made from the Federation Account to the federal, state and local governments based on a formula. Still, the grants to the local governments are paid to the state governments and never get to their intended target.

Based on the research conducted by Acemoglu and Robinson (2012), bad institutions are very persistent and there is no natural process to eliminate them.[2] The effort to make the change from bad to good institutions must be deliberate, properly planned and executed.

Recommendations:

- Complete reform of the election bodies (they are political institutions too) at the state level to make them independent and more competent, or allow the INEC to conduct local government elections.
- Mass education: the electorate must hold the governors and local governments accountable. This requires continuous education of the electorate in english and local languages.

[2] J.A. Robinson & D. Acemoglu, *Why Nations Fail* (2012).

Political elites also need to understand that weak political institutions at the local government level can only contribute to their failure at the state level.

- Amend the law and fund local governments directly. Local governments must be mandated to have quarterly town hall meetings to report on the progress they are making and to take and respond to questions from their constituents. Representatives of that local government at the state and federal levels should also attend such meetings.
- There should be a code of conduct and effective governance for local governments. The code of conduct must be monitored and enforced.

Economic institutions

Economic institutions determine the economic incentive and drivers, plus the incentive to invest, save, to be educated and acquire the relevant skills to innovate, acquire and develop new technologies that will make the society prosperous. Economic institutions supply society with the bare necessities of existence, such as food, shelter, clothing and other necessities of life. They also guarantee the country's material prosperity.

They are also responsible for several areas of the economy. Some economic institutions are responsible for fiscal and monetary policies, the real sectors, investments, competitiveness, contracts and contract enforcement, protection of property rights, the rule of law, and financial markets. Major economic institutions include the Internal Revenue Service (the government tax-collection agency), the Central Bank, government economic ministries and their agencies, and the National Bureau of Statistics.

Economic institutions determine the costs of financial transactions. They spur development in the form of contracts and contract enforcement, standard commercial codes and increased availability of information, all of which reduce the costs of transactions, risk and uncertainty, protection of property rights and the rule of law. Economic institutions also determine whether or not powerful elites are allowed to dominate economic exchange and limit development. Strong economic institution will deliver or assist in providing:

- Property rights
- Political stability
- Honest government
- A dependable legal system
- Competitive and open markets
- Strong economy
- Equal economic opportunities

This raises various questions. Have our economic institutions delivered on these objectives? Has the political class compromised them? Have they produced a conducive environment for businesses to thrive and attract investors? Have they shown consistently strong economic growth and macroeconomic stability? Have they constantly created low unemployment and poverty rate, with a high income per capita?

The answers to these questions should prompt us to adopt and enforce the NCCG in the public sector, embrace meritocracy, set key performance indicators (KPIs) for the economic institutions and engage in periodic reviews of performance. This involves economic institutions at the federal, state and local government levels.

A view of Botswana

I paid a working visit to Botswana while I was a minister in the Nigerian government. There, I learnt how they strengthened the institution for consumer protection and was given a tour of the diamond processing plant. Suffice it to say, it was an eye-opening experience on multiple levels. The discovery of diamonds did not instigate the kind of decline in society that the discovery of oil did in some other parts of Africa. I put this down to the quality of governance and economic institutions in Botswana. These gems' extraction, cutting, polishing and setting provided good jobs and revenues for Government. The government got the most qualified person, an African but not a Motswana, to head what would be the equivalent of the Federal Competition and Consumer Protection Commission in Nigeria. The social impact was also clearly visible. Batswana were happy to stay and be educated in Botswana compared to their Nigerian contemporaries, who have become economic immigrants in many countries.

All these were important lessons for me, and the take-home was that we would do well to add value to our commodities and that meritocracy was essential for success. Botswana was once one of the poorest countries in the world at independence in 1966. It had only 12 kilometres of paved roads, 22 citizens who graduated from university and 100 from secondary school! Botswana now has the highest per capita income in Sub-Saharan Africa and is at the same level as prosperous eastern European countries such as Hungary.

How did they achieve this? By developing inclusive economic and political institutions after independence. Since then it has been democratic, holds regular and competitive elections and has never experienced civil war or military intervention. The government set up strong economic institutions enforcing property rights, ensuring macroeconomic stability and encouraging the development of an inclusive market economy. Even though they have a large mining industry, they have not been plagued with the corruption associated with extractive industries.

Looking inwards: the case of Lagos and Bayelsa

As mentioned earlier, Lagos State has achieved a measure of political continuity and success in the last 21 years. To an extent this is also true of Bayelsa State. In both instances the same political party has controlled political offices since the return to democratic rule in 1999. What remains to be seen is the transformation of the economic base of these two states. Change in this regard will depend largely on the strength of the economic institutions.

Bayelsa State is the site of Oloibiri Oilfield, where oil was first discovered in Nigeria and, as of 2015, was estimated to produce between 30% and 40% of the country's oil. Bayelsa State has over 30% of the gas reserves in Nigeria. It also has arable land that farmers dream of, particularly oil palm, rice, etc. An investor presented a credible plan to me when I was the Minister of Industry, Trade and Investment on how Bayelsa could be turned into a palm State like Malaysia. The company was willing to co-invest with the government to realize this goal. All the government needed to turn Bayelsa into another Singapore in Nigeria was to have strong political and economic institutions that would create the right environment, build enabling infrastructure, such as an airport, a seaport, roads, good hotels, and assure continuity.

Singapore had nothing, no commodities, land, people, money, but Lee Kuan Yew was able to transform Singapore from a third-world economy to a first-world economy within 30 years. This saw its GDP per capita skyrocket to one of the highest in the world. Given that Lagos and Bayelsa states have also had some level of continuity of political leadership like Singapore, is it not fair to ask why we have not seen the same level of transformation or at least signs that the transformation is about to happen after 21 years? It is all down to the strength and quality of the political and economic institutions.

Ideally each state should have a 30-year development plan that clearly sets out its vision for the state and how to get there. It should be reviewed every four or five years to determine how far the state has gone in implementing the plan, what needs to be revised, etc. Everyone in the state should know about the plan and be excited about it. It is the plan for their state and, as critical stakeholders, they should buy into that plan. They should also understand their role in helping to achieve that plan and should get regular updates on the progress the state is making. The State Assembly should enact a law to support it and make it impossible for any new administration to deviate from the plan. We understand that Lagos State has such a plan but how many Lagosians know about it, and how involved were they in developing the plan? What is the progress made to date and how often is it reviewed and updated?

Social institutions

Social institutions are mechanisms for social order, focusing on meeting social needs, such as government, economy, education, family, healthcare and religion. These are regarded as essential to maintaining social order in society.

Formal education, health and religion are also fundamental aspects of any society and the direction these take generally determine the trajectory of the particular society involved.

The federal government took a significant essential step on 19 May 2022 when President Buhari signed a law establishing the National Health Insurance Authority. It is estimated that about 85 million people regarded as poor or vulnerable will benefit from this scheme when fully implemented. A healthy nation is a productive nation. The level, consistency of funding, governance and management structure, quality of appointments, and the successful enrolment of eligible citizens across the country will largely determine the quality of implementation. Nevertheless, the government should be complimented for taking this first significant step. The National Orientation Agency and National Broadcasting Commission, among others, are critical social institutions directly funded by the government.

Have our social institutions produced leaders with competence and the values enshrined in the constitution, our national anthem and the pledge? Chief Obafemi Awolowo once said, 'Any system of education which does not help a man to have a healthy and sound body and alert brain, and balanced and disciplined instinctive urges, is both misconceived and dangerous.' And still on education, Nelson Mandela said, 'Education is the great engine of personal development. Through education, the daughter of a peasant can become a doctor, the son of a mine worker can become the head of the mine, and a child of farm workers can become the president of a great nation. What we make out of what we have, not what we are given, separates one person from another.' These are all to emphasize the importance of the educational system as a critical part of the social institutions that nations must build to succeed.

The family is also a critical part of a nation's social institution. The family's primary role is to nourish its members, protect them, educate them and provide a stable social status. I am what I am today because of the upbringing I had at home and the school that I attended. The environment in which individuals grow up, learn and socialize is essential precisely because it has been shown to affect their prospects later in life. My parents instilled two things in my siblings and I when we were growing up and that they repeated regularly. They told us that they were training us and investing heavily in our education to ensure that we could speak and be heard by our peers anywhere in the world. The second point they regularly made borders on financial independence. They reminded us that they were giving us the necessary tools required through education to be self-sufficient so that when we give to each other as siblings, it is borne out of love, not out of necessity.

They were both completely detribalized. We spoke Yoruba and English at home, but my father spoke or understood at least five other Nigerian languages including Hausa, Nupe, and the local Owo dialect. Our mother, Eunice Omolola, was a princess of Ijebu-Owo, Owo, in Ondo State. Our father was a civil servant who travelled widely and worked in different parts of Nigeria. We were taught that 'wherever you are and happy is your home'. The principle was simple: you cannot and should not be a stranger in your home. The moment you become a stranger, it is no longer your home.

That, to some extent, explains why there are Agangas in Botswana, the UK, Canada, the US and in five states in Nigeria – Lagos, Ondo, Kwara, Edo and Ekiti, all from the same family. There are other families with inter-ethnic and international identities, such as Oshodi, Doherty, Disu, etc., all families with a predominantly Lagos association. Some of my nieces and nephews, for example, are from Botswana (Batswana). But regardless of the tribe, state or country, the common thread that joins us all together and that defines an Aganga are the values of excellence, integrity and service, which were passed down from generation to generation led by our great grandfather, who was in the judiciary and worked as an interpreter to the British. After all, Aganga, according to the dictionary of Yoruba personal names, means 'he who stands his ground in a good cause'.

Birthday letters were a constant feature of my childhood and young adulthood. The letters my mother wrote to us on our birthdays were long, about 15 pages, unfailing. When she passed away, the letter she was writing to one of my older sisters, who was already married and had children, was found on her table. No one was too old to be disciplined or rebuked when you did anything wrong. The carefully constructed and well-articulated letters for our birthdays were our unique gifts from her. The letters were warm and maternal, but they were also a lens through which we could assess our lives during the past year, as observed by my mother. She praised us for what we did well and pointed out areas we needed to improve upon. At an early age she insisted I listened to the news with her from the radio and we would discuss what we heard after the news. Then she would give me three daily newspapers for that day, ask me to read the same story or news item in the papers and then tell her which writing or reporting I preferred and why!

We were taught that contentment is the biggest wealth anyone can have. Of course, we were expected to excel academically, we knew that any grade outside grade one was a failure, but, for our parents, academic excellence was not enough. We also had to participate and excel in sports and other extracurricular activities. For example, every child had to join the Boys Scout or Girl Guides, or Boys Brigade or Red Cross. My mother was a proud member and officer of the Girl Guides and Red Cross. Joining any of these organizations played a major part in our development. At an early stage in our lives, we were taught to be disciplined, patriotic, compassionate, to have integrity, to always do our best, to serve our communities and so many other values.

It was not enough to attend Sunday church services regularly; we were all expected to be in the school choir and also play a role in the church. Our family Christmas carol services were always special because we sang different parts in the choir and were all familiar with the hymns. With benefit of hindsight, I now have a better understanding of why the Bishop of Lagos, Bishop Adetiloye spent some time talking about how my mother left her legacy in the lives of her children and the people she came into contact with, during her funeral at the Cathedral Church of Christ, Marina, Lagos. She followed politics, albeit she was not a politician. Our mother's favourite pet dog was named Lumumba, in memory of Patrice Lumumba, the first prime minister of the Republic of the Congo, who was killed in 1961 at the age 35. Needless to say that she was an Awoist. She loved and took us to watch Ogunde, Duro-Ladipo and Ogungbe plays several times. There were moral lessons in those plays at the time, which she always brought to our attention.

Our father was a complete gentleman and a humble man with friends across the social ladder. He was close to his bosses and peers, who were mainly British, and to his juniors. Both of our parents were caring and generous to a fault. The family institution provides the solid foundation upon which secondary school education and experience builds. These two fundamental institutions form the cornerstone of the larger social institutions and are needed for a child's and a nation's development. Again, parents play an important role in the school selection process. So, when it came to selecting the secondary school I went to, it was not by accident that I ended up in Christ's School Ado-Ekiti. My Mother ranked Christ School ahead of King's College and Igbobi College both in Lagos and persuaded me that it was worth travelling from Lagos to Ado-Ekiti to get a well rounded education that would prepare me for the world. Don't get me wrong, King's College and Igbobi College are excellent schools but Christ School ticked all the boxes at the time. Apart from the strong academic track record, Christ's School had a strong reputation for discipline, character formation and a well-balanced school curriculum that also emphasized spiritual development. The school was known for producing well-behaved and academically bright students who got into and excelled in universities across the country and abroad. It produced many internationally acclaimed scholars and professionals in medicine, law, engineering, architecture, humanities, etc. It is not surprising that today, of all the secondary schools in Nigeria, Christ's School has the highest percentage (10%) of those awarded the Nigeria National Order of Merit. This is Nigeria's highest academic award conferred on distinguished academicians and intellectuals who have made outstanding contributions to academia, growth and development of Nigeria.

It was never my intention to write so much about my family and my personal life when I started writing this chapter. The main point I wanted to get across is the importance of the family institution as part of the social institutions in the life of the individual and in the success of a nation. It is therefore important that there are deliberate policies to promote and support these institutions and educate the citizens about their importance. In some countries there is family support to encourage parents to spend more time with their children at home. The European Union (EU), for example, allows workers with children under the age of eight to apply for flexible working arrangements in order to spend more time with their children. Policies like this recognize the importance of family to a functional state.

The rock of the nation is built upon families. For Nigeria to build a sound and prosperous future, this future must be built upon well-reasoned policies to strengthen the family unit. Policies that emphasize the need for holistic education. Policies that enhance intra-family relationships such as those that provide room for parents, in an increasingly fast-paced world, the space and time to spend quality time with their children to aid their development. In today's world the letter may be written and sent by hand or by email. Never underestimate the impact of a long letter from a loving mother. These unguarded moments are the makings of a man. They are the makings of a woman. They are the ties that bind a family. They are the fuel that has the power to drive forward our society.

NGOs

NGOs are critical institutions and they play a vital role in strengthening political, economic and social institutions by monitoring and reporting their activities, effectiveness and inefficiencies to the general public. They are also influential advocates for the poor, the marginalized and members of society who are discriminated against. Their ultimate goal is the creation of a good society that is progressive, where there is equal opportunity, equity, justice and fairness.

Specialized NGOs often possess the latest data globally on matters such as health, education and human rights. For example, the Damien Foundation tackles two diseases globally: leprosy and tuberculosis. It has data readily accessible to the government as well as treatment protocols that reflect the scientific study of the behaviour of these diseases. Rather than reinventing the wheel, collaborating with these NGOs is a more efficient way to build capacity and achieve desirable outcomes.

However, these NGOs can only be influential if they have solid institutional frameworks. It starts with governance, which we tried to address with the NCCG. They must be openly transparent, independent and supported by local and international communities and multilateral agencies to build more robust and effective institutions. Establishing self-regulatory organizations would also help to improve their credibility, performance and ability to access local and international funds.

Role of NGOs in politics and education

In politics, NGOs help democracy work properly. This is done by making it easier for people to get information about how their country is being run, providing electorates information on the performance of the government and whether parties delivered on their manifestos, helping the public communicate with politicians, making sure people register to vote, highlighting issues around vote buying, exposing corrupt politicians and making sure that governments do not abuse their powers. They also observe and report on elections. Several NGOs do this but they have yet to affect elections significantly. NGOs such as ANAP Foundation did a terrific job getting the youths to register to vote for the 2023 elections, educating the electorate that their votes count and running opinion polls before elections. They have been very effective in this regard.

NGOs in education facilitate access to education. Their conviction is that everyone deserves to learn, no matter their tribe, culture, religion or background. They are also beginning to focus on the *quality* of education, the scope of the school curriculum and the need to make teaching a respectable and well-paid profession. NGOs have repeatedly proven that they can improve global education by encouraging local communities to teach and learn from one another.

Working with governments at the federal, state and local levels, they can target underserved children and take the required steps to reach the 15 million out-of-school children. The out-of-school children include those who are working, roaming the streets, living in slums and those whose culture prevents them from going to school. They can also address the issues of those who live in places without schools and develop programmes to train and retrain teachers.

Role of NGOs in poverty and development

NGOs also have essential roles to play in development and poverty alleviation. Since the late 1970s, NGOs have played an increasingly prominent role in the development sector, widely praised for their strengths as innovative and grassroots-driven organizations with the desire and capacity to pursue participatory and people-centred forms of development and to fill gaps left by the failure of states across the developing world in meeting the needs of their poorest citizens.

One of the areas where some NGOs have had the most significant impact in Nigeria is the economy. BudgIT has become the recognized NGO for analysing the national budget and performance, while the Tony Elumelu Foundation has had tremendous success in identifying and supporting entrepreneurs across Africa. In the health sector, Dangote has partnered with the Bill & Melinda Gates Foundation on eradicating polio, and the Aig Imokhuede Foundation is beginning to make some impact in the area of governance and civil service reform. TechnoServe, a US non-profit organization with a presence in over 30 countries including Nigeria, is rated as the number-one NGO in the world in applying business solutions to reducing poverty.

A Nigerian experiment from 2010 to 2015

In the second term of President Olusegun Obasanjo in office, he made deliberate efforts to strengthen some critical institutions and ministries by appointing technocrats to head these institutions and ministries. President Goodluck Jonathan adopted this approach and had technocrats with relevant experience, exposure and local and international expertise handling these systemically important portfolios. The president set their goals and protected them from political interference.

The results were evident in the stable macroeconomic conditions of that period. Inflation averaged 7%, and food prices were affordable. The foreign exchange rate stabilized between ₦150 to ₦165, and Nigeria became the number-one investment destination in Africa and recorded the highest number of state visits by foreign heads of state. This confirms the link between strong institutions and the economy and was true between 2010 and 2015.

Drilling down further, we see how consistency in policy is a positive force in institutional memory. Even the active politicians in the Federal Executive Council (FEC) were competent and generally accomplished individuals.

President Goodluck Jonathan placed a lot of emphasis on meritocracy but he ensured that the federal character principle was not compromised. This is essential in a diverse and plural country like Nigeria. Competence was the absolute gold standard. Mr Remi Babalola, a highly disciplined and professional agricultural economist, banker and chartered accountant, and Alhaja Yabawa Lawan Wabi, another accountant and former Accountant-General of Borno State, were my two ministers of state in the Ministry of Finance at different times.

At the MITI, we had highly competent and cerebral CEOs and directors in the ministry and in the parastatals. In Chapter 3, we talk about how we transformed the MITI, but it came down to great people. Once leadership and capacity with accountability were introduced, the game changed.

Nigeria became the number-one investment destination because the relevant institutions all played their part well. Customs, for example, quadrupled in revenue. Under Arunma Oteh, the stock exchange was revamped, with Oscar Onyema increasing confidence in the market while introducing transparency and automation. Under Abraham Nwankwo, the Debt Management Office (DMO) successfully established a viable presence for Nigeria in the international capital market (ICM) with a series of Eurobond issuances, thus opening a new path for investment inflows. As Minister of Finance, I personally led the deal roadshow for the debut issuance in 2011.

In finance, we initiated the SWF after decades of producing oil. With the FRC, we developed the Nigerian code of corporate governance and ensured that all financial statements complied with International Financial Reporting Standards. This made it easier for investors to enter the capital market. The Consumer Protection Council became active, and there was a heavy focus on consumer protection; we changed the scope of the agency to include fair trading and competition.

During this period we had several complaints from international and local investors about monopoly and unfair trading, and the micro, small and medium enterprise (MSME) sector complained about the lack of equal access to finance. These are some of the symptoms of weak economic institutions and they were the catalyst for accelerating the expansion of the scope and change of name of the formal Consumer Protection Council to include competition and fair trading. A bill was submitted to the National Assembly to effect the changes. The Bank of Industry (BOI) was also capitalized and restructured to prioritize making loans to MSMEs at single digits. None of these would have happened without having competent people at the helm of affairs of these economic institutions, getting the right support, and lack of interference from the political elites.

Social infrastructure

I remember how my plans for celebrating Christmas in Nigeria in 2010 went. I had been away building a career in Europe for most of my adult life. Although I had family and friends in Nigeria, it had been years and years since I last celebrated Christmas in Nigeria. So I planned a modest lunch and perhaps a visit with a family friend later in the day. It was not to be. Diezani Alison Madueke, my colleague in the Federal Executive, knew very well that this would likely be my first Christmas away from my family back in the UK and insisted that I join her family for lunch. The unforgettable Dr Dora Akunyili also ensured that I reacquainted myself with Nigeria properly. Their thoughtfulness and kindness at the time made my settling back in Nigeria so much easier than it would have otherwise been. In many ways these colleagues brought back memories of Nigerian hospitality as I knew it. There is something to be said for Nigerian conviviality on these special occasions.

Recommendations

Although this chapter already contains several recommendations, I would advocate that the following are prioritized and implemented without delay:

- The FRC of Nigeria must issue the NCCG for the public sector and NGOs as soon as possible, after due consultations. The NCCG for the private sector has been issued and has strengthened corporate governance in this sector.
- The National Assembly should amend the acts that established the agencies and parastatals to make the adoption of the code mandatory for the public sector.
- In addition, the acts should specify the skills, competence and experience (number of years in the profession) required to chair and sit on the board and to be appointed the head (CEO, director-general, etc.), a director and executives of an agency. That was one of the strategies employed to have strong governance and effective leadership at the SWF (Nigeria Sovereign Investment Authority [NSIA]) and which regulators such as PenCom (the National Pension Commission) have used effectively to regulate the pension industry, which is now one of the best regulated sectors. Appoint a commissioner for public appointments to regulate all appointments to the boards and the CEOs of all public institutions. The commissioner and members of the committee will ensure that such appointments are made on merit after a fair, open and transparent process.
- Beyond the Nigerian landscape, African countries should endeavour to establish effective, responsive and democratic institutions that promote accountable and transparent governance and sustainable socio-economic development. The policymakers should concentrate on developing rules and regulations that improve the quality of public institutions in their countries.
- The National Assembly and State Houses of Assembly, working with the Executive, have an important role to play in this. They should review all the laws setting up existing institutions and ensure that only competent people with the required experience and proven integrity can be appointed as the head and executives of the institution and sit on the board. They should remove duplicated roles and ensure an agency is assigned to each of the functions of the political, economic and social institution.

- The Executive should immediately undertake a programme of institutional reform at the state and federal levels. There should be clarity in the mandate of each institution and about how their performance will be determined and monitored going forward.
- There is a need for a complete reform of the social institutions, in particular the education and health sectors, to ensure that every Nigerian has access to good and affordable healthcare, all Nigerians have access to free and qualitative basic education up to secondary school level at least, and that a new financing model is developed for these sectors. School curricula should also address social issues such as corruption, patriotism, religious and ethnic tolerance, etc. The religious organizations, as part of social institutions, should also be engaged to perform these roles as well.

Chapter 3

The backbone of government: civil service

'You must have a structure in your society which makes learning and hard work rewarding. If you have a system where the chap who cuts corners is a man who gets rich and the man who works hard is the chap who is a mug, then you will fail. That is what is wrong in many countries that have not succeeded.'

Lee Kuan Yew

Leaving London, and Goldman Sachs, to take up responsibility as Minister for Finance in Nigeria was a major decision. I was leaving the corporate world where I had worked for about three decades, for another world that was also my own but was unknown to me in appreciable detail. I knew that I was now going into the public sphere for public service. I knew I was going to work with civil servants and I was going to have to adapt to a different set of rules of engagement. Was I ready?

I had cancelled my flight to Nigeria on the morning of my scheduled departure for Lagos. It had first taken a phone call from Chief Olusegun Obasanjo, a respected elder statesman and former president of Nigeria, and an extended conversation with my trusted friend of many decades Oye Hassan-Odukale, to persuade me to call the travel agency back to restore my ticket for the scheduled flight to Nigeria. Oye focused more on my wife and children, addressed all their concerns and gave necessary assurances to get them to buy into the idea and allay their fears. The decision was that big for me; not one that could be taken lightly. Dr Christopher Kolade, a former high commissioner to the UK, and a mentor, and Oby Ezekwesili, who was working closely with President Obasanjo, were also involved in the conversations and played critical roles.

In the end it was a call I could not resist, partly because, as mentioned earlier, since 2006 the NLI had championed the cause of value-centred leadership in Nigeria. Ideals and ideas were refined and significant, but a time comes when one must put one's foot to the pedal and drive home the point – the greatness in Nigeria would come about if and only if its people responded with more than words. Family and friends, colleagues at work and professional allies all had opinions about the move. Ultimately, I arrived in Nigeria with an open mind and a will to serve.

My first duty post was at the Federal Ministry of Finance where I was also the chairman of the Economic Management Team. The world was still adjusting to the international and domestic financial crises. I later had the privilege and opportunity to become the pioneer minister for the MITI after my stint at the Ministry of Finance. With the benefit of hindsight, I am happy to say that I had the opportunity to work with some of the brightest and best people one could find anywhere in the world in both federal ministries during my time. There is, obviously, much room for improvement. Still, I must state that the top civil servants I worked with not only met but often exceeded my expectations for competence and professionalism. This chapter contains my reflections on civil service generally, the agencies and parastatals that I met going in and the interconnected workings of government beyond any particular ministry. I found that I was often joined at the hip with critical ministries, departments and agencies (MDAs).

The civil service as a growth engine

When we had the first NLI class at the Grove in Hertfordshire, UK, I remember someone asking a fascinating question. This individual looked around the room, saw the passion and quality of the people and said, 'Why is our country what it is today with the quality of the people in this room?' There was no immediate response to the question, but I think we all knew what the answer was.

We were all going to have to roll up our sleeves and engage. We would have to engage in public and private spheres. For far too long, the thinking in Nigeria that the civil servant has little to do with the *development* of the country and the growth of the economy has harmed the entire country. The civil service is, in fact, a great engine that modern nations depend upon for delivering public goods and services. If the bureaucracy is understood in this light, we can provide first-rate services to the citizens. Put another way, dreams run on significant public service engines. Everything depends on the quality of the civil service, from planning pipe-borne water to cities to putting satellites in space or train tunnels through a mountain.

We need a leaner, more efficient, meritocratic and better-paid civil service in Nigeria. Getting this done is an opportunity to leapfrog and to prove that many aspects of the civil service in Nigeria and Africa generally can be improved and optimized to deliver more excellent results if proposed reforms are implemented.

The MITI and its transformation from a laid-back and hardly visible or impactful engine of growth into the main magnet for foreign investment in Nigeria and one of the main economic ministries during my time in government is proof that this can be done. The possibilities of this degree of transformation across the entire civil service in the country can only be imagined. Working with world-class benchmarks is no longer an option; it must be embraced. I have, for my part, never doubted that we could succeed in this respect and, in fact, I do believe that, with the right reforms, civil and public service in Nigeria will once again set the standards for Africa.

Encountering the Nigerian civil service

For a government to be successful, the civil service must always be apolitical, professional, embrace meritocracy, be committed to nation-building and be well paid to attract and retain the best. Government is always only as good and effective as the civil service structure on which it runs. Civil servants provide continuity and quality advice to the politicians and public servants who come and go.

There is much to be said about this aspect of excellence and continuity in this book, and we will get to that. Suffice it to say at this point that there is a beautiful tradition of the civil service in Nigeria, but in the words of the late Ambassador Olugbenga Ashiru, a career diplomat, then Minister of Foreign Affairs, the excellent cadre I met represented a 'dying breed' in the civil service. What did this mean? The career diplomats of his time were the very best that the country had to offer and they could compete with the best in the world. I can attest to that because I still met and worked closely with some of those career diplomats on my foreign trips to more than 68 countries to market Nigeria as an excellent destination for investment and to sign trade agreements. They were extremely competent, hard-working, professional, knowledgeable and played a major role in the positive image Nigeria had abroad. It started from the recruitment process, which was rigorous and inclusive. They selected some of the brightest graduates from our top universities based on merit. Each had to learn a second international language within a stated period of joining the Foreign Service and the training was impeccable and demonstrable. By the '90s, the benchmarks of Ashiru's time had all but disappeared. The standards had been compromised and heavily politicized. Values and standards entrenched from the time of such excellent civil servants as the late Chief Simeon Adebo, who distinguished himself first in Nigeria and subsequently at the United Nations, still exist but are on the decline now.

The civil service structure was a huge eye-opener for me. How much of it must be radically improved by various inputs from people to technology? How vital could the synergy between ministries and agencies be? And then there was the sheer amount of innovation that must be carried out to bring government departments to their full potential. I realized all this within weeks of assuming office as the Minister for Finance. By the time I closed the door for the last time at the MITI, I could look back at the changes my team and I had affected but also imagine how much was yet to be achieved.

At the Ministry of Finance, I had an excellent team of career civil servants led by 'super' permanent secretary Dr Ochi Achinivu and special assistants: Segun Ajakaiye (late), Bayo Adeniji, Dr Muyiwa Adedeji, Lanre Fatimilehin, Fola Oyeyinka, Bukky Alakija, Jide Iyaniwura, Yemi Babington-Ashaye and Kelechi Ekugo, who all stood out for their exceptional service. Being my first port of call in government, synergy with these unique and hard-working individuals was critical in ensuring success. I have often been asked to relate my experiences in Nigerian public service. The general impression of many is that it must be full of intrigues and compelling details. No doubt these are present, but also, and more importantly, so are the pleasant surprises of engaging a powerful bureaucratic mechanism – necessary when considering the size and complexity of a country as extensive and populous as Nigeria.

Again at MITI, the teams I worked with – young, cerebral, highly talented people who worked closely with me – and the career civil servants made all the difference. Some exceptional talents joined us from Morgan Stanley, Goldman Sachs and Freshfield in the UK as special assistants. Others came in from the International Finance Corporation, various banks in Nigeria and academia. They were just hungry to serve their country. I drew a lot of my inspiration from these bright, hard-working and selfless young Nigerians. Notable names from the team at the MITI include Ambassador Musa Abdulkadir, a seasoned permanent secretary, Bambo Kunle-Salami, Juwon Sofola, Abi Mustapha-Maduakor, Ladi Odujinrin, Oguche Agudah, Segun Ajakaiye (late), Yemi Kolapo, Lola Visser-Mabogunje, Jide Iyaniwura, Femi Boyede and Dr Biola Oseragbaje. I cannot fail to mention the very dynamic Dr Samuel Ortom, who was Minister of State at the MITI and who went on to be Governor of Benue State. It was as close to a 'dream team' as one would wish for.

This list is not exhaustive, and I shall have much to say about critical players from other ministries who also made some of the successes we recorded possible and remarkable. The MITI, particularly, as hinted at earlier, was joined at the hip with many other federal ministries, of which the Ministry of Foreign Affairs, the Ministry of Justice, the Ministry of Finance, the Ministry of Petroleum Resources, the Ministry of Mines and Steel Development, the Ministry of Agriculture and Rural Development, the Ministries of Power, Education, Science and Technology and the Ministry of Works remain prominent for various reasons. At the MITI, we were proactive and made the effort to establish good working relationships with these ministries. The synergies we created produced the bulk of the impact we recorded at home and abroad.

Facing the elephant in the room

My background in the private sector, particularly at Goldman, had already prepared me to recognize that no matter how bright you are, you are only as good as your team. Good people make great teams. Great teams accomplish goals. However, public perception of the civil service structure and civil servants generally was anything but encouraging at the time. It is generally considered that the civil service is bedevilled by a plethora of negative factors.

After assuming duty in Abuja, it did not take me long to realize that many agencies had drifted away from their original mandates.

Those still with their bearings sometimes struggled with sister agencies with overlapping directives. Someone had to clean the Augean stables. The system must attract, retain and develop the best talent in the civil service.

This is not at the federal level alone; it affects the systems and quality of the civil servants at the subnational level – state and local government. For example, state and local governments significantly affect the quality of schools, roads, hospitals and social institutions. They determine how clean or dirty your environment is. That is why we need the best people running our state and local governments.

Transforming the MITI

It is a significant privilege to serve your country. It is a rare opportunity to be in a position to make changes that will improve the lives of millions of people and help the nation truly realize its potential.

Transformation of the newly created MITI in Nigeria within the space of 47 months (July 2011 to May 2015) from the erstwhile Ministry of Commerce and Industry can provide a reform template that every MDA of government can adopt. The new ministry (MITI) had 17 parastatals under its supervision and had all the ingredients that could transform Nigeria into an 'A' grade economy.

We consulted widely in the first month at the MITI to understand the state of play. The priority during that time was to perform SWOT (strengths, weaknesses, opportunities, threats) analyses on the ministry and its parastatals. Those consulted included: the staff and directors in the different directorates of the ministry; heads and senior management of the 17 parastatals and agencies under the ministry; industry players, including the sectoral associations; and former ministers and development partners. As expected, the feedback was varied and identified several issues and opportunities to transform and reposition the ministry. Some of the issues raised are summarized below:

- An impoverished working environment. For the most part, MITI had electricity only for three to four hours daily on a good day. Some departments bought and maintained their electricity generators, paid for by the individuals. Staff members could only work a few hours a day because there was no constant electricity supply. There was grave and insufficient funding and no facilities such as computers, printers and printing ink to work with. Documents were printed at home or in business centres, etc. Cash backing for capital projects was about 25%–30% of the budget, not sufficient to carry out any capital project. The offices were in old and dilapidated buildings and the conveniences were not functional.

- No clear vision or goals and plans.
- No training programme. Some staff had received no training for more than 20 years! They just took their time, sat for the promotion exams, passed and got promoted to the next level. They were not structured or supported to become service providers to the government and the people.
- High turnover of staff within the ministries. In four years I worked with three permanent secretaries, four different trade directors and three different industry directors. They were always moved to different ministries.
- Staff complained that other ministries had taken over their mandates, and some complained about a lack of confidence. It was not clear where the mandate of one ministry, say the Ministry of Mines and Steel Development or Ministry of Agriculture and Urban Development, ended and the mandate of the MITI, responsible for manufacturing/industrialization started. So, there was always conflicts rather than collaboration between ministries.
- Departments in the ministry and the agencies worked in silos. They were not structured to deliver on their mandate to drive industrial development, trade (international, African and domestic) and the development of MSME. Investment was a new mandate, even though there was no additional funding.
- Poor relationship between the board and management of the parastatals, mainly because of the lack of clarity in their roles, benefits and entitlements and the quality of people appointed to the boards. There was a big expectation gap.
- Poor budgetary allocation. Some agencies or units within the ministry were almost dead or ineffective because of the lack of attention and support, including funding.

The industry players complained about:

- Impoverished and difficult business environment and no one taking responsibility to improve it.
- Policy 'somersault' and inconsistency. It was the first time I had encountered the word 'somersault' in this context. As a result, there was no confidence or trust in the government and the implementation of its policies, which changed with the appointment of new ministers or a change in government.
- No industrial plan, and lack of involvement in policy formulation and critical talks on trade negotiations such as the Economic Partnership Agreement (EPA) with the EU.
- The economy was weak because the MITI, which should have been the primary driver of the economy or one of the main drivers, was very weak and had not been given due recognition by various governments. There was the opportunity to restructure the ministry along the lines of similar ministries in Japan, Germany, Turkey, etc.

All told, it was not all weaknesses and issues. There were many strengths and opportunities as well. For example, the officers and staff came across as capable, hard-working, disciplined, willing and able to deliver on their mandates if given the necessary support. Most of the heads of the agencies were stars in their own right, and with time I discovered they were some of the best in government. It was a delight to work with such a highly talented group.

With the benefit of hindsight, that decision to pick the brains of all the key actors was one of the best early decisions I made in government because, among other reasons, it provided a rich bank of insight and data.

Once the exercise was completed, I wrote to the president to draw his attention to the issues and made some recommendations, and he asked for a presentation to be made to him and the relevant members of the cabinet. We immediately responded to the president, who approved all our prayers. He also directed that funds be made available to the ministry to complete a new office building, improve the working environment, address the issue of the limited supply of electricity and effect refurbishment of the building and offices, among other things. He also directed that the ministry be relocated to a temporary place if that was the best option.

These and several meetings with the staff of the ministry and heads of parastatals and their management staff led to a certain momentum and created a better and happier working environment. Over time the staff responded positively and the synergy produced:

- Restructured departments in the ministry to deliver on their mandates and contribute to the economy.
    - For example, Industrial Development under engineer Tanwa Awobokun was divided into three units: agro-allied industries, solid minerals-related industries, and oil and gas-related industries led by Dr. Francis Alaneme, Adewale Bakare and Kunle Olorode, respectively. Staff training and local and international industry visits were arranged to improve their knowledge and make them experts in their sectors. The heads of the three units compiled a comprehensive list of the companies in their sectors, visited the companies regularly to understand their operations and issues and proactively worked with them to address any issues raised. The permanent secretary organized a training programme for the staff.
    - Gbenga Kuye, the director-general of the Nigerian Export Processing Zone Authority (NEPZA), led different teams to Saudi Arabia and China to have a better understanding of how free-trade zones worked in those countries.
    - Aminu Jalal, the director-general of the Nigeria Automobile Council, led a team to South Africa to gain a better understanding of their automobile policy, how it was implemented over 40 years and lessons for Nigeria.
    - Dr Latif Busari led another team to Sudan, again to assess the implementation of its sugar cane to sugar policy, and lessons for Nigeria.
    - Juliet Onaeko led separate teams to Germany and Brazil to understand their industrial skills training programmes and how they could be adapted in Nigeria.
    - Evelyn Oputu also led a team to Brazil and had discussions with the Brazilian Development Bank, which led to a memorandum of understanding.
    - Parastatals were aligned correctly to the different departments. The trade department focused on international, African and domestic trade.

- The Nigeria Industrial Revolution Plan (NIRP) was developed, working with the Manufacturers Association of Nigeria and other industry players. NIRP is a flagship programme to industrialize Nigeria, grow and diversify the economy and significantly increase and diversify revenue sources for the government. This is based on the fact that no country has ever become rich and transitioned from a developing to a developed economy without having vibrant industrial and services sectors. The NIRP identified 13 products for the export market that could generate significant foreign income for the country.
- Each agency developed a strategic and delivery plan around the ministry's policies and programme; for example, the NIRP, the National Enterprise Development Programme (NEDEP), investment promotions, etc.
- We also developed and implemented the NEDEP, a new and strategic platform to deliver growth within Nigeria's MSMEs.
- A project was initiated to develop a new trade policy based on the NIRP and working with the industry. The last trade policy had been created ten years prior. There was not enough time to present the new trade policy at the FEC before the end of that administration, but I am delighted that the new administration has taken this on board and may soon present an updated version to the Council for approval. That is what continuity is about.
- Revitalized and strengthened the formal vehicles for consulting with the private sector on vital issues such as the EPA. The relevant ministries also joined in these meetings. They played a crucial role in our decision on EPA and policy formulation.
- New KPIs were set and agreed with the MDAs, and a new performance unit, under Ms Lola Visser-Mabogunje, was created in the minister's office to monitor and report performance. This unit was also responsible for managing relationships with the Nigerians in the diaspora.
- Weekly directors' meetings chaired by the minister or the minister of state to get an update on the policies, programmes and plans of the ministry, KPIs, issues and action required. The permanent secretary chaired the meetings in the absence of the minister or minister of state.
- Quarterly meetings of all the 17 CEOs/managing directors of the parastatals, the permanent secretary and the directors or heads of the departments in the ministry to discuss progress

made on the programmes, plans and policies of the ministry, and support required from the ministry or other agencies. The role was to deliver the MITI and its services to Nigerians as one team. In some cases, agencies such as the BOI, the Small and Medium Enterprises Development Agency of Nigeria (SMEDAN) and the Industrial Training Fund (ITF) worked together to develop the MSME sector. This promoted teamwork and assisted us in delivering as one MITI team. Again, this was the first time this had been done in the MITI.

- Following the approval of the president, we engaged with the head of service to include the ministry as one of the professional ministries. This would ensure that staff were not transferred out of the ministry regularly, that they had the opportunity to develop their expertise and support their sectors and that there would be a regular professional and funded training programme in place.
- We reclaimed the ministry's mandate from other ministries but promoted better and closer collaboration with ministries such as those dealing with mining, foreign affairs, agriculture, finance, petroleum, and power, transportation and works.
- Appointments by the president to head the agencies were based on merit/competence within the framework of federal character. There is talent in every state of the federation. Let me share a story with you on how this worked for some appointments. In a diverse and large country like Nigeria, it is important to keep the plurality of the people in mind at all times as a leader. It is impossible to overestimate the impact of fair dealing in positions of power given our history and our aspirations as a country. There was a day when we were deliberating on new appointments. I was already at the MITI at this time. There were three slots to be filled and the norm is for the minister to present a shortlist of at least three credible and competent candidates for each slot and for the president to decide and appoint one. Each region was well represented on the shortlist we discussed but, as it turned out, the most competent person for the first slot was from the south-west, while someone from the south-south was deemed most competent for the second slot. As we were about to go through the shortlist for the third slot, President Jonathan interjected and said the candidate had to be from the north! He wanted all the names on the shortlist

for the third slot to be from the north, then we could discuss each and settle for the best of the three. The appointments were to be announced the same day and the task was to find the suitable candidate from the north. This degree of concern for balance is required in a leader if progress is to be inclusive, without sacrificing merit in the eventual choice. To the credit of the Jonathan administration, the search for qualified and suitable candidates for various offices and functions did yield positive results, proving that there is talent everywhere if we would only look for it.

- Refocused some agencies to play a more significant role in the economy. For example, the Standards Organization of Nigeria encouraged manufacturers to develop their products to meet international standards. This involved developing a credible and internationally accredited quality/standards infrastructure to support the industries and exports. It led to the establishment of two internationally accredited laboratories for the export of agricultural products – the first of such laboratories for agricultural produce in Nigeria. Prior to this Nigeria had one of the highest level of rejects in Africa and many companies exported their products through Ghana. The Consumer Protection Council under Dupe Atoki (now a Judge of the Court of Justice of ECOWAS) raised the bar on consumer protection, and we also started looking at competition and fair-trading rules. This led to the bill to expand the scope of the agency to regulate issues around competition and fair trading and the change of name of the agency to the Federal Competition and Consumer Protection Council. Commercial law under Nima Salman Mann was reformed with a new focus and vision.
- Then followed the drive for investment, which rested on telling the story of Nigeria precisely the way it is and making bold to present, with openness, to the global investment community the opportunities and potential that Nigeria holds for the discerning investors. By 2013/14, Nigeria had become the preferred investment destination in Africa and the number-one country of interest out of the emerging markets, according to *Wall Street Journal*'s Frontier Market Sentiment Index.
- During the period, manufacturing, according to the National Bureau of Statistics (NBS), was the second-fastest growing

sector in the economy, and capacity utilization increased from 46% in 2010 to 52% in 2015 according to the Manufacturers Association of Nigeria.

The ultimate aim is to transform the MITI into the number-one economy ministry, much like the Ministry of Economy, International Trade and Industry in Japan, the Ministry of Economy and Industry in Israel, and the Ministry of Trade and Industry in Singapore.

But reforms are never easy. All these required a lot of sacrifice, hard work, dedication and creativity from the ministry and the agencies. In the process many paid the price for the reforms they undertook in their agencies or departments. And the reason for that is simple. The beneficiaries of the system you are trying to reform are usually influential either inside or outside government, and they will fight back. In one instance the staff barred the director from her office and threatened to deal with her. These threats are not uncommon. We drew strength from each other and from the fact that our reforms would be beneficial to Nigerians. Most of the director-generals and the staff in the ministry wanted to know what drove and motivated me daily, despite the difficult and harsh environment. That was when I shared my own personal conditions of service, which I developed and which spurred me daily for all those years. They were as follows:

- Dearth of financial and human resources demands innovation and making the best use of the few available. You must accept that you will not have the resources to do your work. Therefore you have to be creative.
- Be determined and persistent if you are convinced that agreed actions will lead to an improved society and impact the lives of the average citizen. Focus on what Nigerians can get, feel and see.
- Do the work for the right reasons and do not expect to be praised for doing a great job. Those who actually do the work are not recognized or praised until several years later, if they remember. But do the work anyway and derive your happiness and satisfaction from the inner joy of playing a positive role in the life of millions.
- Be prepared to explain and defend your choices and actions.
- Everyone has a price. Be ready to resign, or be sacked or be moved for your reforms, because the beneficiaries of the

current system have deep pockets, are very influential and will do everything they can to get you out of the way. You are on your own.

A sampling of verdicts on the MITI

As I said earlier, we started the MITI journey by consulting a wide range of stakeholders, including industry players, and the staff of the ministry and agencies. Four years later and in some cases, a few years after leaving government, we went back again to the stakeholders to get their thoughts on the reforms that had taken place over the last four years. Here is a sample of what they said:

The Manufacturers Association of Nigeria (MAN) was part of the transformation and provided regular feedback, which served as a source of encouragement for the staff of the ministry. It was a pleasant surprise when MAN decided to honour me, six years after leaving the MITI as a minister, for work done while in public office. It is common to receive awards when you are in office for various reasons, but to be remembered and honoured by the main and largest association of the industrialists in the country six years after leaving government said and meant a lot. It was an award that I was honoured to receive on behalf of the MITI team because all we achieved can only be credited to the entire team.

Not everyone waited that long. Indeed, 42 months into the transformation of the MITI, Alhaji Aliko Dangote, President of Dangote Group, had this to say:

> I want to commend HE Aganga for coming up with the Nigeria Industrial Revolution Plan. The NIRP is a fantastic and comprehensive industrialization blueprint that will transform the Nigerian economy. It is a well-articulated blueprint that will unlock the potential of the manufacturing sector and the economy in general. Based on our plans and the numbers we have worked on, manufacturers can exceed the minister's target of 10 per cent contribution to GDP by 2015 if we do the right thing.

Jalal Yusuf, Director-General/CEO of the Automotive Design and Development Council, had this to say:

> I worked with the National Automotive Council, later Automotive Design and Development Council, from 1994 to 2017. I worked indirectly with five ministers (1994 to 2006) and directly with four ministers (2007 to 2017). Of all these ministers, HE Olusegun Aganga has the most precise vision, commitment and desire to transform the Nigerian industrial sector. He also pushed the ministry staff and parastatals out of their stupor to achieve their mandates. His legacies include the Nigerian Industrial Development Plan, the Nigerian Sugar Master Plan and the Nigerian Automotive Industry Development Plan.

Dr Waheed Olagunju, Acting CEO of the BOI, testified thus:

> Before HE Olusegun Aganga was appointed Honourable Minister of Industry, Trade and Investment (MITI) in 2011, I had worked closely with the leadership of the Federal Ministry of Industry (FMI), the predecessor of MITI, for twenty-one years prior. Therefore, my antecedents placed me in a position to appreciate the enormous reforms undertaken over the time that Mr. Aganga served as the Minister between 2011 and 2015. From the onset, Mr. Aganga deployed his transformational leadership skills to communicate the rationale for reconstructing the fifty-one-year-old FMI into MITI. Utilizing a participatory model, he embarked upon the team-building process that ensured that team members bought into the vision for the new MITI. After consultations with relevant stakeholders in national and sub-nationals, the organized private sector, and some of Nigeria's international development partners such as the United Nations Industrial Development Organization, the EU and the World Bank, a well-articulated vision was subsequently adopted for MITI.
>
> Over the four years (2011–15), the vision was shared with Nigerians through a robust communication strategy. Accordingly, all stakeholders and the citizenry were focused on the image and mobilised towards its attainment. In the process, many crucial Policies, Plans and Schemes were enunciated. They included the Nigeria Industrial Revolution Plan (NIRP), which incorporated

> the Sugar Master Plan, new Automotive Industry and Textile and Garment Policies, amongst others. The National Enterprise Development Program (NEDEP) was also launched. Relevant agencies under the ministry were actively involved in designing and executing the various initiatives. For instance, the Small and Medium Enterprises Development Agency of Nigeria (SMEDAN), the Bank of Industry (BOI) and the Industrial Training Fund (ITF) led the implementation of NEDEP. The Minister held quarterly formal meetings with CEOs of government agencies to review the performance of plans, policies and schemes. The ministry's novel investment thrust entailed vigorously marketing Nigeria's comparative and competitive advantages to domestic and foreign investors. Consequently, Nigeria accounted for the highest foreign direct investment inflow into Africa in 2012 and 2013.

Many of the leaders of the MITI agencies also attested to the quality leadership and resourcefulness that the ministry enjoyed during the reforms, which are areas in which there is a massive deficit in Nigeria.

Ms Lola Visser-Mabogunje, Special Technical Advisor to the minister, narrates her experience:

> I joined FMITI in January 2013 as Senior Technical Adviser to the Honourable Minister, responsible for performance monitoring and the newly created Diaspora Trade and Investment Desk. In terms of monitoring and evaluation, there was absolutely nothing in place at the Ministry to facilitate my work and it was a herculean task to search for information to establish baseline information for a number of the activities, but we got there in the end.
>
> This was at a time when Former-President Goodluck Jonathan had just introduced the yearly Performance Agreement with the Ministers and Key Performance Indicators (KPI) for the Ministries/Parastatals.
>
> There were a number of challenges which should be addressed:
>
> **Professionalism:** Staff without any knowledge of monitoring and evaluation were often posted to the Policy Planning Research and

Statistics (PPRS) Department to manage the monitoring activities of the Ministry.

Sustainability: Once the staff gets the grasp of monitoring and evaluation, in a number of cases, they were transferred to another Ministry. It meant coming in on Monday to find a new face. This resulted in restarting the whole process again. Therefore, the process could not be sustained due to high staff turnover.

Resources: The Ministry was never allocated adequate resources for monitoring or visits to the agencies.

Diaspora Trade and Investment Desk

The Diaspora Desk was set in the office of the Honourable Minister to assist Nigerians in the diaspora who were interested in investing in the country and in trade, mainly export. This was a completely new initiative by the minister, and I was excited to add it to my portfolio.

On several occasions, HM Aganga met one-on-one with the diaspora trying to invest in the country or who were having challenges with other Ministries. In several cases, I was authorized to go with the individuals to the relevant parastatals and other ministries to resolve the problem.

Under the Nigeria Industrial Revolution Plan (NIRP), the Office of the Honourable Minister collaborated with the Nigerian Export Promotion Council (NEPC) to develop the Nigeria Diaspora Export (NDEX) Program. This Program leveraged on the huge number of Nigerians outside the country to expand market access for Nigerian products. Under this Program, the following activities were carried out:

- Meeting of the Honorable Minister with Diaspora SMEs in London.
- In order to leverage on Diaspora initiatives, especially using Nigerian-owned SMEs in the USA and Europe, the

Honourable Minister advised them to come together and form an economic cluster to enable them import in great quantities and to compete with other nationals who are presently taking over the African product market in Europe. This led to the formation of the Nigerian Diaspora Trade and Investment Association (NDTIA) UK.

- The NDEX Program achieved modest success in the short space of its implementation. Under the pilot phase, yams were exported from the Yam Conditioning Common Facility Centre at Zaki-Biam, Benue State to the United Kingdom by a Diaspora SME. None of these yams were rejected at the point of entry. The NEPC was at hand to assist with logistics issues within Nigeria.
- The Ministry provided support to the organizers of the African Paris Fashion Week and sponsored four Nigerian Diaspora Fashion Designers from the United Kingdom, Netherlands, Switzerland and from Nigeria to the event. These Nigerians sourced their material from Nigeria. The event provided them with the opportunity to exhibit their products. The occasion also enabled them to network with other designers from 26 African countries and also to exhibit their African wares to the large audience drawn from Europe, Africa and the Caribbean.
- To assist with quality control of products exported from Nigeria, the Honourable Minister proposed that the Diaspora SMEs should work with the ministry, SON and NEPC to establish a Consignment Center in Nigeria. Under this initiative products exported from Nigeria will undergo proper quality check before they are exported, and this will minimize rejection of Nigerian products. Questionnaire was designed and disseminated to the SMEs to find out the amount of product they import from Nigeria per year, and those imported from other countries.
- The Government has set up a Diaspora Commission which is an excellent initiative. It is expected that the Commission will work with the Ministry and the Diaspora to develop an action plan on Trade and Investments.

Mrs Uju Hassan-Baba, MITI Director, Legal Affairs, had this to say:

> My role as the director of Legal services in the Federal MITI and working directly under the Minister, HE Olusegun Aganga, was exacting and dictated by his demand for trade and investment advisory services from a legal perspective. The Minister was determined to re-invigorate the Weights and Measures department.
>
> The next critical focus was on initiatives that brought about milestones that influenced investments and trade in Nigeria. Notably, these initiatives were inter-ministerial committees that brought about policies and draft bills geared towards the diversification of the Nigerian economy. In this context, the first draft of the Auto Policy Bill, the legal documentation for the Cotton, Textile and Garment policy, the draft National Competition and Consumer Protection policy and draft bill, the first draft of the Nigerian Industrial Development Plan (NIRP) bill were developed. The critical focus was a plan to ensure continuity of new industrial, trade and investment plans and policies by turning the policies into laws. This led to the first draft Auto policy bill, the legal documentation for the Cotton, Textile and Garment policy, the draft National Competition and Consumer Protection policy and draft bill, the first draft Nigerian Industrial Development Plan (NIRP) bill and the review of the Pioneer Status administration under the NIPC (it was at this time that the ease of doing business mantra took on a new meaning) were developed. The work on the outdated bilateral trade and investment treaties framework, led to the first draft Model Investment Promotion and Protection Agreement (IPPA) that would make it easier for investments to flow into Nigeria. With the unprecedented interest in Nigeria by investors around the world there was a record level of interest by many countries to have or update their Investment Promotion and Protection Agreement with Nigeria.
>
> We were not able to complete the work on weights and measures particularly in the areas of oil and gas because of lack of adequate resources but I will recommend that it is prioritized and properly addressed because of the significant impact it has on the economy.

As I stated earlier, the credit for these verdicts rightfully belongs to the incredible team I had the privilege of working with during my time in public office. It remains the honour of a lifetime to have had these accomplished men and women working with me to bring Nigeria to a higher plane of regard.

Specific outcomes of reforms in the agencies under the MITI

The MITI had a strong and productive collaboration with the Ministry of Foreign Affairs because its minister (the late Ambassador Olugbenga Ashiru) fully understood the direction the MITI was taking, especially in marketing Nigeria to the rest of the world as a viable investment destination. A lot of credit goes to President Goodluck Jonathan, the country's chief marketer.

Figure 3.1: MITI reform achievements

Reform Achievements in the MITI

- Increased manufacturing capacity utilization (from 46% in 2010 to 52% in 2014)
- 50% slash in cost of business registration services
- Nigeria became number-one destination for investment in Africa for two consecutive years (UNTAD) and placed fourth in return on investment
- Revived textile industry
- Auto giants began car production in Nigeria (Auto MCU rose from 10% in 2010 to 50% in 2014)
- $3 billion pipeline investments in the sugar sector
- Nigeria became a net exporter of cement
- MSMEs grew in number and strength (114% increase in number between 2010 and 2014)
- Sub-standard good down to an all-time low (40% to 5% – Standards Organization of Nigeria)
- Consumer now king under the new Consumer Protection Council

- Non-oil export earnings rose (industrial sector contributing 70% of earnings – CBN)
- Number of jobs in MSMEs grew from 32,375,406 to 59,740,212 between 2010 and 2013

Some lessons from the MITI that can be implemented service-wide

There are lessons learned from the MITI experience and other countries, which can be considered for implementation service-wide:

- Have a code of conduct for the directors appointed to the board of the agencies. This should cover fiduciary relationships, meetings, confidentiality, conflict of interest, declaration of interest, gifts and hospitality, secret profit and benefits, outside activities, whistleblower protection, misconduct, and conflict with the code of conduct. The directors should sign an acknowledgement form agreeing to abide by the code of conduct. There should be a process to monitor and enforce compliance. This is where most governments fail.
- Implement the NCCG developed by the FRC in the public sector. The NCCG, which was meant to institutionalize corporate governance best practices, was intended to apply to both the private and public sectors.
- Institutionalize regular professional training programmes and professionalize the ministries that are responsible for the critical political, economic and social institutions.
- Enshrine meritocracy in the civil service, particularly in the recruitment, appointment, promotion and salaries of public and civil servants. Develop measurable KPIs linked to the economy and development for MDAs and hold them accountable. This should determine promotions and reappointments, etc.
- Ensure that ministers with relevant expertise or technocrats are posted to professional ministries.
- Revisit the mandate of the MDAs to ensure clarity and to remove any duplication of roles. There are too many MDAs, particularly regulators, with overlapping mandates.

- Within the framework of federal character, undertake a comprehensive review of all the MDAs to (a) determine the skills, experience and competence required for each head and the management in each agency; (b) determine whether the current board members and management have matching skills, competence and experience; and (c) retain those who meet the requirements, post those who do not meet the requirements to other MDAs where their skills and experience are needed. Make new appointments to fill in the gaps. The National Assembly should amend the acts of all the MDAs to specify the competences, skills and experience required for board and management positions.

Public service and the Nolan Principles

To develop a civil service for the 21st century, Nigeria and other African countries should consider implementing or adapting the Nolan Principles or something similar, review the structure and size of the civil service, improve on accountability and transparency and go digital, embracing the use of technology. The Nolan Principles are also referred to as the principles of public life, and they cover:

- Selflessness
- Integrity
- Objectivity
- Accountability
- Openness
- Honesty
- Leadership

A 21st-century civil service should not only reflect these principles, but it should also use them to rebuild and continually evaluate the system.

Size, structure and transparency in the civil service

An easy way to find out whether the size of the civil service is optimal is to benchmark it against those of selected countries and their population size and GDP. Nigeria appears to have a superior population ratio to civil servants, but it is abysmally behind several countries, including the UK and Japan, relative to its GDP.

One reason the UK civil service remains outstanding is the constant evaluation and review that result in improvements. In some cases, these improvements require restructuring, renaming and sometimes creating new departments to deliver good governance to the citizens. For instance, the UK Department for Work and Pensions was created and made responsible for welfare, pensions and child maintenance policy. A similar agency or ministry should be responsible for poverty alleviation and unemployment and values in Nigeria and other developing countries. At the moment no agency or ministry is accountable for any of these important areas.

It is helpful to mention that the UK is perhaps the first country to have introduced a semblance of disclosure by public officials of their income, assets and financial interests by an Act of Parliament – Public Bodies Corrupt Practices Act (1889). This was formally adopted in 1974 when the House of Commons introduced the Register of Members' Financial Interests. Many countries mandate public officials to make financial disclosures but have no structure, or they lack the will to enforce it. The government publishes information about how it works to allow you to make politicians, public services and public organizations more accountable. The UK government is committed to publishing information about:

- How much public money has been spent on what
- The job titles of senior civil servants and how much they are paid
- How the government is doing against its objectives

There are two issues at stake: financial disclosure and commitment to a code of conduct. For example, before I was appointed as a board advisor to the Queen's Commonwealth Trust in the UK, I had to sign that I would abide by the seven principles of public life (code of conduct), which included selflessness, integrity, objectivity, accountability, openness, honesty and leadership. Regarding honesty, it's about public office holders being truthful at all times. In the UK it is a severe offence for a minister to mislead the House of Commons or the people. Ministers have been forced to resign because they inadvertently misled the House and the public.

Fixing public capacity deficit

Past reforms undoubtedly had many positive gains, but there is still more work to be done in the areas of work ethics, innovation and values. The elements of the reforms are budgetary, financial management, accountability, transparency and anti-corruption, human resource management, operations and systems management. Some specific reforms include:

- The Integrated Payroll and Personnel Information System (IPPIS) has almost eliminated ghost workers' syndrome in the participating federal MDAs.
- The posts of permanent secretaries and directors are tenured for four years. The permanent secretary appointment is renewable once but subject to satisfactory performance. There is a compulsory retirement age for all grades in service, which is 60 years of age or 35 years of pensionable service, whichever is earlier.
- Monetization of fringe benefits, establishment of the contributory pension scheme, intensified war on corruption, introduction of the National Health Insurance Scheme, right-sizing in some establishments through staff redeployment to maximize professional efficiency, downsizing for cost-saving, etc.

What can we learn from other countries?

Japan's civil service

Japan is reputed to have a highly competitive civil service; it is rare to find redundant staff in the national government. Often, there has been a clamour for an increased workforce in specific areas. Japan has the lowest number of government employees per thousand population and a much smaller number of public employees than those in the private sector. This, of course, was after the privatization of the Japan post, and the incorporation of certain Japanese universities and other civil service reforms which significantly reduced the numbers from over 800,000 to about 287,000.

In Japan there are always opportunities for anyone with proven ability to become a civil servant. Japan is proud to have fairness and impartiality in the examination and recruitment system. Every year many bright and promising young people aspire to a career in civil service.

The inferences from the Japanese experience for Nigeria include hiring strictly on merit, avoiding redundancy or overlapping mandates and regard for impartiality in executing policy, all of which Nigeria can benefit from.

Malaysia and civil service reform

Administrative reform in Malaysia began in the 1960s, marked by lawlessness and disorder. The emphasis then was on effective institutional development to support development planning and implementation, and ensuring public sector agencies had the capability and capacity to carry out their responsibilities effectively.

In 1965, with the assistance of the Ford Foundation, public administration reform commenced with the recommendations in the Montgomery Esman Report that led to the establishment of the Development Administration Unit. This unit was entrusted with planning and guiding the reform efforts in the public service, laying the foundation for public sector training policies and programmes and overall administrative and personnel development.

The establishment of the National Institute of Public Administration in 1972 and the Malaysian Administrative Modernization and Management Planning Unit in 1966 were significant administrative reforms in which the former replaced the Staff Training Centre, and the latter is focused on reforms.

A programme-oriented reform led to the launch of Malaysian Incorporated in 1981. Its essence was to run the country as a single business corporation, with the private sector following its growth and expansion, and the public sector providing the support vital for the corporation's success. It was part of the 'Look East Policy' introduced a year later, with the primary objective of adopting work culture, ethics and values from Japan and Korea.

Towards home-grown solutions

The Ministerial Code in the UK is a reasonably detailed document that we would do well to study, understand and adapt for our public sphere.

The Nolan Principles, which have been adopted by many countries, are also a good guide to help Nigeria develop its own. We can no longer depend on outdated guidelines and rules. In the modern world, with its variety of innovations, governance has also evolved, and a failure in the public sphere can prove disastrous for the entire economy and society.

A few thoughts and recommendations

Significant progress has been made in designing public service structures in Europe and Asia. There is room for Nigeria to evolve a system that works for Nigeria, bearing in mind our peculiarities, as was done in the MITI. In addition to the lessons learned from the MITI that were discussed earlier in this chapter, specific changes need to be made to the federal (and state) civil service in Nigeria and many African countries in the following areas:

- Make the civil service smaller and smarter; privatize commercial agencies. The unintended consequence of some redundancy can be mitigated by implementing a combination of measures, such as:
    - Paying off those that want to retire voluntarily.
    - For those desirous of setting up a business and are capable, the SMEDAN and ITF should organize training programmes on business skills and have the BOI provide them loans as seed capital to start the business.
- Restructure to focus on and deliver the government's top priorities and expectations of the governed.
- Emphasize meritocracy, both at entry level and for career advancement. Advertise vacancies and let selection be merit based as in the private sector. This can be strengthened by making the selection criteria predictive. For example, a position requiring professional qualification should prescribe years of experience and possible areas of specialization as was done for the SWF.
- Adopt pay comparable to the private sector's average to attract and retain top talent. Always remember that if you pay peanuts, you get monkeys and you fuel one of the causes of corruption. Invest in modern, qualitative and relevant training programmes.

- Adopt people management policies that not only attract but retain and develop top talent in the civil service. Invest in qualitative training.
- Digitalize work and business processes as well as procedures.
- Create a professional and independent civil service that is protected from any political interference.
- Introduce a robust code of conduct for all public office holders, civil servants and political appointees. An ethics commissioner or an agency should be dedicated to enforcing and monitoring compliance.
- Introduce and maintain a 'gifts' register for civil and public servants. The same should be kept for public office holders, whether elected or appointed.
- Update, expand the scope of and carefully implement the report of the Oronsaye Committee as discussed earlier.
- All agencies should report to the president through the relevant ministry for better supervision, coordination and synergy.
- Appoint ministers with relevant knowledge, skills and exposure to the ministry of their assignment. Also, heads and boards of agencies should be appointed based on merit, while the roles of the board chairman, board members and supervising minister of agencies should be clarified. Adopt the NCCG in the public sector.
- Adopt a performance measurement system similar to the balanced scorecard or performance pyramid used in the private sector.

Reform the Federal Executive Council and National Executive Council

At the federal level, there is a growing perception that the FEC is a contract-awarding or approving body. But it is not, and it is not supposed to be. However, press interviews after every FEC meeting on Wednesdays lend credence to the view that its main preoccupation is the approval of projects or contracts. To be sure, the FEC's role, as contained in the Ministers' Statutory Powers and Duties (Miscellaneous Provisions) Act, is to serve as an advisory body to the President of Nigeria, who serves as the FEC's chair. All ministers are members of the FEC. It should be a forum for discussing and addressing issues that affect the country, such as the economy, standard and quality of the educational system, healthcare system, fuel subsidy, unemployment and poverty, insecurity, corruption, and so on. It has been suggested that, to resolve this problem, there should be a separate day for approval of contracts or a sub-committee of the FEC responsible for the detailed review before making recommendations to the FEC for approval or ratification. The composition of the sub-committee would change from time to time depending on the nature of the contract and expertise required. They should work closely with the Bureau of Public Procurement.

The National Economic Council (NEC) is another government organ that needs to be reformed. The NEC was established by the provisions of the Constitution of the Federal Republic of Nigeria, 1999, as amended; Section 153(1) and Paragraphs 18 & 19 of Part I of the Third Schedule. The NEC is mandated to 'advise the President concerning the economic affairs of the Federation, and in particular on measures necessary for the coordination of the economic planning efforts or economic programmes of the various Governments of the Federation'. Membership of the NEC comprises the 36 state governors, the governor of the Central Bank of Nigeria (CBN) and other co-opted government officials. The vice-president chairs it. While the NEC is a necessary and vital organ of the government/federation, a close examination of the matters discussed, and the composition and structure of the council, suggest that its ability to deliver on its mandate is limited, particularly on the economy. The options are to review the mandate, structure and composition to ensure that the economic ministers are members and that economic programmes of the various governments of the federation are discussed and are well coordinated.

Chapter 4

Focus on number one: the economy

> *'History shows that no country has ever become rich by exporting raw materials without also having an industrial sector, and in modern terms an advanced services sector. The more a country specializes in the production of raw materials only, the poorer it becomes... Industry Multiplies National wealth!'*
>
> **Olusegun Aganga, CON**

Introduction

A former Prime Minister of the UK once said, 'The economy is the start and end of everything. You can't have successful education reform or any other reform if you don't have a strong economy.' The economy determines how rich, prosperous and safe a nation is, how many people are employed, unemployed or underemployed, whether you are able meet your basic responsibilities as a parent providing food, shelter, quality education for your family. It affects all of us, from the person working at a market, to security guards, to businesspeople – small and large businesses. It determines the price you pay for a bag of rice, bread, sugar, cement, etc. It does not discriminate; whether you are a Christian or Muslim, Ibo, Hausa or Yoruba, the effect is the same. That is why it must be the number-one priority of any government and why leaders in the most successful nations in the world appoint competent people to run their economy and head their economic institutions.

One of the reasons economic greatness has eluded Nigeria is that, so far, no election has been won or lost because of the economy. This is because Nigerians do not hold their political leaders accountable for the economy. The political system encourages and rewards short-termism, which means that there is no incentive to commit resources to long-term economic and development plans. In developed countries, the state of the economy is a major factor in winning or losing an election and there are many recent examples in popular democracy. In 'The Nature of Economic Perceptions in Mass Publics', Lewis-Beck, Martini and Kiewiet (2013) reported that the election and re-election of former President Barack Obama of the US was largely determined by the state of the economy.

Nigeria has come a long way from 1960 when it gained independence to becoming the largest economy in Africa, as officially established in April 2014 and maintained to date. The GDP in nominal terms in 1960 was only $4.20 billion, and per capita GDP was $93, but in 2021 the GDP was $514.05 billion and per capita GDP was $2,360. The per capita GDP for 2022 and 2023 are projected to be $2,400 and $2,530, respectively.

In the global rankings, Nigeria has not done badly. Its GDP ranking was 47th out of 195 countries in 2000, then moved up to 24th in 2015 and then down to 31st in 2020. However, it recovered slightly in 2021 when ranked 26th. But the GDP per capita tells a completely different story, as Nigeria was almost in the bottom 30 in 2021 – worse than in 2000.

The state and structure of the economy

The Nigerian economy is the largest in Africa. As stated above, nominal GDP was $514.05 billion and ranked 26th in the world in 2021. It accounts for less than a percentage point of the world economy of $133 trillion. Compared to Indonesia, a country that has a large population (270.2 million) and, like Nigeria, has diverse natural resources, Nigeria's GDP is only about 44.4% of Indonesia's ($1.16 billion). Nigeria's per capita GDP of $2,360 is about 32% of that of South Africa, but the potential for growth are Nigeria's population of over 216.7 million, which is three and a half times that of South Africa (60.8 million), its diverse natural resources and demography. The median age is 18.1 years for Nigeria and 27.6 years for South Africa. These point to the considerable scope for growth that the Nigerian economy has and reflects the divergence between its global GDP ranking of 26th and population ranking of sixth.

Often overlooked in the discourse of the Nigerian economy is the macro structure of the share of agriculture, industry and services in the GDP vis-à-vis the evolution of the advanced and emerged economies. The latter economies in the early stages of their development start with agriculture accounting for a relatively high percentage of the GDP but, as they grow the economy and add value to agricultural commodities, industry or manufacturing and services sectors increase significantly relative to agriculture and the countries become more prosperous, with higher GDP per capita. For Nigeria, between 2012 and 2020, the services sector (mainly trade) consistently accounted for more than 50% of the GDP, peaking at 53.59% in 2016 during the recession and subsequently declining to 52.44% in 2020. Between 2012 and 2015, the industrial sector contributed more to the GDP than the agricultural sector, which was about 40% prior to 2010, as the government of former President Goodluck Jonathan prioritized industrial production.

As Figure 4.1 shows, among the three major sectors of the economy, it is only agriculture that has relatively stable growth during 2012 to 2020, while services and industry experienced growth volatility, and especially so for industry that mimicked the growth pattern of the national economy.

Figure 4.1: Nigerian economy – selected performance indicators

Indicator	2016	2017	2018	2019	2020	2021
GDP, current market prices (US$ bn)	404.65	375.75	397.19	448.12	432.29	420.45
Real GDP growth (%)	–1.58	0.83	1.90	2.27	–1.92	3.40
of which agriculture (%)	*4.11*	*3.45*	*2.12*	*2.36*	*2.17*	*2.13*
of which industry (%)	*–8.85*	*2.15*	*1.87*	*2.31*	*–5.85*	*–0.47*
of which services (%)	–0.82	0.91	1.83	2.22	–2.22	5.61
Non-oil GDP (%)	–0.22	0.47	2.00	2.06	–1.25	4.44
Oil GDP (%)	–14.45	4.69	0.97	4.59	–8.89	–8.30

Sources: World Bank and National Bureau of Statistics, Nigeria

Growing, not fast enough and not as inclusive

The Nigerian economy has been growing steadily since 2000, managed a double-digit growth in 2003 and the growth was consistently above the population growth rate during 2000 to 2015. Since 2016, however, the economy has been slowing down and persistently growing below the population growth rate. The International Monetary Fund (IMF) has projected growth of 2.5% in 2021 and 2.6% in 2022, which will barely equal the population growth rate, but the growth is not inclusive by creating jobs to address unemployment and expand domestic production. Population is not a burden if the economy consistently grows faster than the population and creates jobs. If the economy is not growing fast enough, tough actions are required to slow down the population growth or grow the economy at a higher rate.

Is the Nigerian economy diversified enough?

Six sectors of the economy have been systemic contributors to Nigeria's GDP, representing between 77% and 82% during 2013 to 2020. In the third quarter of 2022, for instance, agriculture accounted for 29.67% of GDP, trade 15.35%, ICT 15.35%, manufacturing 8.59%, mining and quarrying 5.9% and real estate 5.61%, making them the top contributors to Nigeria's GDP. So it is possible to argue that the economy is diversified. These are sectors that should be explored for creation of new jobs.

The real problem with the Nigerian economy is the overdependence on hydrocarbons for foreign earnings and, by extension, government revenue and the failure over the decades to effectively use these resources to develop the non-oil sector – a phenomenon commonly referred to as the 'resource curse'. This reflects in three basic statistics:

- Oil accounted for an average of 87.8% of total exports during 2013 to Q1 of 2022 and is thus a very strong contributor to Nigeria's foreign earnings (NBS).
- Oil revenue averaged 68.86% of total federally collected revenue during 1999 to 2020 (CBN).
- Oil and gas production, on average, accounted for about 10% of GDP for most of 2013 to 2020 (NBS).

Given Nigeria's high dependence on imports of all categories, the high concentration of the source of foreign exchange is major cause of weakness and vulnerability.

Government revenue size and structure

Federal, state and local governments in Nigeria rely largely on oil revenue, which accounted for 68.9% of total federally collected revenue during 1999 to 2020, averaging annually ₦4.42 trillion or $10.78 billion. In 2020, the 36 states and the Federal Capital Territory (FCT) received 76.23% of their revenue from the Federation Account, the balance of which varies with the vagaries of the oil market.

Being resource-rich is, however, not a sentence to misery as often portrayed. This is demonstrated in the case of Indonesia, which is also resource-rich and has a large population but where oil and gas account for less than 35% of its export value, while the remaining 65% is from a wide range of products and commodities.

Government revenue in Nigeria is also relatively small, reported at 8% of GDP in 2019 (IMF), down to about 5% in 2020 and 3.6% in 2021 because of the collapse of oil prices and dwindling production.

Average crude oil prices declined by 59.9% between 2014 and 2020, production by 20.4% and exports by 25.63%, thereby dampening oil revenue in real terms and also relative to non-oil revenue. The increasing relative share of non-oil revenue is also traceable to efforts to diversify government revenue, adoption of information technology in tax administration, increases in some tax rates (including Value Added Tax), fall in oil prices and consolidation of treasury activities into a Treasury Single Account (TSA) that stopped the practice of disparate bank accounts by government MDAs.

Figure 4.2 illustrates the level of dependency of the 36 states and the FCT on Federation Account Allocation Committee (FAAC) allocation, showing that only three states (Lagos, Ogun and FCT) have internally generated revenue (IGR) of 50% and above of their total revenue. This reflects better fiscal operations, a wider tax base and improved efficiency of tax collection and administration. The FAAC distributes revenues pooled into the federation account between the three tiers of government (federal, state and local) using an agreed distribution formula.

Figure 4.2: Federal allocation as % of total revenue of states of the federation, 2020

Groups	States	Dependency Ratio
1	Lagos	21–30%
2	Ogun, FCT	41–50%
3	Kaduna, Osun, Oyo, Rivers	51–60%
4	Anambra, Cross River, Edo, Enugu, Kwara, Ondo, Plateau, Zamfara	61–70%
5	Abia, Bauchi, Delta, Ebonyi, Imo, Kano, Kebbi, Kogi, Nasarawa	71–80%
6	Adamawa, Akwa Ibom, Bayelsa, Benue, Borno, Ekiti, Gombe, Jigawa, Katsina, Niger, Sokoto, Taraba, Yobe	81% and above

Source: National Bureau of Statistics, 2021

The tax/GDP ratio

The ratio of tax revenue to GDP is 6.1% in Nigeria, which is far below the Sub-Saharan average (18.6%) for 2019/2020 and fell behind countries such as South Africa, Ghana, Rwanda, Kenya Angola and Zambia. Among the reasons for this dismal fiscal structure are the small tax base, poor compliance with tax laws and revenue leakages, either because of official exemptions or outright fraud. Nigeria also has one of the lowest tax/GDP ratios in the world because of the structure of the economy, where MSMEs account for an estimated 48% of Nigeria's GDP. Most MSMEs are nano, micro and small businesses that do not make sufficient profit to pay high tax or they are not in the tax net. Also, most of the players in agriculture (the dominant contributor to the GDP) are MSMEs and they make an insignificant contribution to tax revenue. Efforts should be made to improve on tax compliance and to bring MSMEs into the tax net by offering creative incentives that assist microbusinesses to become small businesses, the small to become medium and many medium to become large businesses. In addition, peasant farming must turn into commercial agriculture and farmers be assisted to increase their income through commodity exchanges, improved yields and value added. Tax revenue can also be increased through granting titles for landed properties and bringing the assets into the tax net.

There is a need to periodically review policies such as pioneer status, waivers, tax concessions in the free-trade zones and similar policies. With more than 45 taxes and levies collected by different MDAs and into different accounts, the ratio reported might be understated.

The blight of recurrent expenditure

The level of recurrent expenditure has been a major challenge to the Nigerian government, as it keeps increasing year after year. For example, between 2011 and 2019, recurrent expenditure as a percentage of total expenditure rose steadily from almost 70% to about 80%. This was an area of major concern for me when I was the Minister of Finance, and it led to the establishment of a Recurrent Expenditure Review Committee, headed by Professor Anya in 2010/11. Majorly, the issues are the structure and cost of governance, government ministries and parastatals that at times have overlapping responsibilities, the size of the civil service, the number of political office holders and special assistants, high salary and allowances paid to members of the National Assembly, system rigidity (unwillingness to change), subsidies, and waste and leakages. Tough decisions need to be made to reduce recurrent expenditure and create more room for capital expenditure.

Managing Nigeria's public debt better

Another area of concern is the rising debt burden, which has manifested in the very high debt service to revenue ratio, particularly in the six years to 2022. The steady rise since 2015 is due to more aggressive borrowing for infrastructure renewal and expansion, and for meeting statutory and recurrent expenditure of government due to low revenue. This reached epidemic proportions during January to April 2022, when debt service exceeded total revenue by 19%!

Nigeria's debt stock was 34.98% of GDP in 2020, which was low when compared to other countries, such as Japan 266.18%, the US 131.18%, Brazil 101% and the UK 95.5%. The real problem with Nigeria's debt profile is twofold:

1. The high level of the debt servicing cost to revenue is partly because the GDP does not convert proportionately into public revenue to pay back the loan. The four countries mentioned above all have debt servicing cost to revenue of less than 10%. The UK has a debt to GDP ratio of 80% and debt servicing cost to national income is only 1.9% (Q3 2021).
2. Much of the funds borrowed are not for productive infrastructure that will attract domestic and foreign investments to expand the economy and increase government revenue.

Nigeria should focus attention on the debt servicing cost to national income, which could have a devastating impact on the economy and country. In addition to public debt, the macroeconomic environment has been very poor and unpredictable since 2016.

A look at the external sector

Nigeria's annual imports bill rose from $2.43 billion in 1985 to $88.74 billion in 2019 and dampened to about $71.63 billion in 2020 as a result of the COVID-19 pandemic that hobbled global supply chains. As the monthly import bill increased, initially of non-oil commodities and later for both refined oil and non-oil goods and services, the national currency (naira) depreciated and had to occasionally be devalued against Nigeria's major trading currencies.

Ineffective diversification

Nigeria has not been able to effectively diversify the economy and revenue sources, or to improve on the size and quality of the government revenue. There is no plan and policy continuity. For instance, the administration of former President Olusegun Obasanjo came up with the National Economic Empowerment and Development Strategy. Late President Umaru Musa Yar'Adua came up with the Seven-Point Agenda. Former President Goodluck Jonathan came up with the Transformation Agenda driven by the different economic ministries, including the NIRP and the NEDEP for MSMEs developed by the MITI. The incumbent President Muhammadu Buhari came up with the Economic Recovery and Growth Plan, Economic Sustainability Plan and the National Development Plan (2021–25).

Borrowing the terminology from the hedge fund sector, it is fair to say that Nigeria is 'long' on plans but 'short' on implementation. Poor execution can be attributed to gap in leadership, because, so often, government activities are only beneficial to a select few in the country and there is no culture of continuity.

Exchange rate management

The exchange value of the Nigerian naira has been a major issue of discourse in economic circles and the general business ecosystem ever since Nigeria became a net importer of non-oil commodities and subsequently net importer of all categories of items. This fuelled the demand for foreign currencies and reflected in a rising import bill.

The response over the years had been to repeatedly devalue the naira to close the gap (premium) between the exchange rates at the Central Bank window and the bureau de change. But, like a moving target, the exchange rates at the alternative segments of the foreign exchange (FX) market had always adjusted upwards and away from the official rate.

Between 1999 and 2012, the currency was fairly stable, as the premium was below 5% (the recommended maximum threshold for exchange rate stability) in nine out of the 15 years. The period from 2013 to date saw a persistent depreciation of the naira in the alternative FX market segments and official response by the monetary authorities to devalue the domestic currency, following the typical Bretton Woods recommendation of narrowing premium to the 0% to 5% band. This is a superficial solution that is not sustainable, as proven in Nigeria's case since the mid-1980s.

The approach has been to work within the financial pillars of exchange rate management. That is, foreign earnings from hydrocarbons, income from non-oil exports, remittances from the diaspora, foreign investments (portfolio and direct) and external borrowings. Domestic manufacturing is weak and needs to be deliberately revived for Nigeria to produce most of what its people consume, as we had in the late 1970s and early 1980s.

The twin challenges of rising and high inflation and exchange rates can be decisively addressed if there is effective coordination of policies at the design and execution stages such that every government ministry, department and agency whose mandate has a bearing on economic activity value chains work together. Government MDAs including the CBN should stop working in silos and effectively collaborate to ensure successful policy implementation and strengthen the value of the Naira.

The successful efforts with fertilizers, sugar, cement and now refined petroleum products should be replicated in other key sectors. The benefits will go beyond exchange rate stability to include job creation, poverty reduction and inequality reduction.

Interest rate sterility

In Nigeria, interest rate as the main or only tool for controlling inflation, is not effective because of the high level of poverty, a large number of low-income earners, the cash economy, a poor credit culture, the undeveloped mortgage system and a poor savings culture. Moreover, the large-sized informal sector, poor data production and management, the low degree of transparency in transactions, and the transmission of monetary policy to target variables through interest rate is quite weak.

Effective management of inflation in the Nigerian economy requires more than a muddle-through, with proper attention to the distortions associated with inflation. Interest rates, inflation, exchange rate and public debts are discussed in detail in Chapter 5.

In summary, the signs of a weak economy that point to what needs attention are listed in Figure 4.3, a number of which apply to Nigeria and other African countries, and demand a sense of urgency from the political leadership.

Figure 4.3: Signs of a weak economy

- Import-dependent economy
- Export of primary products without value addition
- Consistent rise in interest rates (cost of borrowing)
- Fall in real wages
- High dependency on foreign earnings without building productive capacity
- High incidence of poverty
- High rate of unemployment
- High rate of emigration of skilled professionals
- Weak governance structure
- High degree of insecurity
- Weak regulatory framework and contract enforcement

We will now turn to some of the areas that Nigeria needs to address to build a strong and inclusive economy that is globally competitive.

Industrial development/manufacturing value addition

Strong industrial and services sectors based on areas of competitive advantage are fundamental for sustainable economic growth. This can be achieved by the execution of the NIRP, which was designed to move Nigeria from being an exporter of raw materials to an industrialized nation. The plan also identifies 13 items that can become a major source of foreign income as we walk towards implementing the zero-oil policy.

The NIRP/national plan

In addition to the national plan, Nigeria needs an integrated national economic long-term and medium-term plan that the whole country, regardless of the ruling political party, will buy into, to ensure continuity in its implementation, periodic review and updates every five years, and an effective framework for delivery, monitoring and reporting. The ideal is to have a 20–25-year plan that is reviewed and updated every five years. Cases in point are Singapore's economy that was transformed over a 30-year period and the automotive policy of South Africa, which was first developed in 1960 and has been reviewed and updated every five or seven years since.

In order to focus on building strong industrial and services sectors based on Nigeria's competitive and comparative advantage, the NIRP should be revisited. Obviously, resource endowment does not translate into inclusive economic growth that brings a high quality of life and standard of living.

In 1980, China was the seventh-largest economy with a GDP of only $305.45 billion, while the US was then at $2.86 trillion. China averaged 10% annual growth for many years and now has the largest economy in the world with a GDP (in PPP terms) of $25.27 trillion. The economic reforms in China started in 1978 under Deng Xiaoping and his reformist allies and it took 35 years of rigorous implementation of its industrial revolution plan for China to become an industrial powerhouse.

There is a combination of reasons why China was able to achieve this rapid economic growth, but most economists agree that two main factors played a significant role: large-scale capital investment, which was financed by foreign investments and domestic savings, and accelerated productivity growth. Industries and the small and medium-sized enterprises (SMEs) were the major contributors to the productivity growth. That is why Nigeria must focus on the industrial, services and MSME sectors and ensure disciplined implementation of the plans.

MSMEs

All over the world, MSMEs are the primary drivers of employment and economic growth. In China and Brazil, MSMEs employ 75% and 70% of the workforce, respectively. The last survey conducted by the NBS and SMEDAN in 2020 identified 40 million MSMEs, employing 76.5% of Nigeria's workforce, accounting for 49.78% of the GDP and 7.64% of exports. The majority (99.8%) of these enterprises are nano or microbusinesses, and only 10.6% of them operate formally with registration and paid employment.

Enough attention has not been given to this sector, particularly since 2017. According to the surveys by the NBS and SMEDAN, the number of enterprises in the sector grew by 20 million from 17 million in 2010 to 37 million in 2013. Between 2013 and 2017 it grew by only four million, and in 2020 it fell by about two million to 39 million, partly due to the effects of the COVID-19 pandemic. The nano and microbusinesses were most affected as their number fell by about three million by 2020. This is inconsistent with global the trend in the sector, where the enterprises grow in good and bad times but grow faster when there is downturn in the economy.

Nigeria already has a comprehensive plan, the NEDEP, which was launched in 2014 along with the NIRP. This can be updated and implemented as part of the long-term plan. It covers the entire ecosystem of the sector nationwide, working closely with the SMEDAN, ITF, BOI, the state and local governments and the private sector, under the supervision of the National MSME Council, which was set up in 2014 but was discontinued when the new administration arrived in 2015. The Council was made up of the relevant MDAs and the private sector and worked alongside the Presidential Jobs Board, a body set up to facilitate the creation of a minimum of three million jobs annually and to bring the rate of unemployment below 10% through a combination of policies, intervention, providing enabling environment and supporting both government and private sector projects that have the potential of creating a large number of jobs. This should be complemented by state MSME councils and job boards.

Policy formulation and implementation critical for sustained economic growth – lessons learned from South Africa and the automotive policy

The size of a nation's economy determines its greatness. A country can only have a great economy if a developed industrial sector diversifies the economy and sources of revenue, and a vibrant MSME sector creates jobs. It requires development and implementation of policies consistently over time. The automotive, cement and sugar policies can be used to illustrate this.

Automotive policy

Nigeria's automobile industry was a vibrant industry due to high demand for automobiles in the 1960s and 1970s, which propelled the government to partner with Peugeot, Volkswagen and Mercedes-Benz Group AG to set up assembly plants in Nigeria. Policy changes and economic downturn have adversely affected the industrial sector, leading to its near total collapse as Nigerians opted for affordable pre-used imported vehicles.

In 2014, the MITI and the National Automotive Council of Nigeria, now the National Automotive Design and Development Council, with the support of the president, decided to revive the automotive industry after the sector was discussed exhaustively at one of the presidential Honorary International Investors Council (HIIC) meetings. There were several reasons for this:

- Nigeria had a high and rising import bill for motor vehicles, rising from about ₦6.2 billion to ₦1.2 trillion, with the prospect of it increasing further as the population expanded. This was going to become a balance of payment problem and adversely impact on the FX rate.
- Potential value added of locally assembled vehicles was estimated at about ₦200 billion, which should further increase with vigorous implementation of the local content programmes.
- At full capacity, the sector had the potential to create 70,000 skilled and semi-skilled jobs with 210,000 indirect jobs in the SMEs that would supply the components.

- Earn foreign income from exporting to other African countries, as Proforce is already doing with its armoured vehicles. The auto policy was very comprehensive and had many parts to it, including:
  - Using the levy generated to provide single-digit loans to new car buyers working with a financial institution.
  - Auto spare parts industrial parks for original equipment manufacturers (OEMs) and local manufacturing to increase the percentage of local content. A car has over 2,000 parts.
  - An auto skills training park in Badagry, Kaduna and Nnewi for the training of skilled manpower for the sector.

The development and finalization of the policy involved wide consultations, a study of four countries that have developed and implemented a successful automotive policy, and a retreat with local players and stakeholders in the South African auto sector, a country that has successfully implemented an automotive policy. I also met with the global CEOs of the leading brands in Nigeria and I recall the global head of Nissan assuring me that, if the policy was well thought through, he would publicly announce to the world that Nissan would set up a car assembly plant in Nigeria. He did so about a week after the policy was approved by the FEC, and many other OEMs followed his lead.

The number of vehicles assembled locally increased steadily in response to this policy. When subsequently the new government suspended the policy and reduced vehicle import tariffs from 35% to 5% for both cars and vehicles for goods, aimed at reducing the rising cost of transportation and to boost mass transit, the number of vehicles assembled locally in Nigeria started to decrease and investors started pulling out again.

When compared to South Africa and how developed the industry is there, it is obvious why Nigeria must take a look at this sector again. Egypt, Morocco and Uganda are close to achieving their goals as regional centres for the automotive industry, while Ghana and other African countries implemented their automotive policies many years after Nigeria and have attracted a lot of attention and interest. With the Africa free-trade zone in place it is obvious that Nigeria is the target market.

South Africa has one of the most advanced automotive industries in Africa, with a market share of 54.3%, a workforce of about 110,000, 6.9% of the country's GDP, 4.4% of manufacturing GDP, 2.5% of retail

GDP, 30.1% of manufacturing output, and 13.9% of total exports, which was about R12.2 billion ($858.54 million) in 2020. Unlike Nigeria, South Africa has an automotive policy that it reviews and enhances periodically and that it has implemented rigorously for more than 60 years. Its first automotive policy was introduced in 1960 and it was last reviewed in 2020, which produced the South African Automotive Master Plan (2021–35). This plan set objectives of 60% local content, global competitiveness, transformation of the South African society, sustainable development and shared prosperity. That is what it takes to build a robust industry – consistency and continuity.

Cement policy

The backward integration policy on cement was developed and started during the term of President Obasanjo. When I came in 2011, as usual all efforts were made by the stakeholders, especially those importing cement, to persuade me to cancel or suspend the policy. Businessmen came to my office crying (literally) about why it must be suspended and how the economy was suffering. I decided to speak to the former ministers and consulted with the investors, all stakeholders and ministry officials and concluded that there was no basis for suspending or cancelling the policy.

The ministry adhered to it strictly, introduced transparency and a monitoring process that involved the investors, encouraged the investors to set up a cement association, which the late Joseph Makoju, a man of integrity, chaired. No one was allowed to see me individually, I spoke to the industry through the association. Goals were set for the industry and we started monitoring investment, jobs created, contribution to GDP, etc.

And the result, after four years of rigorous implementation, production capacity increased from 11 metric tonnes to 32 metric tonnes, over ₦19 billion had been invested, creating direct and indirect jobs and, in 2013, I was delighted to announce that Nigeria had become a net exporter of cement. We worked very closely with the Industry Association and in 2014 we set new goals: increase export, reduce cost of production, reduce cost of distribution and price to consumers, and develop and promote a national concrete road programme that would ensure safe, dependable and durable roads. The players in the industry are now some of the biggest tax payers in the country. That is what continuity holds and fair decision-making does for a country.

Sugar policy

Nigeria has a huge market for sugar, with demand estimated at about 1.5 million tonnes, but the nation continued to import sugar despite the huge potential across the sugar value chains. To address this, the National Sugar Development Council (NSDC) was established in 1993 and by an Act of the National Assembly in 2004 to achieve at least 70% self-sufficiency in sugar. But it was not until 2012, when I became the minister of MITI, that the NSDC's Nigeria Sugar Master Plan (NSMP) was finalized and approved by the government, while implementation commenced in 2013. The NSDC Act was amended in 2015 to give legal backing to the NSMP.

Kenana Sugar Company in Sudan was incorporated in 1975, the same year as Savannah Sugar Company in Nigeria, while Elgunaid was established in 1966, and NISUCO Bacita in Nigeria in 1964. However, while the two companies established in Sudan grew from strength to strength such that Sudan was well on the way to achieving self-sufficiency in sugar and becoming an exporter of the commodity, both Savannah and Bacita were run-down and had to be privatized.

As part of our efforts to market the NSMP and attract investments into Nigeria's sugar sector, I visited Sudan in 2014. I was very impressed with the sugar cane plantations, processing factories, research centres, the irrigation infrastructure and the communities of about one million people supported by the sugar industry in Sudan in 2014. These were exactly what we set out to achieve with the NSMP through the NSDC. Sadly, I understand that there has been a downturn in the Sudan sugar industry. The NSMP was expected to deliver:

- 1.79 MT/annum of sugar
- 116 million litres/annum of ethanol
- 37,378 permanent jobs
- 79,803 casual jobs
- 411.7MW of electricity
- \$350–\$500 million foreign exchange to be saved on sugar importation
- \$65.8 million savings foreign exchange on fuel imports annually (E10 mandate)

Some progress has been made since the plan was approved, albeit slow. The full delivery of the outcomes will depend on the consistency and quality of implementation as well as the macroeconomic environment, in particular the exchange rate.

SWF: a mechanism for economic diversification, development, savings and stabilization

SWFs play a prominent role within the global financial ecosystem. The number of SWFs has increased in the last three decades, with sovereign investors in more than 50 countries, and combined assets under management exceeding $8 trillion. The largest funds are held by resource-rich countries and East Asian economies. Most SWFs have economic diversification as a primary mandate in addition to providing a buffer against commodity risk.

One of the high points of my time in government in Nigeria was the actualization of the NSIA, which has been the vehicle for managing Nigeria's SWF since 2011. At the time I was appointed Minister of Finance, the world was just beginning to recover from the global financial crisis. Given my professional background, one of my first priorities was to assess the sovereign risks and put strategies in place to prevent similar crisis in future.

I also assessed the size, quality and sustainability of revenues, the quality of spending and the loan portfolio. I inferred that to build a strong and resilient economy that would deliver sustainable and inclusive economic growth, we had to manage our risks better and address the other issues identified. The entire financial ecosystem was overdue for comprehensive reform. We needed to manage our loan book better, only borrow to fund infrastructure projects that would expand the economy and allow us to pay back our debt, and set up sinking funds to repay the loans; there was room to optimize the value and economic returns for a larger proportion of our borrowings. The economy was not diversified and resilient enough to absorb a major shock, among other things.

We relied almost entirely on one source of revenue, sale of crude oil, which is a finite asset, and we had no influence or control over the price of oil. When you dig deeper you also realize that at that particular time, of all the OPEC (Organization of the Petroleum Exporting Countries) and commodity-dependent countries, Nigeria, Iraq and Ecuador were the only ones in the world without a SWF. Even countries like Ghana, which had just found oil, were already in the process of setting up a SWF. I also anticipated at the time that, with the discovery of oil by many countries, the supply would outweigh the demand in a matter of time. Climate change would also have an impact, so we had to take some bold actions immediately.

President Obasanjo's administration had taken some critical risk management steps by introducing the oil-based fiscal rule and the Excess Crude Account when Dr Ngozi Okonjo-Iweala was the Minister of Finance. However, the Excess Crude Account is a stabilization account that would not achieve the goals of a SWF. In addition, it was not a legal vehicle (many state governors saw it as illegal) and was unfortunately perceived by some Nigerians and the international community as a vehicle for corruption, because there were no rules for withdrawals, funds were 'shared' at various NEC meetings to the state governments and there was no transparency or accountability about how the amounts shared were spent. President Yar'Adua also tried to set up a fund, but due to a combination of factors it was not passed by the NEC and the National Assembly. We therefore decided to set up a SWF that would achieve the following:

- Help reduce the country's vulnerability to significant external shocks resulting from global oil price fluctuations.
- Ensure intergenerational equity, as oil and gas are finite assets.
- Support domestic development efforts by investing in critical and trade-related infrastructure.
- Serve as a catalyst for attracting additional local and foreign investment.
- Provide a powerful signalling effect to credit agencies and external investors in terms of improved fiscal management, with an associated positive impact on Nigeria's sovereign credit ratings.

Creating the SWF in under a year in 2010/11 was a tough task that involved:

- Structuring the fund to reflect the Santiago Principles, achieve the set objectives and to comply with the constitution.
- Drafting the bill and make presentations to the NEC about five times to secure its approval for the SWF and to set aside a seed capital of $1 billion.
- Presentation of the bill and meeting with the attorney-generals of all 36 states of the federation in Abuja to obtain their approval.
- Presentations to FEC for approval.

- Seek legal opinion from a Supreme Court judge to confirm that the bill and method of funding were not inconsistent with the provisions of the constitution.
- Presentations and meetings with the Senate and House of Representatives, as well as appearance at public hearings to present the bill and respond to the many questions.

Some told me point blank that it was impossible, and others argued that a section of the Constitution required all revenues to be paid into the Federation Account and distributed. While this is true, other sections of the Constitution supported the creation of such a vehicle but, more importantly, it was possible to structure a SWF that complied with all sections of the Constitution, including the section on paying all amounts into the Federation Account and distributing it. It only required creativity and political will. Generally, it required patience and attention to every detail and side comments. Three of my special assistants (Bukky Alakija, Dr Muyiwa Adedeji and Fola Oyeyinka) spent most of their time on this initiative, working with the advisors, relevant ministries, the CBN and the National Assembly to harmonize the bill and to get the act gazetted.

We wanted the SWF to be a tool for economic development and diversification and a vehicle that would meet international standards, become one of the best in the world and attract investments. We were specific on the qualifications required to sit on the board and hold key management roles, we assured transparency and accountability, which involved publication of annual reports in newspapers, and presentations of the report to a council, which included NEC members, etc. Within two years of operation, the NSWF won an award for its governance structure and operations, reflecting the quality of the thought that went into its structuring, the Act and the appointments of the management team.

The bill was passed into law on 17 May 2011 and signed into an Act on 27 May 2011 at 4.30pm, which was the last working day of the administration and the President's last major approval for the term.

All this happened because of the total support and leadership of President Jonathan. Also, it was a joy to work with Mr Adoke, who was the Attorney-General of the Federation at the time; Dr Ngozi Okonjo-Iweala, who supervised the operationalization of the fund after she took over from me when I moved on as the pioneer minister for the MITI; Dr Bukola Saraki (chairman of the governors' forum at the time); and other progressive state governors, who included Governor Peter Obi, Governor Murtala Nyako and Governor Liyel Imoke, who rallied strong support for the vision.

It was disappointing, though, that apart from the initial $1 billion seed money made available to the NSIA at inception, the regular funding plan within the law setting up the fund was not adhered to. If this had been adhered to strictly and some governors had not gone to court challenging the law, the fund would have exceeded $20 billion by now and the impact on the economy would have been significant. In time, one hopes, this will be corrected, given the clamour for savings when there was a sustained fall in oil price recently.

The following is an extract from a report published by one of Nigeria's business newspapers, *BusinessDay*, three years after the SWF was established:

> Positive rating of Nigeria's Sovereign Wealth Fund, July 21, 2014
>
> 'The establishment of the Nigerian Sovereign Investment Authority (NSIA) in May 2011 by the Federal Government with seed capital of $1 billion has turned out to be one of the most significant economic policy decisions taken in recent times. The NSIA was founded for the purpose of managing the Nigerian Sovereign Wealth Fund (NSWF) into which the surplus income produced from Nigeria's excess oil reserves is deposited.
>
> 'It is worthy to note that within a very short time of existence, the NSIA is now rated second globally by Linaburg-Maduell transparency index administered by Sovereign Wealth Institute. Linaburg-Maduell Transparency Index was developed at the Sovereign Wealth Fund Institute by Carl Linaburg and Michael Maduell, and is a method of rating transparency in respect to sovereign wealth funds.
>
> 'In the official statement announcing the second quarter ratings, the Institute singled out NSIA for special mention, stating that the NSIA has been upgraded to nine points out of a possible ten from a score of four in the previous rankings.

'The NSIA, which was ranked alongside sovereign wealth funds from the USA, France, South Korea, Brazil, and Malaysia, is the only African sovereign wealth fund so ranked. More significantly, the improved transparency ranking was due to NSIA's commitment and adherence to the highest prescription of Santiago Principles with respect to corporate governance, investment strategy, disclosures and SWF best practices.'

Among its achievements since creation, the NSIA has been involved in:

- Structuring and deployment of capital received from the Presidential Infrastructure Development fund on three major projects: the second Niger Bridge, which has stalled for decades, the Lagos–Ibadan Expressway and the Abuja–Zaria–Kaduna Kano highway.
- Investment in fertilizer plants to assist farmers, increasing output by more than 12 million bags of fertilizer.
- Investment in fintechs.
- Collaboration with the Fund for Agriculture Finance in Nigeria, a fund that provides tailored investment capital and technical assistance to commercially attractive agriculture SMEs across Nigeria.
- Investment in a world-class cancer centre at Lagos University Teaching Hospital, advanced diagnostic centres at Federal Medical Centre Umuahia and Aminu Kano Teaching Hospital.
- A credit guarantee/insurance scheme, which mobilized funds into the economy.
- Co-invested with the African Development Bank (AfDB) and UFF (now signature Investments), a specialist in agri-investment.
- Financed the hyperscale data centre in Lagos through Kasi Datacentres.

I will discuss two similar funds, by other countries, to show what is possible and what Nigeria may be missing.

Mubadala Development Company: the UAE's economic diversification

Mubadala is a highly successful global telecom company and a subsidiary of the UAE's SWF. Its primary objective is to generate strong returns by investing in areas that will benefit the community, and develop and diversify different sectors of the UAE's economy. To promote tourism, Mubadala invested in hotels and museums, and in Formula One racing with the Abu Dhabi Grand Prix. To advance its healthcare, Mubadala partnered with and brought the Cleveland Clinic to Abu Dhabi. In education, the company has attracted prestigious international universities such as New York University to the UAE. The fund also invests in the energy, healthcare, telecom, utilities and education sectors to produce the best minds and skills to drive the economy.

Saudi Basic Industries Corporation (SABIC)

SABIC is a Saudi Arabian multinational corporation that was established in 1976 with investment of $1.8 billion. Today, it is the second-largest diversified chemical company in the world, being a market leader in the production of methanol, polycarbonate, polyethylene, polypropylene, glycols, fertilizers and granular urea. It is owned and funded directly by Saudi Aramco (officially, Saudi Arabia Oil Company) from oil revenues but the concept/goals are very similar to those of the SWF or a subsidiary of the SWF. Its mandate is to pioneer and drive gas industrialization in Saudi Arabia by adding value to the gas produced.

The company had total assets of $78.7 billion as at end of December 2020, while the aggregate production was 60.8 million tonnes. It employed about 32,000 people and generated $31.2 billion in sales revenue in 2020 despite the impact of COVID-19. With 68 plants worldwide, 20 innovation centres and over 9,946 global patents (2019 and 2020 annual reports), the company also has the SABIC Academy, which trains all SABIC staff as well as hosting classes for university students. All this meant that Saudi Arabia had a long-term industrialization plan and SABIC (funded from oil revenues) pioneered and drove gas industrialization.

Having operated successfully for several years, SABIC expanded into steel manufacturing, focusing on the export market, as local demand was inadequate. The SWFs in Saudi Arabia and their partners invested in some of the industrial zones in 35 industrial cities and in the technology zones too, the investments exceeding $133 billion and employing 528,000 people. This was the model that Nigeria tried to replicate with Eleme Petrochemicals but failed and then sold the company to Indorama, which turned around the company; its sales and profit increased over 30 times.

Nigeria's NSIA can achieve the same remarkable success as SABIC in the Ogidigben oil and gas free-trade zone, if given the opportunity. In fact, I visited SABIC, one of its academies and some of the oil and gas free-trade zones in Saudi Arabia and initiated discussions to invite them to invest in Ogidigben free-trade zone and also arranged for NEPZA to undertake a study visit to the free-trade zones and develop a working relationship with their counterpart in Saudi Arabia.

Nigeria: low-hanging trade fruit

Apart from a very low manufacturing value added, the major problem with Nigeria's export of non-oil commodities is the quality and standards. Poor compliance with phytosanitary measures has caused Nigeria to have one of the highest level of rejects of agricultural produce exports to Europe and the US. This results from the excessive use of agrochemicals that exceed the maximum residual level permitted, use of banned agrochemicals and presence of aflatoxin in agricultural commodities. This is also a local consumer protection issue, as sanitary and phytosanitary measures are there to protect humans, animals and plants from disease, pests or contaminants.

Government agencies whose mandates relate to standards and quality must be revamped. These include the Standards Organization of Nigeria, the NEPC, the Department of Weights and Measures of the MITI, the Federal Competition and Consumer Protection Council, and Federal Produce Inspection Services, among others. To address some of these issues, the Standards Organization of Nigeria established two internationally accredited laboratories in 2014 and we commenced a comprehensive quality infrastructure programme with the United Nations Industrial Development Organization (UNIDO) and the EU. This needs to be completed and enhanced.

Nigeria may not be able to match the skills of the dominant countries in global trade, but it can at least produce for Africa and ensure that the WTO trade facilitation agreement is fully implemented to get the desired benefits of the agreement. To this end, the top-ten high-valued items imported by the top-ten economies in Africa were identified (Figure 4.4), and the aim should be to produce and export to those countries. This trade strategy will not only boost trade but also improve the balance of payments and foreign reserves. This strategy has been adopted and successfully implemented by the Asian economies for decades.

Figure 4.4: Top-ten African economies (Nigeria excluded) and their top-ten imports

Country	Top-ten Imports
South Africa	Mineral fuels (including oil); machinery (including computers); electrical machinery and equipment; vehicles; pharmaceuticals; plastics and plastic articles; optical, technical and medical apparatus; other chemical goods; organic chemicals; inorganic chemicals.
Algeria	Mineral fuels (including oil); fertilizers; inorganic chemicals; sugar and sugar confectionery; fruits and nuts; salt, sulphur, stone and cement; iron and steel; machinery (including computers); organic chemicals; fish.
Morocco	Electrical machinery and equipment; vehicles; fertilizers; clothing and accessories; fruits and nuts; vegetables; fish; inorganic chemicals; aircraft and spacecraft; salt, sulphur, stone and cement.
Kenya	Mineral fuels (including oil); machinery (including computers); electrical machinery and equipment; vehicles; iron and steel; plastics and plastic articles; animal/vegetable fats, oils, waxes; cereals; pharmaceuticals; articles of iron or steel.
Angola	Mineral fuels (including oil); gems and precious metals; salt, sulphur, stone and cement; fish; machinery (including computers); wood; copper; food industry waste and animal fodder; aluminium; iron and steel.

Ethiopia	Machinery (including computers); mineral fuels (including oil); electrical machinery and equipment; vehicles; animal/vegetable fats, oils, waxes; cereals; iron and steel; plastics and plastic articles; pharmaceuticals; fertilizers.
Ghana	Gems and precious metals; mineral fuels (including oil); cocoa; fruits and nuts; ores, slag, ash; animal/vegetable fats, oils, waxes; wood; meat/seafood preparations; rubber, rubber articles; aluminium.
Tanzania	Gems and precious metals; copper; ores, slag, ash; fruits and nuts; oil seeds; vegetables; coffee, tea, spices; tobacco, manufactured substitutes; cereals; fish.
Côte D'Ivoire	Cocoa; mineral fuels (including oil); rubber, rubber articles; gems and precious metals; fruits and nuts; ores, slag, ash; cotton; wood; meat/seafood preparations; animal/vegetable fats, oils, waxes.

Source: Research by BAA Consult 2022

Time to deliver double-digit inclusive growth

Nigeria has all the potential to become one of the top-ten global players in gas industrialization, which is one of the 13 sectors identified by the NIRP as sources of foreign earnings for the country. As of 1 January 2022, Nigeria had about 208.62 trillion cubic feet (TCF) of proven gas reserves, in addition to which the US Geological Surveys estimate 600 TCF of undiscovered potential. The combined 808 TCF is approximately equivalent to 136 billion barrels of oil, which is significantly greater than the oil reserves of 37.046 billion barrels. The gas reserves are expected to increase from 208.62 TCF to 220 TCF within the next ten years and to 250 TCF thereafter. Nigeria clearly has a competitive and comparative advantage in gas.

As demonstrated by Indorama, the petrochemicals industry can be one of the major drivers for sustained double-digit growth in Nigeria.

It has the potential to grow to about 20% of Nigeria's GDP, become a major earner of foreign income, reduce the pressure on foreign reserves, and to contribute significantly to exchange rate stability, employment generation and entrepreneur development. I recall a global head of one of the international oil companies telling me that Nigeria does not understand or appreciate enough the quantity and quality of gas it is endowed with.

The government is a major driver of inclusive growth, but more effective through policies and programmes that create an enabling environment and incentivize private participation in key sectors of the economy. This has been done successfully by the Nigerian government in oil and gas, petrochemicals, telecommunication, cement, development finance and in the way the SWF was established, among others. These successful models and policies can be replicated in other sectors of the economy that have capacity to create a large number of jobs. Specifically, Figures 4.5 and 4.6 provide summaries of the Indorama Eleme Petrochemical Limited and Nigeria Liquefied Natural Gas.

Figure 4.5: Indorama Eleme Fertilizer & Chemicals Limited (IFL)

The privatization in 2006 of Eleme Petrochemicals by the Nigerian National Petroleum Corporation birthed IFL, whose core investor is Indorama Corp. and has become a success story in privatization. The company has operated the world's largest single-train urea plant within Nigeria since June 2016 and it is the largest fertilizer producer in Sub-Saharan Africa, with a combined production capacity of 8,000 tonnes per day in granular urea and an annual capacity of 2.8 million tonnes. This world-scale urea complex comprises urea-ammonia facilities, a captive port terminal, and 83 kilometres of gas pipeline and associated infrastructure facilities. The gas pipeline connects the plant with the feedstock supplier at a design capacity of 235 million standard cubic feet per day to support the natural gas requirements of the two urea lines.

The company has a unique shareholding that includes an ownership stake of 7.5% by local communities and 2.5% by employees, the latter enabling staff commitment and enhanced productivity. Rivers State Government and the FGN also have stakes in the company.

The surplus production after supplying the domestic market is exported to over 20 countries in Europe, Asia and Africa, as Nigeria offers excellent logistics as well as seasonal advantages to best serve regional markets in the west and south of Africa, and the natural export markets in South and North America. All the urea exports are handled by the captive port terminal, located 16 kilometres from the complex, with a capacity to handle handy, supramax and panamax ships.

The firm has 41 new grades of polyethylene and polypropylene, and it is the market leader in petrochemicals, controlling about 85% of the market. The company leverages partnerships with licensors across the US, Canada, France and Italy, which boosts its export reach, as the products are of international standard.

Figure 4.6: Nigeria Liquified Natural Gas (NLNG)

NLNG was established in 1989 to harness Nigeria's enormous natural gas and its potential, starting with production capacity of 22 million tonnes of liquified natural gas and five tonnes per annum of natural gas liquids. The public–private partnership model brought remarkable success:

- A board structure that is transparent and accountable.
- Board and management appointments based on merit.
- One of the fastest-growing global oil and gas entities, expanding from Train 2 in 1999 to Train 6 in 2019, and currently working on the Train 7 project.
- It has earned over $100 billion over the last 20 years and paid over $18 billion dividend, over $9 billion in taxes and about $15 billion as feedgas payments.
- It has over $17.5 billion worth of assets.

An effective legal instrument that institutionalizes the firm: guarantees protection of the interests of all stakeholders as enshrined in the Nigeria LNG (Fiscal Incentives, Guarantees and Assurance) Act. Cap87, Laws of Federation of Nigeria 2004.

Ownership: the government (through the Nigerian National Petroleum Corporation) owns a minority share of 49%, while the majority shareholding of 51% is owned by private participants, namely Shell (25.6%), Total LNG (15%) and Eni (10.4%).

Local content: the firm is committed to local content development that empowers indigenous contractors (including local and community vendors) to access contracts on merit.

Independent board: the 12 board members act independently in setting the strategic direction and making decisions for the firm.

CEO outside of political influence: the appointment of the CEO is carried out by the board, based on merit, without political influence, with emphasis on qualifications and experience in oil and gas.

Financing: all the key projects of NLNG are mix-financed with self-funding and international borrowing based on the company's credit rating.

Global governance standards/shareholder committee best practices: the code of corporate governance promotes best practice that enhances transparency and accountability to all the key stakeholders.

Skill transfer: Nigerian technicians are being trained and have access to career development opportunities.

Critical enablers

The drivers of national competitiveness, namely: investment, a friendly business environment, skills acquisition, availability of cheap and long-term financing linking technology and innovations to industries, infrastructure and standards are already addressed in the NIRP. But there are other critical enablers for economic diversification and national development, which are often not properly identified as such and linked to economic diversification and development.

A strong and stable macroeconomic environment

Money follows money. One of the biggest predictors of how much money an economy attracts at the end of the day is a strong and stable macroeconomic environment. This is why Nigeria must strive to re-establish a stable macroeconomic environment so that both 'hot' and more 'sticky' money can come into the system, establish and revive industries and create jobs. A situation where rising inflation, exchange rate and runaway food prices is the order of the day cannot foster the kind of stimulus our economy needs. Between 2011 and 2015, Nigeria saw a relatively stable macroeconomic regime, which was the magnet for many new investments in the country at the time. If the country did it then, it can be done again.

Security of lives and property

Without question, security is a paramount national consideration. The irony in Nigeria today is that, as a country, we fought for and secured peace (through the Economic Community of West African States Monitoring Group) in Liberia, Sierra Leone and the Congo, where Nigerian soldiers on peacekeeping missions proved to be great examples through significant sacrifice. It is time to invest in a modern security framework for the country that pre-empts insurgency, crime and unrest.

National values system

History has shown that the most successful companies and countries in the world have some core values, which have become part of their culture. It is *people* who make the laws and enforce them, develop and implement the economic plans and policies. So, if the values of integrity, hard work, patriotism, industry, spirituality, compassion and contentment are not embedded in the culture and do not form the foundation on which the economic programme is built, the nation is bound to fail woefully. It is time Nigerians realized that religion and tribal linings are tools for division that allow the mediocre to run the economy.

Civil service reform

The civil service is the backbone of the government. In the period of the economic transformation of Singapore, the civil service was one of the first institutions that Lee Kuan Yew addressed. He forged a system of meritocracy, a highly effective and non-corrupt government and a civil service with a reward system that recognized hard work, performance and integrity. Civil servants are critical to the formulation and implementation of policies but are often ignored in the process. They are powerful and can do and undo. In many ways they determine the quality of the plans and policies and their implementation.

Nigeria needs a smaller and professional civil service that is well trained and paid very well in order to attract and retain the best talent. This should reverse the current pattern of a bloated civil service whose members are paid less than a living wage and are ill-equipped.

Economic institutions and agencies

Government agencies are the implementing arm of the ministries and are therefore critical to any economic diversification plan. At a minimum, competent technocrats that have a reputation for delivery should be appointed to the boards and management of these agencies. KPIs should be set and a comprehensive review of their performance conducted every four years before renewal of terms.

In 2013 a committee set up by the FRC was inaugurated to harmonize existing codes of corporate governance and to develop codes of corporate governance for private, public sectors and non-profit organizations for the first time in the country. We engaged the best and drew from the best practices around the world. The work was completed before I left office in 2015, but I felt we needed further consultation, particularly with the NGOs, before implementation. It has now been issued and adopted by the private sector. We do have an NCCG, which compares with the best in the world and will have a dramatic and positive effect on our economic institutions if fully adopted by the public sector.

Drastically improve quality of spending and investment

Getting value for taxpayers' monies spent or invested confers the right on taxpayers to hold political office holders to account. Concerted efforts should be made to eliminate any form of waste, misappropriation and leakage, including the menace of uncompleted projects.

Investing in our most important asset

Investing in people should begin with reforming health and educational systems to make education more relevant to the economy and the schools focused on character formation, technical skills acquisition and educational excellence. This approach to education and skills acquisition has been successfully implemented by Germany and Poland.

Population control

The number and demographic advantages of Nigeria's population are of little value if and when productivity is low and the economy remains relatively small. Most of the youth population is unemployed and thus they do not have enough disposable income to become important consumers of goods produced locally. Every year Nigeria adds roughly 5.5 million people to its population, which is about the population size of Congo, Namibia, Liberia, Mauritania and the Gambia, among others. In 1960 the population of the UK was 52 million and that of Nigeria 46 million, but by 2015 the UK's population was 62 million and Nigeria's was 185 million. It is projected that by 2070 Nigeria's population will be 550.37 million and the UK's 75.81 million!

When the population persistently grows faster than the economy, it leads to unemployment, poverty and insecurity. It is time to introduce population control measures such as sustained and effective reproductive education, at least in the interim, backed up with policies that will turn the quantity advantage into productive advantage. This could be through sustained and effective reproduction education in local languages and easy access to birth control.

Political arrangements

Nigeria's current political and governance structure as constituted is not sustainable and needs restructuring in order to accelerate economic diversification and development. As operated, the presidential system is rather expensive for Nigeria and does not encourage competition between the different states.

Funding infrastructure

Inadequate economic and trade-related infrastructure in which electricity adds about 30% to the cost of production remains a problem that must be addressed. The problem has persisted due to a poor infrastructure development plan and implementation, low priority given to production and trade infrastructure and poor funding.

There are many infrastructure financial instruments, strategies and incentives that can be explored, including private finance initiatives (PFIs), public–private partnerships and diaspora funding. Nigeria and other African countries that suffer resource paucity for the design and delivery of development projects in their pursuit of inclusive growth do not always have to borrow for this purpose, especially offshore loans that are expensive and come with other attendant concerns. If these countries take advantage of the large and growing population of migrant workers and their home remittances, there are two possible ways to get the diaspora population involved in national development. The first and increasingly popular way is a diaspora bond, and the second is a diaspora fund to finance economic/trade-related infrastructural development.

The success that Nigeria recorded with its maiden issuance of a $300 million diaspora bond in 2017 illustrates this potential. This instrument can be further explored by ensuring that the proceeds are project-tied. For example, the bonds can be floated to fund new projects in power, railway and road, eliciting confidence through transparency, accountability and opportunity for the investors to take ownership. There is 'citizenship pride' when their investment is tied to specific national projects.

Nigeria should consider working with the diaspora to explore these opportunities, which will also help reduce external borrowing. India adopted this instrument to meet matured financial obligations during financial crises, whereas Israel issues diaspora bonds on a yearly basis to fund developmental projects, while Ethiopia raised funds from the diaspora for a major hydropower project.

Data is golden

Availability of up-to-date and credible data has been a major problem in developing countries but the situation has improved in many, including Nigeria, over the last 12 years. Government sits on a lot of important data and in Nigeria much of this is generated by the NBS. Unfortunately, there is no established machinery for interrogating, interpreting and using these data and surveys to formulate policy. The NBS has produced details on the economy, sectoral contributions to the GDP, inflation, the drivers and causes of inflation, poverty levels, unemployment at national and state levels, by age group, gender, etc. The NBS and SMEDAN also undertake and publish surveys on the MSME sector every three years. This survey provides data and information on the number of MSMEs at state and national levels and by sector and gender, the challenges they face, government policies that have or have not worked for the sector and more, but no one acts on them. If anything, the usual and only reaction of government is to argue about methodology and discredit the information if it shows the government in a bad light. My team and I engaged with the NBS under the leadership of Dr Kale first when I was in finance and later in the MITI. We were amazed at the amount and quality of the data available. We became regular users and it was one of the reasons why our presentations to investors were dynamic, credible, different, fresh and impactful. We were also regular users of the MSME survey, a sector that accounts for a large proportion of Nigeria's GDP and workforce.

It is time for developing countries to understand that data analysis and use is critical to developing a 21st-century economy, understanding and addressing issues on the economy, poverty, unemployment, insecurity, etc. Knowledge, relevant skills and innovation are the global currency for the 21st-century economies. The director-general of the NBS should be encouraged to make regular presentations to the FEC, where decisions can be taken and ministers held accountable. Governments must invest in generating credible and up-to-date data and employ professional data analysts to help analyse and direct information to the relevant MDAs.

Economic partnership and strategy

China remains the highest trading partner (imports) for products that Nigeria can produce if it focuses on its industrialization plan. Sub-Saharan Africa has the highest cost to export compared with all other regions and the highest cost to import with the exceptions of Latin America and the Caribbean, based on border compliance, and South Asia, based on documentary compliance.

Ideally, trade policy should be driven by the industrial policy and Nigeria should have a well-defined strategy and policy for domestic trade, intra-Africa trade, trading with the rest of the world and with the major trading partners, including China. It is obvious that China has a strategy for Africa and Nigeria, focusing on infrastructure development and export of their products, which they have successfully implemented. The question is, do Africa and Nigeria have a strategy for China and other major trading partners?

Africa needs a strategy for its main trading partners, including China, Europe, the UK and the US. I recall that on one of UK Prime Minister David Cameron's trips to Nigeria, he and President Goodluck Jonathan directed the UK Minister for Trade and Investment (Lord Stephen Green) and me to design a programme that would double the trade between the two countries by a target date. This was achieved. This encouraged Lord Green and me to agree to work on a diaspora-led programme that would deepen and increase the volume of trade between both countries. This is just a small example of what can be achieved when there are specific plans for major trading partners.

Despite the challenges, Nigeria is still on track

In 2005, Goldman Sachs' Global Economics Paper No. 153 identified the 11 countries that could have BRIC-like (Brazil, Russia, India, China) potential in rivalling G7 nations over time. These countries were Bangladesh, Egypt, Indonesia, Iran, Korea, Mexico, Nigeria, Pakistan, the Philippines, Turkey and Vietnam. These were the next 11 most populous, highest-potential, emerging economies after BRIC countries. They were referred to as the 'Next Eleven' or 'N-11' by the oracle, Lord Jim O'Neill and his team at Goldman. While these countries are significantly smaller than G7 and even BRIC members, Goldman Sachs estimated that the N-11 could reach two-thirds of the size of the G7 economies by 2050. As one of the N-11, Nigeria was predicted to become a top-20 economy by 2050. The conditions the N-11 required to achieve this potential included:

- Maintaining and entrenching macroeconomic stability.
- Continuing reforms to improve business climate and tackling corruption.
- Improvements in financial depth to mobilize local and international capital.
- Urbanization that supports economic growth, particularly by underpinning productivity growth, as has already been the case in China and was beginning to materialize in India.
- Increase in energy and infrastructure investment.
- Investing in education and health as human capital is a critical aspect of long-term growth. The right investment in health could lead to life expectancy of about 75 years.
- Adoption of technology, including growth in mobile phones as important drivers of long-term growth.
- Focusing on drivers of growth at the micro level, such as cost of doing business, legal framework, political climate, etc.

In April 2006, President Obasanjo invited the NLI and its moderators from the Aspen Institute in Colorado to run an NLI-style seminar for him and his cabinet and some heads of government agencies. That led to a follow-up presentation on the economy and N-11 to him, his economic ministers and the CEOs of the large companies in Nigeria on 26 April 2006. I was accompanied by one of our senior economists at Goldman, Ben Broadbent, who is now Deputy Governor for Monetary Policy at the Bank of England. It was at that meeting that Vision 2020 was declared. Ben had indicated in our presentation that, according to the Goldman research, Nigeria was on track to become a top-20 economy by 2050 if it carried out the expected reforms. But Mr President was not having any of that. He said Nigeria could and would do better. Nigeria would work towards becoming a top-20 economy by 2020. This was how Vision 2020 was declared. It was easy to go along with the president at the time because the country had already started many critical reforms and the economy was moving in the right direction, with a strong president and cabinet.

Between 2010 and 2015, African countries had high prospects for strong growth as seven out of the ten fastest-growing economies in the world were in Africa. Nigeria was one of that seven. The continent was known for a stable and strong macroeconomic environment, low debt to GDP ratio and higher returns on investments. There was so much optimism for Africa as the next frontier from 2011–14, which was at a time when developed countries were suffering from financial crisis, very high debt to GDP ratio, low growth and return on investment. This was the period that the MINT economies emerged – Mexico, Indonesia, Nigeria and Turkey.

Nigeria, being one of the seven economies in the top-ten fastest-growing economies, had so much promise, blessed with abundant human and natural resources. So, what happened? What prevented African countries from sustaining the growth and emerging as the next frontier as expected?

An immediate explanation often offered for the poor performance of African economies is unprepared and poor quality of leadership. Most political leaders in Africa tend to focus on war, conflicts and retention of power rather than on the economy. This is compounded by weak economic, political and social institutions as discussed earlier. In short, Africa was not ready to take advantage of the situation then despite the fact that investors were looking for new homes.

The main lessons from this period are that Africa needs to address the leadership and structural issues in order to strengthen the political, economy and social institutions. China was in the same position up to 1980 when, despite its population, it was poorer than Sub-Saharan Africa. China's GDP/capital was less than Nigeria, Malawi, Burundi and Burkina Faso.

It is now 18 years since the research was published and the question is: are the N-11 nations on track to becoming top-20 economies or have they missed the boat?

Lord Jim O'Neill, the architect of BRICs and N-11, in his assessment in 2018, said that he still believed that Nigeria, Vietnam and perhaps Iran had great potential but must address the serious obstacles to becoming a $1 trillion economy. I have already discussed some of these obstacles above and in this book.

If we focus on Nigeria alone, the numbers tell us that, despite the serious obstacles and recent economic hardship, Nigeria has made some notable progress since 2005. The GDP of Nigeria in 2005, when Goldman published its research paper, was $169,645 million and it was ranked 38 in the world out of 195 countries. This compares to a GDP of $514.05 billion in 2021, the highest in Africa. It was also ranked as the 27th-largest economy in the world in terms of nominal GDP, and the 24th-largest in terms of PPP. The GDP per capita of Nigeria in 2005 was $1,222 and it reached $2,421.62 by the end of 2021. In the near term, the Nigerian GDP per capita is projected to trend around $2,441 in 2022 and $2,452 in 2023.

Yes, Nigeria did not make the top-20 in 2020 but it and President Obasanjo were close enough. Nigeria should be commended for this achievement given that the original prediction was for the year 2050, but it is still not near where it should be, given the fundamentals and potential. If anything, Goldman and Lord Jim O'Neill were right to include Nigeria in N-11 because it has demonstrated that it has great potential and that, if it addresses the areas identified in this book, it has a bright future and the Jewel of Africa can be reclaimed.

Lessons from China

China, before its economic transformation, had a high rate of poverty, a command economy dominated by the government and trade-protective policies. Industrial production was controlled, and resources allocated by the central government. The country had poor leadership during the Great Leap Forward of 1958–62 when there was famine that resulted in the loss of 45 million lives. As the economy opened up to the global market from 1979, investments into the Chinese economy increased significantly.

The Chinese economy has doubled every eight years, lifted over 800 million people out of poverty and ranked first using the PPP metric for its GDP. China is the largest manufacturing economy, merchandise trader, highest holder of foreign reserves, the commercial partner of the US and largest foreign currency holder of US Treasury securities. As the economy attained maturity, the growth rate of real GDP slowed from 14.2% in 2007 to 6.6% in 2018, necessitating a new economic model that focused on innovation, private consumption and services to trigger sustainable long-term growth. In the new model, China set the target of upscaling manufacturing in ten critical sectors towards reducing dependence on foreign technology and to boost its market globally.

Huge investment in physical and human capital repositioned the country for rapid growth, as special economic zones were established. The economic reform included removal of trade barriers, enhanced global competitiveness and incentivized foreign direct investments. In response to the financial crisis of 2008, the Chinese government injected a $586 billion stimulus package to finance infrastructure, along with an accommodative monetary policy that increased bank lending. This helped to moderate the rate of economic slowdown.

The two key drivers of Chinese economic growth are huge capital investment funded by domestic savings and foreign investments, and a significant boost in productivity, based on the Industrial Revolution Plan. China is among the leading net global lenders due to high gross savings that far exceed its domestic investment. Reforms in agriculture result in rapid improvement in productivity and opportunity to shift manpower to manufacturing and service sectors as well as enhancing private sector participation.

China's industrial and investment policies allow state-owned enterprises (SOEs) to dominate key sectors such as petroleum, mining, telecommunications, utilities and transportation, which together account for about 50% of non-agricultural GDP. SOEs constitute 50% of the 500 largest manufacturing companies in China and 61% of the top 500 service sector enterprises. Chinese merchandise exports rose from $14 billion in 1979 to $2.5 trillion in 2018, while merchandise imports grew from $18 billion to $2.1 trillion. The economy faces challenges on the environment, corruption, relative lack of rule of law and ageing workforce and population, partly because of the one child policy, which has now ended. The Made in China project set goals to achieve 40% of domestically manufactured basic components and basic materials by 2020 and 70% by 2025.

Governors and local communities also have a role to play

The example of Offa

Offa is a town with a population of about 120,000 in Kwara State, Nigeria. In many ways, both the traditional and modern leaders in that town have shown how to transform the town and make it compliant with the 21st century.

Accelerated transformation calls for everyone's hand to be on the deck. It cannot be left to the central government alone. Individuals, regional and local governments and communities have a significant role to play, and I think Offa has set an example that other traditional leaders and indigenes of local communities can emulate. Offa has a ten-year economic development plan developed by the Offa Descendants Union through its Economic Development Committee led by Dr Waheed Olagunju, a development expert. This is based on the vision of Oba Mufutau Gbadamosi, the traditional ruler of Offa, for the economic and social transformation of Offa. The union is already building a multipurpose industrial park as part of that plan. The information technology hub of the park has already been commissioned. Offa Metropolitan Club, led by Dr Sarah Alade, a former deputy governor and acting governor of the CBN, comprises some active and retired Offa indigenes in Nigeria and the diaspora who have completed the construction and equipping of an ultra-modern medical health centre within the complex of Offa General Hospital. The centre will offer some specialized medical services currently not being rendered by existing public and private health delivery institutions in Offa and neighbouring communities.

One can only imagine what would happen to the economy, jobs, poverty level, insecurity and development of the nation if this example set by Offa indigenes led by Oba Gbadamosi were replicated across the country.

The Oba of Lagos, Oba Rilwan Akiolu, is another traditional leader who has taken a very keen interest in attracting investments into Lagos and in ensuring that Lagosians take full advantage of the job opportunities created by government policies. In every call I had with him, he talked about jobs for Lagosians and investments for Lagos and was always available to meet with investors. He was on top of those policies and the job creation opportunities.

I was also particularly impressed with the level of support the Sugar Council and Flour Mills received from the Emir of Bida, Yahaya Abubakar, when Flour Mills decided to embark on the construction of the sugar cane to sugar plant in Sunti, Niger State.

State governors have become very competitive in attracting businesses to their states. That is a welcome development as they now link this effort to increasing the states' IGR. For example, the former governor of Ogun State, Governor Ibikunle Amosun, and his Commissioner for Industry, Trade and Investment, Bimbo Ashiru, over the period became masters in the game. Close to 300 new industries were established in Ogun State with the state working very closely with the federal MITI. The incentives were good, state support was always there and the governor and commissioner were both very proactive. There is no doubt that President Jonathan was in Ogun State far more than any other state to commission new factories. I was there more than 15 times also to commission new factories. I remember on one occasion one of the companies had a security problem. As soon as it was brought to my attention, I called the governor and was pleasantly surprised that he picked up my call immediately even though he was outside the country on official duties. I told him about the issue and he said I should leave the matter with him. Within about ten minutes, I received a call from the investor/industrialist to say that the matter had been resolved with the governor's intervention. That is how proactive they were and how state governors and their commissioners can make a huge difference by working closely with the MITI and other relevant federal ministries.

Apart from the investor-friendly environment, Ogun State had some unique advantages: proximity to the ports and Lagos, a big market and at the time the Commissioner of Finance, Kemi Adeosun, had started a quiet but profound re-engineering of Ogun State finances, working with Bimbo Ashiru under the guidance of the governor. This led to a significant monthly increase in the IGR from ₦700 million in 2010 to about ₦5 billion in 2015. Most of that additional revenue went into infrastructural development. On one of my visits to Ogun State, the governor took me round to see the development taking place. Ogun State (Abeokuta) was like a construction site – roads, flyovers, bridges, etc. My security detail who grew up in Abeokuta was in tears because of the transformation taking place.

Former Governor Peter Obi of Anambra State was another development-oriented governor. Innoson Motors, the celebrated automotive manufacturer/assembler in Nnewi, and PAN in Kaduna were some beneficiaries of his foresight and commitment to local industries. Innoson was one of a kind. The local content of his cars was close to 60% and he believed he could rival any OEM in the world given the right support. Well, he got that support from the government and in particular Governor Obi, who ordered all the cars the state needed from Innoson and PAN, paid them in advance and helped construct a road to Innoson's factory. Trust us Nigerians, with our taste for foreign goods and cars! There were complaints, as most people expected to receive imported cars, but Governor Obi insisted that we must buy what we produce locally. That is how nations grow; that was how the Asian countries developed their economies. He was an extremely good champion of local patronage, a key requirement to support industrialization and boost the local economy.

Governor Babatunde Fashola and his Commissioner for Industry, Trade and Investment, Sola Oworu, were also very active. In fact, they both played very important roles in the citing of the Dangote Refinery and Petrochemical Complex in Lekki, Lagos.

Conclusion: the future remains bright

It is obvious, despite previous shortcomings, that the Nigerian economy has enormous potential that can be converted into valuable and tangible gains in job creation, industrial revolution, vibrant agribusiness and resilient services in the context of macroeconomic stability. The good news is that, as a country, Nigeria is not starting from scratch. We did it in the '70s and early '80s and we can do it again and do it even better this time. We have made tremendous progress in some areas. I will give some examples:

- There was a time when Nigeria spent a large proportion of its foreign earnings on the importation of cement, but today more than $9 billion has been invested in the cement sector and that industry today supports more than 1.6 million jobs. In 2013 I had the privilege of announcing that Nigeria had become a net exporter of cement for the first time in its history.
- Dangote petrochemical and refineries is a game changer. I and my ministry worked closely with Aliko Dangote and his team at the start of the project when I was in government and I remain an advocate because I know the impact it will have on our economy. When completed and operational next year, it will have the largest single-train refinery in the world. It will not only help to produce what we consume, but it will also export its products as well. Hopefully this will put an end to all the issues around petroleum subsidy, pressure on foreign reserves and the inadvertent impact on inflation and exchange rates.
- Flour Mills is leading the sugar cane to sugar production in Sunti, Niger State. When the policy is fully implemented, four other northern states (Kwara, Nasarawa, Jigawa and Adamawa) will benefit immensely from this policy.

- Proforce in Ode Remo is producing and exporting armoured vehicles for the military, while the likes of Innoson in Nnewi, PAN in Kaduna, Elizade, Stallion and Coscharis and others are championing local assembly of cars.
- Coleman Cables, based in Arepo, Ogun State, has grown to become Africa's second-largest electrical and telecommunications wire and cables manufacturing company.
- The fintech sector, Nollywood and music industries, led by young and enterprising Nigerians, have recorded unprecedented growth in the last few years.

Nigeria has all that is required to become the China of Africa, 'Africa's factory' and even more. When we achieve this, the African Continental Free Trade Area (AfCFTA) will work better for Nigeria and the rest of Africa.

Chapter 5

Investment: making Nigeria the top destination again

'... people are now focused on the MINT – Mexico, Indonesia, Nigeria and Turkey. They are the four countries that international investors are really focused on for growth and investment.'
Michael Andrew, Global Chairman, KPMG International

Attracting investments to any country is serious business that should always be approached as such. I have personal experience from my time at Ernst & Young and Goldman Sachs, too numerous to recount here, about just how critical everything about investments is or can be. A particular event, before I relocated to Nigeria to serve as a minister, relates to my first impression of the government of Nigeria after a long time working abroad. Umaru Yar'Adua was the president and commander-in-chief at the time. I had been out of the country, working in Europe for about 20 years at the time. I came to Abuja for the first time ever with the Goldman Sachs team. It was a senior team comprising the heads of Europe and South Africa. Coming out of the airport I clearly remember the half-hour drive to town. The roads were wide and paved, there were well-spaced trees planted by the road and it felt like going through wooded areas in other developed countries. When eventually we got to Aso Rock, there was a sense of organization, unhurried and orderly from our arrival point. We were then led down the gangway leading up to the reception within the villa, where we were to hold the meeting. At the time, the walk down the gangway seemed long to me, and I am sure also to my colleagues, but the ambience was stately and it was pleasant. In the meeting room, government representatives sat on one side and the Goldman team on the other. What struck me immediately was how orderly it all was. It was a huge contrast to the common image of Nigeria. And as soon as the president came into the room, everyone stood up without prompting. This was new to me.

After the president sat down, he motioned for us to all sit down as well. There was a quiet charisma to President Umaru Yar'Adua, a man of few words but one who had a powerful impact when he spoke. We had a good meeting and the president instructed the Ministry of Finance to work with us. Then he wrapped up the meeting. He rose and left the room, before we all quietly did the same. He left a strong impression on everyone, and I personally was proud to be a Nigerian in the villa on that day. We had met a very serious man who obviously did his homework and knew what he wanted from our working with his team. There was no hint of disorder or the chaos that, in other contexts, people readily associated with Nigeria and Nigerians. In retrospect, I am glad that this visit to Nigeria was in its good order, quietly dignified, classy and efficient, something that set Nigeria apart. The team left that meeting with the impression that we had to deliver. These things matter because they add to the sovereign goodwill of the country and determine how seriously investors engage with the country.

A necessary function

For sustained growth, increased productive capacities, more and better-paid jobs and larger private sector participation, the government must attract private investors into the different sectors of the economy by creating an investor-friendly environment, where good governance, the rule of law, security of assets and people are guaranteed. The delivery on the national plan depends almost entirely on the quality and quantity of the investments the government is able to make and attract from local and international investors. In fact, nations depend heavily on investments from the private sector because government has limited resources and many priorities. Nigeria's National Development Plan 2021–2025 seeks to achieve a broad-based real GDP growth rate of 5% on average during the plan period, generate 21 million full-time jobs and, through an inclusive growth, lift 35 million people out of poverty. In this chapter, the link between all these and a robust economy are further explored using the experience from 2010 to date.

The economy thrives when investors are treated as royalty. With the benefit of hindsight, this was the empirical, measurable, lived reality in Nigeria between 2010 and 2015. Those years were truly remarkable in terms of the sheer range, quality and quantity of investments that flowed into the country. The macroeconomic environment was such that no less than the *Wall Street Journal*, Reuters, Bloomberg, Moody's, Forbes.com and the *Financial Times* – the most mainstream of mainstream media worldwide – had Nigeria on their radar.

A bit of a backdrop will help to situate and contextualize the rise of Nigeria during this period as a prime investment destination globally and as the number-one destination for investments in Africa. The global financial crisis of 2007 to early 2009 had its effects on the economy and in particular on the capital markets and banking sectors, and the recovery was slow. It took coordinated and concerted action by both the monetary and fiscal authorities to put Nigeria on an even keel. I salute the courage and foresight of then governor of the Central Bank, Sanusi Lamido Sanusi, my predecessor Dr Mansur Mukhtar, Ms Arunma Oteh, the director-general of the Nigeria Securities and Exchange Commission, and Dr Abraham Nwankwo, the director-general of the DMO, who had done a lot of the work. I was appointed in April 2010 to work with the team to finalize the plans and operationalize the Asset Management Corporation working with the CBN.

Why Africa?

Despite its challenges, Africa remains the last frontier for investors. The facts speak for themselves. In 1990, Africa's GDP was about $800 billion, but today it is over $2.7 trillion and it is expected to be about $29 trillion by 2050. In the 1990s, foreign direct investment into Africa was about $6 billion to $7 billion a year; by 2015 it was in excess of $50 billion annually. However, as expected, there was a decline in 2021 because of the effects of COVID-19 on the global economy. In 2000, Africa's exports to the rest of the world were about $150 billion; today, exports well exceed $500 billion a year. In fact, according to UNCTAD's (United Nations Conference on Trade and Development's) 2019 report, total trade from Africa to the rest of the world averaged $760 billion in current prices, and the share of exports from Africa to the rest of the world ranged from 80% to 90% in Africa's total trade during 2000–17. The new AfCFTA provides new opportunities for investors in a continent that has an abundance of natural resources, a fast-growing middle class and a population of about 1.4 billion that is set to double by 2050.

Why Nigeria matters

At the centre of the continent's economic story is Nigeria. With a GDP of about $514 billion, Nigeria is the largest, and for many years was one of the fastest-growing economies on the continent. It is endowed with abundant natural resources and large arable land as discussed in Chapter 4. The demographics are in Nigeria's favour, with a population of 216.7 million that has a median age of 18.6 years. Nigeria is the sixth most populated country in the world and it is projected that it will surpass the US before the middle of the century, implying a huge market. There is also a labour workforce of 80 million people, which will make it the ninth largest in the world.

We invested time over a three-year period beginning from 2011 to tell the Nigerian story to local and international investors. It was a story that had previously been delegated to third parties who had little understanding of the Nigeria and Africa we know and the opportunities in the continent. We met with hundreds of local and foreign investors and businesses, spoke with various governments and engaged the larger public. Our efforts paid off. In 2012, UNCTAD reported that Nigeria, for the second year running, was the number-one destination for foreign direct investment in Africa and provided the fourth-highest returns for foreign investments in the world. So, how did Nigeria become the number-one destination for investment in Africa?

Making Nigeria the number-one destination for investment in Africa

As we say at Goldman, it was a team effort. It started with the macroeconomic environment, but many other factors came into it. There was a strong, stable and predictable macroeconomic environment:

- The exchange rate was stable, predictable, relatively low at about an average of ₦150 to the dollar and the FX was available.
- Inflation for most of the period was single digit – about 7%.
- Debt to GDP ratio, at about 12%, was one of the lowest globally, and debt servicing to national income was relatively low too. There was fiscal space to operate within.

- Average GDP growth was about 7%. One of the fastest-growing economies in the world – top-ten.

Nigeria had many other things going for it as well. It was the number-one economy in Africa. It had emerged stronger after the global financial crisis relative to other developing and developed economies, maintained a level of fiscal discipline not seen for decades and had a diverse pool of resources to further fuel its growth. The Nigerian stock market was buoyant, following the implementation of a very successful reform programme at the Nigerian Stock Exchange and a change of leadership. The market rose by 47% in 2013, and the world came to know more about Nigeria's huge, vibrant and resourceful population of about 170 million, three times the population of South Africa then, but now about 216.7 million. Nigeria then had the sixth-largest population in the world with a median age of 18.6 years. By 2070, Nigeria is expected to be the third most populated country in the world, after India and China, and the middle-income class estimated at 23% excited investors.

In terms of natural resources, Nigeria was the tenth-largest producer of crude oil globally, with more than 37 billion barrels of proven reserves being the 11th-largest oil reserve in the world. It also had the eighth-largest gas reserve. In addition, it had more than 44 exploitable minerals in commercial quantities and about 84 million hectares of arable land where any commodity could be grown, with less than 40% utilized. For example, Nigeria is the fourth-largest producer of cocoa in the world and also the largest producer of cassava. Cassava is mostly produced in 25 states of the federation, including all the states in the south-east, south-west, south-south and north-central geopolitical zones, and in Taraba and Adamawa states in the north-east geopolitical zone. Cotton is produced in 11 northern states of the country and it is the second-largest producer in Africa. Oil palm thrives in all the southern states of the country as a major economic tree but is produced mainly by 16 states. Before the emergence of petroleum, revenue from palm oil export was a major source of foreign exchange earnings for Nigeria. Production was much higher than Indonesia's or Malaysia's and it formed a substantial proportion of the capital development fund for the former Eastern Nigeria. Today Nigeria is the fourth-largest producer of palm kernel oil in the world. It is also the second-largest producer of sorghum in the world. This is produced throughout the 20 northern states of the country. Rice paddy is grown in all ecologies across the country, from the Sahelian Yauri through the inland valleys of Badegi to the delta regions of Ogoja, while sugar cane is grown in about 17 states.

Access to Nigeria means access to the entire ECOWAS (Economic Community of West African States) region. Nigeria is a strong member of ECOWAS, accounting for about 60% of the population, 78% of the GDP and 50% of its manufacturing capacity. We had a structure and a delivery team. Even though it was informal, I was the chief marketing officer but I had an active marketing director in the person of President Goodluck Jonathan. He knew and appreciated the value of investors and he always made himself available for investors' meetings at home and abroad. We visited at least 40 countries together, and I went to 68 countries in total, telling the Nigeria story. I was not alone as the chief marketing officer; I had strong marketing officers led by the Nigeria Investment Promotion Corporation(NIPC) and ably supported by other agencies, such as the FRC of Nigeria and the BOI. The NIPC had enabling laws, including visas for investors on arrival. The FRC supervised the adoption of the new financial reporting standards, which made it easier for investors to analyse and compare companies' financial statements.

We also had a strong partnership with the Ministry of Foreign Affairs. This partnership was the key to our success. Working with the Foreign Affairs Minister, late Ambassador Gbenga Ashiru, was not only productive but a dream. All the foreign missions bought into the vision and made investment a major priority. They went all out to find and court foreign investors, and organized highly successful investment conferences.

To further equip them, the MITI organized a meeting with all the ambassadors in Asia, which was hosted by the ambassador in India. The idea was to have separate meetings for the embassies in Europe and in the US. The meeting in India was very well attended. Each ambassador gave a briefing on the country they were posted to, identified opportunities for Nigeria and bottlenecks delaying the flow of investments into Nigeria, plus the support they required from the relevant agencies, led by the NIPC, while other relevant agencies gave presentations on the support available for investors. My team reported on the economy, investment opportunities and new policies in place. The meeting agreed on the next steps, follow-ups and the strategy for attracting investments into the country.

Incentives

Nigeria had and still has some of the best incentives in the world, with foreign investors able to own 100% of their investments in the country, generous tax holidays for investments in key sectors, robust capital allowances and a law that allows foreign businesses to repatriate 100% of profits and dividends. Some of these incentives are not matched anywhere in the region. And in recognition of the varied levels of investment in different parts of the country, Engineer Mustapha Bello, a former Executive Secretary of the NIPC, and this team started putting together a package of incentives to encourage investments into less industrialized parts of Nigeria.

Security

Insecurity and investments do not go together. Although there was some level of insecurity in a small part of the country at the time, generally there was security of lives and property in most parts of the country. My visit to Japan brought this clearly home to me when I had a meeting with some Japanese investors and the issue of insecurity was raised. They told me not to worry about the Boko Haram threat because they already knew the situation, where to invest and which areas of the country to avoid. They then showed us a map of Nigeria, which they shared with any Japanese investor considering investment in Nigeria. The map showed the different states in Nigeria in three colours: red, amber and green. The red indicated the no-go areas, amber indicated states you should avoid and green indicated good areas to invest in and stay. They were very relaxed about security issues because most of the states were in green. Apparently, they had similar maps for the countries they invested in and assured me that Nigeria was not alone. I received similar assurances from some American investors who had done their homework.

We also strengthened one-stop investment centres at NIPC to substantially reduce the cost of entry into the country. The centres simplified procedural steps for obtaining business approvals and brought together all government agencies under a single roof. We introduced visas on arrival for investors and reduced the cost of business registration for SMEs by 50%, and 25% for larger businesses. The president's HIIC was a masterstroke. The NIPC, was then the secretariat of the HIIC and I was the host. Working with the NIPC and the HIIC coordinator, Baroness Lynda Chalker, we revamped the agenda and made the meetings more productive and targeted, and we secured the president's commitment to attend all meetings, which were held twice a year.

Members of the HIIC included foreign investors, former presidents and ministers of some selected countries and local investors, with membership cutting across Europe, the Middle East, Africa, Asia and the US. At those meetings, some ministers, mainly the economic ministers and investors, were invited to make presentations on the economy and the progress made on the transformation agenda, new policies that investors should be aware of, etc. We got feedback on what international and local investors are looking for, their views about Nigeria, how we could address the concerns and policies or initiatives that we should be considering.

Several of our policies and initiatives came from those meetings. For example, at one of the earlier meetings, the HIIC identified Nigeria's image abroad as a problem. At the next meeting, we invited experts, who included investment bankers, renowned economists, credit rating agencies, investors, media and social media experts, to discuss the issues, how other countries had dealt with similar issues and how Nigeria should respond. The Ministry of Foreign Affairs also attended and presented papers at these meetings. One of the findings was that we had delegated the telling of the Nigerian story to people, mainly foreigners, who knew little about the country and that we must now take responsibility for telling our own stories based on facts. This took me to about 68 countries, telling our compelling story. It was an easy sell because Nigeria is indeed a blessed nation endowed with many resources, great weather and with many opportunities. The unique partnership with the Foreign Affairs Ministry to deliver 'Team Nigeria' was hugely successful. I will give you some examples.

Canada

It was the first time that Nigeria had such an event in Canada, and it was very well attended by quality investors. It was obvious that the ambassador, late H.E. Ojo Madueke, and his team had done a marvellous job. Numerous people spoke, but when I finished my presentation on 'Why Invest in Nigeria', all the delegates rose to give a standing ovation. That was how successful most of the events were. We had one-on-one meetings with quality investors and quite a number visited Nigeria after the event. It was the catalyst for the first trade and investment agreement with Canada.

China

In Beijing we were prepared for about 150 investors but more than 400 turned up. We had a record number of requests for one-on-one meetings with the president from credible investors.

Kenya

The event in Kenya was historic; it was tagged the 'East meets West Investment Forum'. President Kenyatta, a very pragmatic and active president, authorized that a five-year (multiple-entry) visa be granted to all the Nigerian investors who attended the event. Passports were collected and some got their multiple visas before they left Kenya. This was his response to complaints by Nigerian investors on how difficult it had been to travel within Africa because of the time it took to get a valid visa. A follow-up event was held in Abuja as part of the maiden flight from Kenya to Abuja.

London

The BOI led by Ms Evelyn Oputu and assisted by Dr. Waheed Olagunju hosted another highly successful investment forum in London, around the Olympics, which led to numerous investments in Nigeria. It was easily the best event Nigeria has ever hosted in London and it had a lot of impact on the image of the country. It also highlighted the quality of the ministers in President Jonathan's cabinet and the government's commitment to attracting investment. The comments from Rezia Khan of Standard Chartered Bank, Regional Head of Research, Africa, summarizes the strong and positive feedback we received from participants:

> 'This wouldn't be the first Nigerian investment conference that London has seen, but it's easily the best. This conference really stands out in one respect, because it's been able to instil a sense of optimism that change is on the way, that reforms are

> happening, that it's all going to drive positive development in the future. So hugely encouraging from that perspective and easily the best investment conference on Nigeria that has been hosted in London.'

There was so much talk about Nigeria, the investment opportunities and quality of leadership that it was not surprising that Nigeria experienced unprecedented numbers of state visits by presidents and investors during that period. These included President Rousseff of Brazil, who visited twice; the presidents of China and France; US Secretary of Trade Spritzer, who led an energy trade mission to Nigeria in May 2014, after I met with Klans Schwab in South Africa to present Nigeria's case. Heads of government of Poland, the UK (twice), Germany and Kenya also visited Nigeria.

The momentum was so strong that the World Economic Forum agreed that Nigeria should host the African version for the first time in May 2014. This was the first and only time that Nigeria hosted the event. More than 900 world leaders, top business executives, entrepreneurs and other influential figures attended that global executive gathering in Abuja. About 13 heads of state and government, including Chinese premier Li Keqiang, attended the event.

Telling the Nigerian story based on local and international convincing data made our case for investment credible. It was not just about telling or making up stories, it was far more about the use and interpretation of local and international credible data to get a compelling message across. I was privileged to have three young, extremely clever and hard-working senior special assistants who understood what I wanted to say and how to the different audiences, and who used compelling data and graphs to get the message across. The presentations were all different, depending on the audience I was targeting. That meant we were always working on our slides, even when on the plane. I do not know where Bambo Kunle-Salami, Juwon Sofola and Abi Mustapha-Maduakor got their energy from! They were inspirational and selfless in their service to the country. They gave me so much confidence in the younger generation that, given the opportunity, they will excel anywhere they are required to serve their country. With such quality of young leaders, the future of the country is bright.

The partnership with local private investors was also key to our success. We developed a strong symbiotic relationship and partnership with these investors, with a strong understanding that an investor should be recognized and treated like a king or queen. There are several reasons for this, as international investors follow the lead of local investors and look for opportunities to partner with them. They want to know whether local investors have confidence in the country and economy, are investing in the economy and have done well by investing in the country without a 'godfather'.

Our impact and success did not go unnoticed by governments, investors, international research institutions, etc. The UK government invited me to speak at the investment forum that was organized around the Olympics in London.

The *Wall Street Journal* said:

> 'In absolute terms, Nigeria is still the clear leader... nearly 3 in 10 companies have Nigeria on their watch list.'

The Economist Intelligence Unit (EIU) had this to say:

> 'Of all the African markets, investors believe Nigeria will offer the best overall prospect for investment returns over the next 3 years.'

Further, Michael Andrew, Global Chairman, KPMG International, also declared in March 2013 that:

> 'People are now focused on the MINT – Mexico, Indonesia, Nigeria and Turkey. They are the four countries that international investors are really focused on for growth and investment.'

These following quotes also summarize the theme of the press reports at the time:

> 'If it [Nigeria] were to show the same increase in its growth-environment score over the next decade, many investors will look back and say why the hell didn't I invest in Nigeria.'
>
> Lord Jim O'Neill, Global Head
> of Economic Research Goldman Sachs

> 'Nigeria was identified as a top pick by some of the most influential investors in emerging markets finance.'
>
> July 2010 Reuters Emerging Markets Summit – São Paulo

There were several lessons learned in that period but I will mention only a few that I consider relevant to this chapter:

- The world and indeed Africa want Nigeria to succeed. A successful Nigeria will have a strong positive impact on the image, respect for and the economy of Africa. Investors, particularly Africans, wherever we went, enjoyed the story, wanted it repeated over and over again, were proud to be Africans and desperately wanted Nigeria to succeed and pull the rest of the continent up. It is true that if you are not in Nigeria, you are not in Africa.
- We must tell our stories ourselves. No one can tell the story or narrative better than the subject of the story.
- The structure of delivery matters. The change of focus and name of the ministry to the MITI and the transfer of the NIPC from the presidency to the ministry was a masterstroke. We also created the role of Regional Investment and Trade Officer in Asia, a diaspora desk with direct links with trade/economic officers in foreign missions, who fully bought into 'Team Nigeria' in all embassies abroad.
- It all starts with a stable, strong and predictable macroeconomic environment, and we had this. High inflation, a high and unpredictable foreign exchange rate and insecurity make it extremely difficult to attract investment.
- It works better when there is synergy between ministries and the relevant agencies. For example, the synergy between the MITI and the Ministry of Foreign Affairs, starting from the two ministers, was critical to our success. It was indeed a team effort. It was a joy and a dream to work with my former colleague, the Minister of Foreign Affairs, late Ambassador Olugbenga Ashiru. He was a seasoned diplomat who got it right from the start and we worked like Siamese twins.
- Good and well-thought-out policies attract investments and investors. We saw that in the automotive, sugar, cotton, textile and garment, and local content policies. The emphasis of the NIRP on value addition, producing what we consume and

consuming what we produce, rather than remaining a country that exports raw materials and jobs and imports finished goods, also paid off.

- Poor implementation or inconsistency in the implementation of policies is damaging to the reputation of the country. Investors lose confidence and it often leads to loss of investments.

Nigeria fintech investment global attraction

In 2021 alone, 63% of foreign direct investment that came into Nigeria went to Nigerian fintech. The development of the fintech industry has been a bright spot in the Nigerian economy, with the potential to get brighter. The sector has been gaining momentum, as agile and innovative start-ups move to take advantage of increased technology penetration and high levels of unmet needs in the traditional banking sector to seize market share. In the past three years, fintech investments in Nigeria have grown by 197%, with the majority of the investments coming from outside the country.

Fintech companies have led with innovation in product development, designing useful, convenient and affordable financial products and services for millions of Nigerians. In the process, they have created a multiplier effect across the economy, unlocking new business models beyond financial services, fuelling the growth of e-commerce and moving the needle on progress towards the country's development goals.

Despite these impressive gains, the impact created by fintech is still only a fraction of its potential. Most fintech companies have targeted early adopters, individuals who are already making use of banking and other financial services and are willing to try out new ones. But opportunity knocks for those who can find ways to deliver new and better services to the underserved and unbanked or use technology to solve some of the problems in developing and developed countries. Nigeria still faces a significant financial-inclusion challenge, with more than 40% of the country's adult population without a bank account.

Nigeria is now home to over 200 fintech standalone companies, plus numerous fintech solutions offered by banks and mobile network operators as part of their product portfolio. Between 2014 and 2019, Nigeria's bustling fintech scene raised more than $600 million in funding, attracting 25% ($122 million) of the $491.6 million raised by African tech start-ups in 2019 alone – second only to Kenya, which attracted $149 million. However, the sector is still relatively young. As Africa's largest economy and with a population of over 200 million – 40% of which is financially excluded – Nigeria offers significant opportunities for fintech across the consumer spectrum, notably within the SMEs and affluent segments and, increasingly, in the mass-market segment.

Nigeria is classified as a developing fintech creator economy compared to its more mature global peers such as the UK, Singapore, Australia, Sweden and India. Nigeria's fintech revenues are anticipated to reach $543 million by 2022, spurred on by rising smartphone penetration and the country's large unbanked population. In 2019, Nigeria officially recognized its first fintech unicorn (a start-up company that is valued at more than a billion dollars), with Interswitch achieving a valuation of $1 billion based on a $200 million investment from VISA. In 2021, Flutterwave became Africa's fourth start-up to achieve unicorn status. It is now valued at $3 billion. The Nigerian fintech ecosystem has so far maintained its growth trajectory within the continent, with Jumia, Interswitch, Flutterwave, Opay, Andela, and Paystack being six out of the eight unicorns in Africa as of January 2022. I expect that another five unicorns will be created in the next eight years.

Where is Nigeria today?

Nigeria's capital importation has been on the decline, from $23.99 billion in 2019 to $9.66 billion in 2020 (during COVID-19) and further down to $6.7 billion in 2021. A similar pattern has been observed in other emerging markets that rely on foreign investment to grow their economies. About 61% of the investment inflow is foreign portfolio investment (hot money), while only 20% is foreign direct investment (sticky money). The rest is other transient forms of capital, including loans. The naira is taking a battering on the FXs, and inflation is rising rapidly, as discussed in Chapter 4. This is problematic, because the foreign direct investment required to create jobs and develop the economy is significantly low.

However, the fundamentals remain strong in terms of natural resources, large workforce and potentially large market. To reclaim its number-one position as the destination for investment in Africa and to compete globally for investments, there are certain steps that Nigeria must undertake, and these are discussed below as critical enablers.

Critical investment enablers

A strong and stable macroeconomic environment

This is a necessary and important prerequisite for economic development and for attracting investments. It is one of the factors we leveraged on when Nigeria became the number-one destination for investment in Africa. Some of the most important macroeconomic indicators are inflation, interest rate, exchange rate and public debt.

Inflation

Food and core inflation figures determine the headline inflation numbers. In 2021, inflation in Nigeria rose to 15.62%, up from 13.2% in 2020, compared to about 9% in 2015 and an average of about 7% between 2010 and 2015. By the end of 2022 it was 21.34% (see Figure 5.1). The NBS attributes the upsurge to the continuous surge in food prices, constraints on domestic supplies, worsening exchange rates, the removal of oil subsidies and increase in electricity tariffs. The goal to pursue is a return to single-digit inflation.

Official statistics show that price rises are faster for food and non-alcoholic beverages, indicating that improving the supply of food items and local production is key to moderating inflationary pressures. We must also note that there are several long-standing constraints, including poor infrastructure, which worsens the problem from the supply side. For example, poor quality of roads, multiple roadblocks/taxes/checkpoints and other transportation modes means that the speed of distributing goods and services is low and the cost is high. A significant percentage of hauled goods are lost due to accidents and collapses of the vehicles, and there is significant spoilage due to longer haulage period. As a result, when the remaining goods arrive at their destination markets, they are sold at around the full price of the full quantity that was dispatched. This is a clear source of inflation.

Addressing the problem of inflation is not just about the Central Bank, it must involve the government ministry in charge of road and transportation development (ministries of works and transport) and the MITI. Of course, in addition to the Ministry of Agriculture, the ministry responsible for water resources has a critical role in ensuring that farming is all-season through irrigation and canalization, and not largely rain-fed as is currently the case. It also means that the Ministry of Transport must prioritize trade-related infrastructure.

Figure 5.1: Nigeria – inflation rate (average consumer prices) 2015–21

2015	2016	2017	2018	2019	2020	2021	2022
9.0%	15.7%	16.5%	12.1%	11.4%	13.2%	15.62%	21.3%

Source: Central Bank of Nigeria, Statistical Bulletins, Various Issues

For a country that is highly import-dependent, particularly for consumer goods, a deterioration of the naira exchange rate would push inflation up. The naira/dollar exchange rate has been deteriorating almost consistently since 2015. The peak official rate was ₦197.8/$ in 2015; ₦361.3 in 2018; ₦358.8 in 2020; ₦403.5 in 2021; on 29 November 2022 it was ₦444.67, and the unofficial rate on the same day was ₦820. A worsening exchange rate means worsening imported inflation. In addition, there is the component of imported inflation that arises from inflationary momentum in the European, Asian and American countries of origin of the imports because of worldwide disruptions in supply chains caused by the COVID–19 pandemic lockdowns, the Ukraine–Russia war and now the energy crisis.

But Nigeria can greatly reduce the risk of exposure to this type of imported inflation. It still depends on imports for which substitutes are readily available from its abundant natural resources or that can be produced locally, such as processed food, petroleum products, plastics, raw materials, auto parts, etc. Part of the defect is obviously policy based: the lack of or poor implementation of policies and plans such as the NIRP, lack of sufficient discrimination in the imports of capital goods versus raw materials or versus consumer goods. Nigeria continues importing so much food when it has an abundance of agricultural potential, variety of climates and vegetations, variety of soil types suitable for grains, tubers, fruit trees, animal husbandry, etc. Food import-driven inflation is, therefore, a challenge to the Ministry of Agriculture.

Specific attention needs to be paid to effective migration from subsistence to commercial-scale agriculture. In doing this, though, measures must be taken to include the smallholder farmers in the value chain, rather than displace them. On the capital goods and raw materials, the Nigerian Raw Materials Research and Development Council and several other research institutes, such as the Federal Institute of Industrial Research Oshodi (FIIRO), have a major role to play if they are encouraged, properly resourced and supervised, and stay within their mandate. I visited the FIIRO many times to see how it could play a role in the implementation of the NIRP, and I was impressed with the work that Dr Gloria Elemo, the director-general at the time, was doing.

Importation of petroleum products in 2018 constituted 12% of Nigeria's total imports valued at ₦1.623 trillion. According to OPEC sources, in 2020 Nigeria's petroleum imports were ₦2.945 trillion. A related item, plastic products, accounted for 7.7% or ₦1.032 billion imports in 2018. Nigeria was the 17th-largest petroleum products importing country in 2020, yet the irony is that Nigeria is the sixth-largest oil-producing country in the world. The fact is that Nigeria has no business importing petroleum products when its fossil fuel resources (oil and gas) places it at an advantage to be an exporter of processed products from the mineral.

Of course, importation of petroleum products relates to removal of subsidies, which the NBS identifies as a major cause of inflation. Rather than import petroleum products and import inflation therefrom, Nigeria ideally needs to develop and improve its domestic refining capacity to satisfy its domestic demand for the products. This is a sure path to fighting inflation in the medium to long term. The good news is that the Dangote refinery will be completed soon and it is on track to produce enough for the local market and for export. It was one of the game-changing projects we envisaged under the NIRP and why I and my ministry including NEPZA were involved right from the beginning. It is a major investment, would boost both local and international trade and earn foreign income for the country. The whole complex, including the fertilizer plant, is located in a free-trade zone – one of the policy instruments under the MITI implemented through the NEPZA.

Beyond the tariff on electricity, perhaps a greater problem is that of its inadequacy in terms of quantum and stability of supply. For quality of electricity, Nigeria ranked 136 out of 137 countries in the 2017 Global Competitiveness Index. Poor electric power supply means that industrial production, in particular, is discouraged. Industries that forge ahead must rely on self-generation of power, thereby complicating and increasing their cost of production while losing the benefits of economies of scale that accrue from an external multi-customer power supply firm. As a result, cost of production is high, production level is sub-optimal, product prices are high, while the products are globally uncompetitive. As in the case of road infrastructure, therefore, inadequate electricity is a structural driver of inflation. The Ministry of Power needs to deploy imaginative models of licensing independent power plants. Models, such as the one that enabled the success story of Geometrics Power Limited in Aba, should be replicated for other industrial and commercial clusters. The new arrangement with Siemens, which has started, should improve the situation particularly the transmission, drastically.

Nigeria's inflation is also a monetary and fiscal phenomenon. Broad money supply rose by over 81% from ₦21,288 billion in 2015 to ₦38,627 billion in 2020. A related source of monetary operations-induced inflationary pressure is monetary financing of fiscal deficits: CBN net claims on government rose by 590% from ₦835 billion in 2018 to ₦5,768 billion in 2019; it then rose by another 48% to ₦8,559 billion in 2020. Monetary authorities, therefore, need to rein in the explosive growth of money supply. In any case, maintaining price stability remains a paramount objective of central banks the world over.

Viewed from the purely fiscal angle, the fiscal deficit to GDP ratio, which was minus 1.6% in 2015, became minus 2.28% in 2018, minus 3.3% in 2019 and minus 4.0% in 2020. The Ministry of Finance, Budget and National Planning can contribute to the remedy for surging inflation in this respect. Among other opportunities for this solution is to address the underperformance of public revenue. Nigeria's public revenue to GDP ratio at about 7% is among the lowest in the world and can be significantly increased.

In summary, if only one thing has been made clear with the above brief excursion, it is that the task of controlling inflation and achieving a strong and stable macroeconomic environment is not that of the Central Bank alone. There needs to be a co-joining of efforts by the real sector public entities: the ministries of Agriculture, Industry, Trade & Investment, Works/Transport, Power, Science and Technology, as well as the monetary (CBN) and fiscal authorities (Ministry of Finance, Budget & National Planning). To achieve the common objective, each of the entities will need an appropriate target from its platform, which when combined would add up to the common goal. Coordination is, therefore, imperative.

Exchange rate

A realistic and stable exchange rate is an essential component of a strong and stable economic environment. I have already noted that a deteriorating exchange rate, particularly in an import-dependent economy, would weaken the economy by contributing to domestic inflation and discouraging investors because of the uncertainty it causes, not only in the valuation of their assets but also in their ability to legitimately repatriate their earnings or even exit their capital as the need arises. Therefore, building an environment that attracts stable investment to support huge and sustainable economic growth requires working towards a stable exchange rate.

As previously noted, the Nigerian currency has been weakening in recent years. The major explanation for this is that the Nigerian economy is not diversified in respect of exports. Nigeria's forex earnings are dominated by oil and gas. As such, quantity shocks as experienced over the last two decades from insecurity in the oil-producing regions of the country and price shocks in the international oil market cause major drops in forex earnings and lead to depreciation pressure from the supply side.

Figure 5.2: Naira/USD exchange rates 2015–21

	2015	2016	2017	2018	2019	2020	2021
Naira per USD	196	305	305.5	306.5	307	380	403

Source: Central Bank of Nigeria, Statistical Bulletins, Various Issues

The exchange rate at the official market closed at ₦451.67/$1 on 20 December 2022 but the black market rate (unofficial rate) was ₦736/$1. Diversification into value-added non-oil exports, rather than a few primary products and commodities, is the appropriate strategy to support a strong and stable currency. Indeed, the NIRP, introduced in 2014, did identify 13 items that Nigeria can produce and export competitively as a top-ten exporter globally. An export-led industrial economy is what is required. This should simultaneously aim at limiting imports, particularly of consumer goods, to only items for which direct or close substitutes cannot be produced locally, with food self-sufficiency as part of the building blocks for a strong national currency.

Diaspora remittances provide another window for Nigeria's quest to diversify and strengthen its foreign exchange inflows; these were about $23 billion in 2019 and $17 billion in 2020. At the global top, in 2020, diaspora remittances as a percentage of the GDP were 4% for Nigeria, 3.1% for India and 6.7% for Bangladesh. Nigeria's diaspora inflows are mostly consumer-oriented – sent to family and friends as gifts, payment of school fees, settlement of hospital bills or, at the near-investment end, for the acquisition of residential houses. The opportunity is, therefore, to design frameworks and platforms that can attract remittances into direct investments in projects and investment-funding platforms. The Ministry of Industry, Trade & Investment should partner private sector funds and investment managers to launch such a fund or programme. India has had similar programmes for years and Ethiopia used the diaspora fund to partly fund its hydro project.

A balancing item in the architecture of foreign exchange maximization is foreign loans, the inflow of proceeds adding to the country's pool of foreign exchange and helping to strengthen the exchange rate. However, care must be taken to direct foreign loans into projects that either directly or indirectly would generate the cashflow for servicing and amortizing the loans.

It is appropriate to, at this stage, undertake a situation audit of the principles, practices and technicalities for Nigeria's activities in the ICM. After all, it should be expected that there have been significant changes in both the local and global landscape, which need to be reflected in a modified framework.

On the demand side, high and price-inelastic import dependence complements the supply-side pressure to cause the naira depreciation. The common sense solution is to produce as much as possible of the goods we consume and consume what we produce. In addition, local capacity for significantly increasing the local content in the assembly of vehicles and other mechanical spare parts, as provided for in the automotive policy, should be boosted through focused support to local initiatives that are already existing in places such as Nnewi and Coal Camp in Enugu. Processing machines such as rice and cassava processing plants produced by the country's technology research institutions, for example the FIIRO, should be producing en masse through effective collaboration between research institutes and the private industry. These measures will reduce demand for foreign exchange.

It is obvious from the above that, when you look at the exchange rate levers on both the supply and demand sides, while the Central

Bank must play a productive role, particularly in maintaining an appropriate balance among exchange, inflation and interest rates, a desirable exchange rate requires achievement of real targets by the industrial, agricultural and infrastructure sectors, which are under different ministries. Each of these ministries must understand that its action or inaction affects the exchange rate, and the government must ensure that targets are set and are well coordinated. The exchange rate is only a nominal variable whose value and movements depend on the real variables.

Interest rates

Interest rate is essentially the price that enables economic agents with surplus funds (surplus units) to make them available in exchange to economic agents who are in deficit of funds relative to their existing or planned activities (deficit units). A logical interest rate architecture facilitates savings, investment and growth of the national product. That is why it is important to review the interest rate structure as part of the quest for a strong and stable macroeconomic environment that would facilitate investments and support sustainable economic growth and development.

The most formalized and most traditional way through which this exchange occurs is the banking system. Hence, the focus on bank deposit rates and bank lending rates, vis-à-vis the Central Bank's Monetary Policy Rate (MPR) and the inflation rate. The MPR, being the rate at which the Central Bank lends to deposit money banks, serves as a point of reference for banks' deposit and lending rates. In lending to the various grades of customers, a bank would mark up on the MPR – differing mark-ups reflect the riskiness of the different groups. Also, in lending to its customers, a bank considers its average cost of funds and, particularly, the interest rates it pays on customers' deposits of different tenors, which are usually much lower than the MPR. It must ensure that the interest rate spread, that is the lending rate minus the average deposit rate, is not too wide as to discourage depositors. The bank must strike an optimal balance between what it pays to depositors and what it charges borrowers.

When the inflation rate is well above single-digit, the monetary authorities have a big problem because in an attempt to ensure a positive real interest rate, they would have to fix a high MPR, which would trigger a high level for the other interest rates, including lending rates. Such development would discourage industrialists and other businesses from investing in the economy, as their cost of funds becomes high. Because a central bank would desist from that line of action, a price distortion is invariably introduced into the financial system and the role of the price (in this case interest rates) to drive efficient allocation of resources is impaired.

Figure 5.3: Nigeria – money market indicators (%) March 2022

Inflation	15.5
Monetary policy rate	11.5
Savings deposit rate	1.28
3-month deposit rate	4.41
6-month deposit rate	4.53
12-month deposit rate	5.82
Prime lending rate	11.84
Average lending rate	11.84
Maximum lending rate	26.61

Source: Central Bank of Nigeria, Statistical Bulletins, March 2022

What this anecdote of relative data shows is that there are several incongruencies in the structure of interest rate in the Nigerian money market. The major source of that distortion is the rate of inflation, which is significantly above single-digit. Achieving and sustaining the inflation rate at single-digit for an appreciable length of time will offer the opportunity for a logical realignment of the various interest rates, in such a manner that they could serve as dependable signals for maximum mobilization and rational allocation of funds in the system. What is needed is the implementation of all those initiatives already proposed under the section on inflation. A final note is that in developing nations where there are structural issues, high dependency on importation, poverty and low savings, a non-existent mortgage system, and where interest on borrowing is a relatively small proportion of the high cost of production for most companies, relying on interest rates mainly to moderate inflation is not as effective.

Public debt rate

Maintaining a healthy public debt portfolio is an important determinant of investment inflows and sustainable growth of the economy. A country suffering from unsustainable debt will experience capital flight as well as capital atrophy; this was the case for Nigeria in the 1980s and 1990s before the debt trap was exited through debt relief in 2005 and 2006.

Although Nigeria's debt to GDP ratio at 27% (in 2021) is not a major concern, given that it is lower than the country-specific conservative threshold of 40%, and even much better than the IMF threshold of 55% for countries in Nigeria's peer group, there are two big areas of vulnerability. One is the debt service to revenue ratio and the other is the utilization of the proceeds of foreign borrowings. Nigeria's debt service to revenue ratio for 2021 was over 90%; this is much higher than the peer-group threshold of between 12% and 15%. In 2022 the ratio exceeded national income. This means that debt servicing is crowding out resources that would have been used in other areas, particularly for growth-generating investments. This condition reflects at least two pathologies. One is that the country is not generating enough revenue relative to the size of the economy. Accordingly, comprehensive, transparent and efficient revenue collection and management and the diversification of the economy through accelerated, consistent and disciplined implementation of an industrial plan are the clear remedial actions required in this regard. The second area of concern is that the speed of debt accumulation seems to be very much faster than the speed of economic growth and revenue generation of the economy – a variant of absorptive capacity. This is evident in Figure 5.4. Over the five years, 2016–21, the public debt stock rose by 128%. There is a need to be less impulsive and more cautious and purposeful about procuring new loans.

Figure 5.4: Nigeria's public debt stock 2016–21

	2016	2017	2018	2019	2020	2021
Amount ₦ trillion	17.360	21.725	24.387	27.401	32.955	39.556
Growth (%)	–	25	24	12	20	20

Source: Debt Management Office Publications

The second big issue around Nigeria's ballooning public debt is utilization of the proceeds of both domestic and external borrowings. First, there are enough indications that much of the loan proceeds are directed to recurrent expenditure rather than growth-generating capital expenditure, which is a complete departure from the policy of the DMO and the Ministry of Finance presented to the FEC when I was Minister of Finance that proceeds from borrowing must be used solely for infrastructure development that would expand the economy. I also insisted that sinking funds be established to repay the capital when due and to service the debt to avoid putting the burden on future generations. Second, there is the challenge of ensuring that the entire public finance management ecology is efficient, transparent and accountable, so that borrowed funds are neither used to refill leaked public funds nor directly leaked out. Unless borrowed funds are fully protected from leaking out and are fully utilized for investment and growth, borrowing will be dysfunctional. These anomalies would show in poor and deteriorating debt ratios, which would serve as warning indicators to investors to keep away from the country. The economy will get weaker and less stable.

When I went to China to seek and negotiate the loan for the Abuja–Kaduna standard railway (the first standard rail gauge in the country) and commenced the process for securing the finance for the Lagos–Ibadan railway, the clear intention was to concession the railway to the private sector and use the proceeds to service the debt and repay the loan. Government is not and should not be in the business of operating a train service. If this had been adhered to strictly, we could have avoided the inefficiencies and the leakages, as Nigerians found out after the unfortunate train attack in 2022. As part of my negotiations with the Chinese company engaged to build the railway, they were to set up a company to manufacture the spare parts, etc., transfer technology and restrict the number of Chinese employed on the project to an agreed number.

The Nigerian government should review the state of its public debt condition to ensure the country is on a path of debt sustainability – a path that makes public debt an asset in support of investment, growth and development, rather than a drag on the economy.

In this regard it is relevant to recall that in 1996 the federal government commissioned an appraisal study of projects funded with ICM loans. The results of that exercise were very revealing about how external borrowing could be a misadventure. Now, 26 years after that audit exercise and 16 years after the country's exit from the debt trap, it is long overdue and appropriate to conduct another comprehensive audit of all the projects funded by external loans – ICM loans (Eurobonds), multilateral loans and bilateral loans, including Chinese loans. Moreover, the country should establish a standard for conducting such audit exercises every five years.

Closing note on the macroeconomic environment

In summary, to achieve and maintain a strong and stable macroeconomic environment that would support economic development and attract investments, there is a need to design a macroeconomic framework that will be supervised by a strong macroeconomic management team within the economic management team that is led by the vice-president and is accountable to the president. The macroeconomic management team would take responsibility for addressing the macroeconomic correlates of a strong and stable economy as identified and outlined in the foregoing, using dedicated task teams constituted from various relevant ministries identified above, departments and agencies, and who are charged with specific targets and with specific delivery timelines.

The financial system

According to IMF's Article IV 2021 Report, Nigeria's financial sector is stable. However, given the rapid developments in the global financial system, and especially the enigmatic thrust of fintech, it would be necessary to adopt a more dynamic approach by carrying out a comprehensive review of the financial system, so as to develop a strategic plan for the years ahead. The required review is the type that was conducted by the World Bank in 2000, that is 23 years ago. This position is with full recognition of the Financial Sector Strategy 2020, which was launched in 2007; two years after its target date and it is apparent that the big and confident leap forward projected has not materialized.

The review of the financial system will include the review of the CBN's mandate, governance structure and independence to determine whether it is fit for that purpose and to ensure that it is apolitical. The primary objective will be to have a central bank that is or matches the best central bank in a developing economy. On independence there should be clarity on what it means and how the CBN is measured based on the role it had to play to control some macroeconomic indicators. For example, it was only in 1997 that the Bank of England was granted independence, but it was very specific. The independence was to set interest rates, and it was given a single target to keep inflation at 2%, plus or minus one percentage point. With inflation much higher than the 2% target, there are calls to review its independence again.

In Japan, the Bank of Japan (the central bank) maintains 'close contact' with ministers so that monetary policy is mutually harmonious with government economic policy. The approaches adopted by the UK and Japan have their pros and cons. Nigeria needs to find what works for it, given the nature of the economy and drivers of the macroeconomic environment.

The review of the financial system would also look at how the government can further support the banks to ensure that they play a more effective role in the economy, charges to account holders are transparent and justified, and that they are supported to become key players in the fight against money laundering and corruption.

Finance

The cost of funds in Nigeria is high, typically more than 20%. Also, available tenures on credit facilities are too short and cannot be used for long-term competitive businesses. The short-term facilities in Nigeria are best suited for trading. There is no access to development finance for infrastructure. Anecdotally, it would be clear that, given Nigeria's huge infrastructure deficit as summarized earlier, together with its massive commercially exploitable resources, its finance needs are significant. Indeed, speaking at the November 2021 Glasgow COP26 event on improving global infrastructure, Nigeria's President Muhammadu Buhari stated that the country needs about $1.5 trillion over ten years to close its current infrastructure deficit.

In terms of addressing the challenge, there are two broad sources to look at: domestic and external. For the domestic market, efforts should be directed at broadening and strengthening the systems, networks, platforms and frameworks, including regulatory and coordinating frameworks, supportive of raising long-term debt, and non-debt capital. And that should be targeted at both public and private sector financing needs.

In the period from 2005 to 2017, a lot of progress was made in developing the domestic debt market by various public and private sector organizations, spearheaded by the DMO, with similar strides in the equities market by the then Nigerian Stock Exchange (now Nigerian Exchange Limited) and the FMDQ (Financial Markets Dealers Quotations). Although there is some evidence that a good foundation has been laid, the country's ranking in financial market development remains unacceptable. The 2018 Global Competitiveness Index report presented the picture thus, among other components: availability of financial services, 102; affordability of financial services, 129; and venture capital availability, 133. It should be useful to now undertake a comprehensive and in-depth review of the domestic capital market so as to come up with initiatives towards its optimal contribution to capital formation and financing, going forward.

For the external private capital market, it should be recalled that, under my guidance as Minister of Finance, the DMO in January 2011 successfully issued the first Nigerian sovereign debt in the ICM. The debut $500 million was for ten years and was 2.65 times over-subscribed at a coupon of 6.75%. The initiative created a sovereign benchmark, which Nigerian corporates have leveraged to access long-term capital in the ICM. Of course, the Nigerian government has since established a permanent presence and reputation in that market and has been severally accessing needed long-term capital from it. Indeed, it has 30-year bonds in the market, the first of that tenor having been issued in 2013, thus showing the country's advances in that market.

But it is appropriate to, at this stage, undertake a situation audit of the principles, practices and technicalities for Nigeria's activity in the ICM. There have been significant changes in both the local and global landscape that need to be reflected in a modified framework.

Account should also be taken of the conventional non-private foreign debt sources that include the multilaterals (World Bank, International Fund for Agricultural Development, European Development Bank, European Investment Bank, AfDB, African Export-Import Bank, etc.) and the bilateral arrangements with China, France, Japan, etc. These two require a review for appropriate repositioning.

Nigeria must review the legal framework for alternative financing sources such as private equity and venture capital funds, and development funds for infrastructure development. The country's development financial institutions, such as the BOI, Bank of Agriculture and NEXIM (Nigeria Export-Import Bank), are unable to meet the needs of Nigerians because they are grossly undercapitalized. Strategies must be put in place to expand these institutions and assist them to access cheap external funds, including raising funds from the capital markets. We started that process with the BOI and have discussed the success in Chapter 4. The CBN also has to develop a financing model, working with local banks to unlock new sources of cheap long-term capital for investing in critical sectors of the economy.

Urgent need for risk capital

For infrastructure, for example, it is a lot easier to raise equity and debt of about $3 billion after the developmental studies have been completed, but it is almost impossible to raise the $4 million required to undertake the development studies and establish a business case. There are two possible solutions to this: the government needs to create a strategic investment vehicle for this purpose and for the accelerated industrialization of identified sectors and/or make adequate budgetary allocation to address sectoral risks, as in the case of mining, where certain credible studies must be completed to attract credible junior miners, before the major miners come in. If well structured and managed, these vehicles will generate high-risk adjusted returns for the country. Some multilateral institutions have also tried to help address this, but the approach is often wrong and therefore it does not lead to the desired outcome.

The lack of risk capital and management expertise significantly curtails the growth of the MSME sector in Africa. And yet this is a sector that has the greatest potential to grow the economy and create jobs in Africa. There is a need to deepen and transform the private equity and venture capital sectors in Nigeria as enablers for the attraction of global capital, including risk capital for small and growing businesses in the economy. Private equity capital, at its most basic, is typically longer-term, relatively patient capital that is provided in exchange for an equity stake in existing high-growth but undercapitalized and/or underperforming companies. Venture capital, on the other hand, is usually seed capital invested in start-up businesses at the earliest stages of their development. Both have been invaluable for the promotion of innovation and technological advancement, not just in high-risk businesses but across all sizes of business, particularly in emerging markets, which for different reasons have been considered by providers of finance to be high risk. Some of the world's best-known and innovative businesses and brands have been private equity or venture capital financed.

Infrastructure

The status of a country's infrastructure is a major determinant of its productivity, industrialization and competitiveness of its goods and services in the global market, which in turn determines its growth, employment generation, export capacity and external balance (balance of trade and balance of payments), domestic prices and external value of the local currency (exchange rate). In essence, a developed state of a country's infrastructure is an all-important enabler of economic growth, economic diversification and competitiveness. Apart from attracting direct investment (foreign and local) and stimulating diversification, adequate infrastructure is necessary for the blossoming of MSMEs, which are an engine for sustainable and inclusive growth.

Accurate diagnosis of and prescription for enhancing the various components of infrastructure is imperative for the establishment of a strong, stable, productive macroeconomic environment.

The current Global Competitiveness Index 2017–2018 edition, which reported the relative positions of 137 countries, provides a summary of the abysmal state of Nigeria's infrastructure. Overall, the country ranked 132 out of 137 countries. For quality of electricity, Nigeria ranked 136; for quality of roads, 127; for air transportation, 125; and for mobile telephone subscriptions, 117.

Poor electric power supply means that industrial production, in particular, is discouraged. Industries rely on self-generation of power, thereby complicating their production focus, while losing the benefits of economies of scale that accrue from an external multi-customer power supply firm. As a result, cost of production is high, production level is sub-optimal, product prices are high, while global market position is uncompetitive. In some cases the lack of constant supply of electricity adds close to 20%–30% to the cost of production.

Poor quality of roads and other transportation modes means that the speed of distributing goods and services is slow, affecting the quality of goods and pricing, as previously discussed. I remember some industrialists telling me that it is cheaper and sometimes quicker to import a product from China than to transport goods from Lagos to some parts of northern Nigeria. As MITI Minister, I received the prices of some commodities in each state every month. When I investigated the reasons for price differential of the same commodities, such as rice and cement, it was always attributed to the high cost of transportation within Nigeria and the lack of appropriate trade-related infrastructure.

Even in the case of telecommunications, where the industry is making commendable progress, contributing 12.61% to GDP in the last quarter of 2021, up from 8.5% in 2015, the country's ranking in mobile-cellular telephone subscriptions is as poor as 117. This shows that, given the population of the country, its landmass and economic potentials, there is still huge untapped capacity based on the low level of the requisite infrastructure.

Accordingly, Nigeria needs to address its huge infrastructure deficit urgently and strategically. It needs to take deliberate and definite steps to attract investments to the sector. We had the opportunity to do this on the Lagos–Ibadan Road and a few others but missed the opportunity for sub-sectors such as roads for which concession should be encouraged. For electric power, imaginative models of licensing independent power plants, such as the one that enabled the success story of Geometric Power Limited in Aba, should be replicated for other industrial and commercial clusters. The privatization of electricity generation and distribution under President Jonathan was not a bad idea. He was determined to address the issue and he personally chaired the meetings in his first year before the privatization. In that year he assembled a team of technical advisors and multilateral institutions to develop the privatization road map, which was subsequently executed by the National Council on Privatization, chaired by the vice-president. The whole concept of the privatization and how it was designed was considered an innovative and an effective solution to the problem but, as usual, there were weaknesses in the implementation. Nigeria must learn from this.

Given the nature and stage of Nigeria's infrastructure backwardness, it is pertinent to broaden the discussion to include soft infrastructure, particularly education and health. This is because the human being is both the agent and target of growth and development; they are producers and consumers of the goods and services that summarize the endgame of the economic drama. In primary education and health, Nigeria ranks a frightening 136 out of 137; in higher education and training, it ranks 116. Its primary education enrolment ranking is 132, infant mortality is 133, while overall life expectancy is ranked 133. The quality of mathematics and science education ranks 118.

One of the consequences of this, is that the best brains are going abroad, contributing to the economy, education, health, commerce and governance of those countries, leaving Nigeria largely in the hands of people who are less capable of running and developing the country. A strategy for enabling a strong, sustainable economy through transformation of both the hard and soft infrastructure condition must, therefore, include a simultaneous and interactive transformation of the human development factor, as discussed in Chapter 6. In respect of education, for example, there is a compelling need to establish the conditions for sustainable funding, a major cause of the collapse of the education system at all levels. The existing model of sharing of responsibility for basic and tertiary education among the three tiers of government, as well as between the public sector and the private sector, needs to be rationalized.

Competitiveness: investment and economic growth go together

To attract investors into the country, Nigeria must become more competitive. Competitiveness drives productivity and will determine the long-term prospects of our economy as we saw in Asia. Investors are not in love with China for the sake of it. They go to China because it is cheaper to produce there and they know they can get world-class skills and technology, without paying too much. That is competitiveness. In 2005, landed costs to manufacture in China and deliver to the US were 25% to 30% less than manufacturing in the US. This led to a huge reallocation of capital and capacity towards Asia. Recent analysis suggests that the gap has narrowed to 10% to 15%, but the gap remains. Although Germany lost its clothing and fabrics manufacturing to cheaper locales such as China, India and Turkey, German companies have innovated and moved up the technology curve to stay competitive. They now have a commanding share of the global market for complex machines that weave, braid and knit textiles, riding the investment boom in low-wage countries. Germany's former textile sector went high-tech, shifting its speciality to industrial textiles for the automotive and aerospace sectors. The Germans have used innovation to be competitive and I must say that it is not just about becoming competitive, but staying competitive.

Nigeria must act quickly. As regional markets consolidate, economic blocks strengthen and trade barriers are removed through multilateral and bilateral agreements, it is becoming more important to be competitive than ever before. The effects of agreements such as the AfCFTA, Common External Tariff, EPA and Preferential Trade Agreement mean that Nigerian businesses are now open to competition from all over the world. Nigeria must enhance its governance and regulations by promoting leaner and easier to implement business regulations, leveraging on technology and innovation. This will also involve working with the Organisation for Economic Co-operation and Development (OECD) to review all relevant investment laws, regulations and policies in Nigeria and update them in line with international best practice. The establishment of a functional competitiveness council will also assist.

National competitiveness councils

The common denominator of successful approaches is close cooperation between the public sector, business and civil society – the three key actors. Over the past few years, national competitiveness councils (NCCs) have proven to be one of the most successful approaches to institutionalizing public–private dialogue and action on competitiveness. Recognizing that competitiveness can only be enhanced through joint action, many countries have created NCCs and many of these play a major role in economic policymaking in their country, such as in the US and Ireland. That was the catalyst for setting up the first NCC with Dr Chika Mordi as the pioneer CEO, and Tony Elumelu and Aliko Dangote as substantive co-chairs. I chaired the interim NCC when it was first established but the idea was to transfer leadership to the co-chairs once the council was fully established.

In general, the purpose of an NCC is to provide a platform for constructive public–private dialogue on economic competitiveness, provide objective information on the state of competitiveness in the country and raise awareness of the strong link between national competitiveness, business performance, economic growth and the population's prosperity and well-being to the government, businesses and the public. In addition, councils can help clarify the role of the business sector in improving competitiveness and help mobilize and channel support of this part of society.

Nigeria must focus on the following main drivers of competitiveness, which include:

- Strong and stable macroenvironment
- Organized and reliable financial system
- Availability of finance for reliable infrastructure
- Innovation – linking innovation to industry
- Conducive business climate
- Governance, regulations, laws and standards for produce and products produced
- Market access

Innovation is a differentiation factor. The triple helix model advocated in the NIRP links research in academia and research institutes with the industry. According to the World Economic Forum: 'Going forward, traditional distinction between countries being "developed" or "developing" will become less relevant and we will instead differentiate countries based on whether they are "innovation rich" or "innovation poor."' It is vital that leaders from business, government and civil society work collaboratively to create enabling environments to foster innovation and to create appropriate educational systems.

In the Global Competitiveness Index 2017–2018, Nigeria's summary ranking based on assessment of 12 'pillars' was 125 out of 137, showing a very unfavourable overall business climate. A conducive business climate is a prerequisite for investment, and Nigeria has made several attempts to improve its business environment. From the time of President Obasanjo, committees were established; President Jonathan intervened and supervised the clearing of the ports, among other things, and President Buhari appointed a special assistant to focus on the ease of doing business. But the competitiveness ranking and the experience of the private sector suggest that there is still a lot of work to be done.

Among the institutional components that impede movement to a more favourable business climate are the following with their rankings:

- Diversion of public funds, 133
- Intellectual property protection, 127
- Public trust in politicians, 130
- Favouritism in decisions of government officials, 125

Moreover, the constraints caused by pervasive insecurity across the country over the last ten years is reflected in the following rankings:

- Business cost of terrorism, 133
- Organized crime, 110
- Reliability of police services, 123

This is in addition to the well-known lapses and deficiencies in relation to the efficiency of the structure and procedures of taxation, the sanctity of contracts, the speed and transparency of commercial dispute resolution, local and informal taxes, etc.

The way forward is for both the government and the private sector to appreciate that beyond the old factors, which have been too long in waiting for solutions, the inception of different types of insecurity and terrorism in the business space presents a spectre of terminality. It would, therefore, amount to gross irresponsibility to treat such problems with levity and still expect any future accelerated growth of the economy or the attracting of investments into the country.

The OECD should be engaged to assess Nigeria's investment climate in line with international best practice. The OECD PFI Framework is the only multilateral-backed instrument to improve the investment climate, building on good practice from OECD and non-OECD countries. The review is in five areas:

- Investment policy
- Investment promotion and facilitation
- Trade policy
- Competition policy
- Corporate governance

There may be a need to strengthen the Presidential Enabling Business Environment Council to ensure that it is inclusive of all relevant government regulatory agencies, mandated with removing regulatory and administrative barriers, and ideally NIPC should serve as its secretariat.

Sovereign risk management is a winner

Sovereign risk refers to the probability that a sovereign will fail to meet its foreign debt payment obligation due to an aggregation of various factors, where the factors may not only be related to economic, but also to political, cultural and other spheres. It is time for a robust sovereign risk management desk, particularly with the high level of borrowing over the last six years.

Accordingly, sovereign risk management refers to the package of activities around identifying and addressing the various risk elements that could predispose a country to failure to meet its obligations, with a view to preventing, minimizing or moderating the impact of such risks. Sovereign risk management parameters would include universal elements as well as country-specific elements that reflect the realities of the country in question.

For example, for a developing economy such as Nigeria, parameters for sovereign risk assessment would include:

- Political and social conditions, including security – militancy, separatist agitations, etc.
- Quality of leadership and governance structure
- Rating agencies evaluation
- Size, growth rate and structure of GDP
- Size, sources and diversity of national income
- Debt, public finance, financial system and monetary policy
- Regulatory and legal conditions, pending litigations, etc.
- Health emergency and disaster risk management.

There are some salient points to consider here:

- Certainly, from the investor's point of view, sovereign risk management is all about the economic health of the subject country, but that economic health depends on almost everything else.
- Sovereign risk management is conventionally defined in the context of the concern and interest of foreign creditors, but in reality, it is also pertinent to foreign direct investors.
- Because sovereign risk management is about the health of the economy, even local creditors, local direct investors and,

indeed, all other stakeholders are as concerned with the sovereign risk factors as foreign interests are.

For developing economies, inflow of external resources is no doubt a pre-eminent source and strategy for financing rapid economic transformation. Therefore, the slant of sovereign risk management definition and framework towards foreign investors is justifiable. For example, because of the dangerous dominance of Nigeria's foreign exchange earnings by oil and gas, one of the most prominent risk management initiatives undertaken by the country was the introduction of the oil-based fiscal rule and the introduction of the Excess Crude Account or stabilization fund in 2004; this later formed part of the SWF created in 2011.

Continuity and consistency in the implementation of sectoral policies as a green light for investors

Working with the industry and investors in developing sectoral policy makes it a lot easier to attract investments to the relevant sector. It is even better if these policies are enacted into law. This gives increased confidence to investors that there will be continuity in the implementation of the policy. Unfortunately, when policies are discontinued by a new administration or the quality of implementation is poor, the country loses, but, more importantly, investors will lose their capital and lose confidence in the country.

Develop structures and vehicles to attract investments

As discussed in Chapter 4, SWFs and other structures have been used effectively to attract investments and diversify the economy. Economic zones and free-trade zones have also become very important in national development for some decades now. In 1975 there were 25 countries with free-trade zones in the world, employing 800,000 people globally. However, by 1997 there were 93 economic zones in the world employing 4.5 million people. As at the beginning of 2007, there were over

2,700 free-trade zones around the world, providing employment for approximately 63 million people. According to UNCTAD's report in 2019, the number has grown to more than 5,000 free-trade zones. The acceleration in industrial cities over the last few decades is striking, as the world continues to develop more industrial cities, clusters and economic zones to intensify the industrialization process, accelerate their export programs and attract investment.

At the heart of the Chinese economic and industrial revolution lies the strategic use of special economic zones, or industrial cities. In 1979 the Chinese adopted and started implementing the 'open door' policy to liberalize and industrialize its economy. This policy was anchored on the development of special economic zones in the country. Just two years after this policy was introduced, these zones accounted for a significant percentage of the total foreign direct investment going into China, with Shenzen as one of the most successful zones. By 2021 China's 21 free-trade zones contributed 17.3% of its total foreign trade and 18.5% of its foreign investment inflows.

Nigeria adopted this policy a few decades ago, creating two agencies: NEPZA and the Onne Oil and Gas Free Zone Authority. It licensed over 30 free-trade zones but only about five that were set up by the private sector are considered to have been successful. Again, this was as a result of the poor implementation of a policy that has worked so well in other countries. The successful free-trade zones include:

- LADOL, where the first floating, production storage and offloading unit was built in Nigeria.
- Dangote Free Zone, which has the second-largest refinery in the world, and a petrochemical plant.
- Onne Free Zone, has one of the most efficient ports and infrastructure.
- Lagos Free Zone, where a new port has been constructed.
- Eko Atlantic, which is expected to have Nigeria's first international financial centre.

There has also been some success in the Calabar free-trade zone, established by the federal government, and Lekki free-trade zone, set up by the Lagos State and some Chinese companies.

The newly created Infrastructure Corporation of Nigeria, set up by the CBN, SWF and Africa Finance Corp, is another effective vehicle for addressing Nigeria's infrastructure deficit and for attracting investment into the country.

Market access and local patronage – consume what you produce and produce what you consume

Nigeria has a huge internal market, given its estimated population of 216.7 million people, and access to the ECOWAS. A large internal market is a major strength for the world's top-two economies, US and China, as a well-exploited internal market provides stability to the economy by maintaining an assured core demand for locally produced products. In other words, the natural population quantitative advantage should be converted into competitive advantage deliberately, through fiscal and civic measures, encouraging sufficient reliance on and patronage for locally made goods by the government and the citizens. This has not been so in Nigeria, as local patronage of local products is scandalously low, even when there are policies approved by the government through the FEC that promote the culture. It is very common for the three arms of government to buy imported cars and foreign goods when there are policies in those sectors for local patronage. Sadly, there are no consequences for not complying with the policies and relevant laws. Nigeria's money must work for Nigerians.

How do you increase demand for local goods and encourage investors to invest in those sectors? On capital goods importation, there is room for intelligent rationalization. For example, given that a local company, Innoson Group, is doing well in producing cars, buses and trucks locally, with a high percentage of local content, is it not appropriate to have a mechanism in place to ensure that at least the public sector (federal, state and local governments) is mandated to comply with the government policy of patronizing that firm and similar firms? That would lead to more employment and encouragement of local invention and innovation. It would affect the demand for goods produced locally and encourage investors to invest heavily in those sectors, thus creating and supporting profitable businesses that will pay more taxes. It sends a strong message to investors that there are many investment opportunities in Nigeria with relevant raw materials in abundance and the market. The AfCFTA also provides a unique opportunity for eventual export of Nigerian-made cars and support for the country's external balance sheet.

What is certain is that, by not patronizing local products, the Nigerian government and people are exporting employment and prosperity, while importing unemployment and mass poverty. These concerns are relevant to the objectives of a strong, stable and predictable macroeconomic environment, because of the relationship between Nigeria's exports and imports. For a country with a high export revenue concentration ratio, the strategy of import minimization and export maximization is more imperative. These are some of the issues that the NIRP and smarter plans were designed to address if and when implemented.

Conclusion

No one can tell Nigeria's story better than Nigerians. That should be the job of 'Team Nigeria', beginning with the president as the chief marketer and provider of an enabling environment. The MITI must also work with the other ministries, in particular the foreign missions through the Ministry of Foreign Affairs. A strong and stable macroeconomic environment, business friendly environment, laws and strong institutions as regulators, investment in energy and trade-related infrastructure are all essential to attract investments.

The investment fundamentals remain strong and, despite the challenges, Nigeria and Africa remain the last frontiers for investors. The time to invest is now. As the challenges are addressed, there will be more competitors for investing in Africa. The experience in the telecom sector comes to mind. Ask MTN, which had a first-mover advantage when the telecom industry in Nigeria was opened up for international investors many years ago. Most of its competitors waited and refused to invest in Nigeria because they thought it was too risky. Meanwhile, MTN focused on its strategy in Nigeria and turned the business into one of the most profitable in the group. Seeing how successful MTN has been, its competitors decided to enter the Nigerian market but it was too late. Few wanted to sell, and the ones that wanted to sell were too expensive.

Chapter 6

Managing our resources better: eliminating leakages and waste

> *'It is time to do away with the leaking basket. Blocking leakages, eliminating waste, getting value for money, efficient and effective programme management are all as important if not more important, than revenue generation at this stage of our development. Africa cannot afford the current level of leakages.'*
>
> **Olusegun Aganga**

Over the period when I was in government, I developed an appreciation for landscapes, skylines and first impressions at airports around the world. The view from the air as you approach for landing very often is an indication of what to expect in the country one is visiting. Some countries have carefully cultivated landscapes literally visible from space. Order, efficiency, beauty and productivity all go together, as a rule of thumb. There are places, such as Dubai, where there has been such incredible transformation over the years that the aerial view 30 years ago and the aerial view today suggests that one is arriving at a different destination altogether.

In my role as the Minister of Industry, Trade and Investment, I travelled to about 68 countries in four years to represent or/and market Nigeria to investors, and in many cases I accompanied the president on state visits, because trade and investment is always on the agenda for such meetings. Over the period, I found out that first impressions, starting from the aerial view through to the baggage reclaim, immigration, the state of the airports and the drive from the airport, tell a story about the country. The chaos or order and calmness experienced as you collect your luggage and walk out of the airport tell you about how organized the country is, how welcoming the people are and, more importantly and more relevant to this chapter, how the country has invested public funds and managed public assets.

Very few countries in the modern world have the range of endowments Nigeria has. It bears reiterating that, with 84 million hectares of land, up to 93% of which is arable, well-watered savannah and forests, a topography that has at least three plateaus that are the envy of the world, we have everything it takes to grow every crop on the planet. The sheer abundance of human talent and material resources in Nigeria means we can become the processing and industrial powerhouse of Africa. We are a gas-producing country, we have oil sufficiently to transform into the foremost hydrocarbon hub in Africa. If we were to take an inventory of minerals and metals, there would be little on the periodic table that we do not already have, some in commercial quantities. Why are the people and country so poor then? There are numerous answers to this question, but huge waste and leakage is one obvious reason.

The latest data from government and oil industry sources in 2022 suggests that up to 70% of Nigeria's crude oil is stolen. There are many abandoned or uncompleted projects around the country, such as the old Federal Secretariat Complex in Lagos; Ajaokuta Steel Complex in Kogi; NITEL in Lagos; four moribund NNPC refineries; abandoned residential quarters spread all over the federation; moribund aluminium smelting complexes; Lagos and Abuja stadiums; abandoned National Machine Tools facilities; the Defence House in Lagos (formerly Independence Building); the former naval headquarters building in Marina Lagos; thousands of kilometres of uncompleted roads, culverts and bridges; 'parked' and redundant national satellites in space; and water projects at Mambilla, and Ogere Gorge Dam. There are also other abandoned hydroelectric power projects across the country. The abandoned nuclear research facilities at Ile-Ife and Sokoto, moribund river-basin projects across the nation, uncompleted and abandoned grain silos across the country – these are but a few of many projects that describe the kind of waste that, as a country, we have to stop. We must also ensure, going forward, that these do not recur.

There is also the high cost of governance, which is not just about the salaries and other allowances paid to legislators. It is about the huge cost that the presidential system of governance, as practised now, imposes on the economy. The cost of maintaining the bloated and inefficient civil service, the cost of assistants attached to members of the National Assembly and the executive, the severance pay and other payments for life to ex-governors who served for only eight years at best, the cost of maintaining redundant agencies. All of these combine to staggering amounts for which the country is not getting value.

Poorly negotiated government contracts or agreements at national and subnational levels, poorly understood and executed treaties and protocols – all these have added to the waste liability for Nigeria in the form of judgement debts and must be budgeted for. There are so many forms of these – from hydroelectric power contracts, to roads, to oil and gas servicing contracts, to badly handled property leases and investments abroad. Again, these highlight the necessity to have a modern civil service that is smart and knowledgeable and has respect for law and order. The situation has resulted in several court cases that were disclosed by the Federal Attorney-General and Minister of Justice to be at least 648 as at August 2022!

Our past of prodigal waste should make us sit up and task both citizens and leaders about how to turn the whole country around immediately. At federal, state and local government levels, the aggregated number of abandoned projects between 1960 and the present are well in excess of 25,000. This is a very conservative number considering that a 2022 forensic audit report on just one agency, the Niger Delta Development Commission (NDDC), revealed that there were 13,777 projects that were uncompleted, and most have their execution substantially compromised. These numbers are not exaggerated. Still, resource management is a critical issue globally, cutting across countries, regions and continents. It is a phenomenon that goes beyond Nigeria and Africa, although quite worrisome in the region. Leakages and wastage are pervasive as a result of poor governance. Development and sustainable and inclusive economic growth in Nigeria and Africa depend on the effectiveness of efforts to significantly reduce or eliminate these leakages and manage public assets and funds better.

There are two ways of addressing the issue of abandoned projects. We could sell the convertible assets and put the proceeds to value-adding projects and programmes. Alternatively, as canvassed by the Association of Capital Market Valuers, give those assets to facility managers to manage them and generate revenue for the federal government. Either way, this should boost government revenue and bridge some of the revenue gap and challenges that the government is facing at present.

There are several reasons for the rather high and unusual level of leakage and waste, including:

- The lack of continuity of projects. Every new administration, regardless of whether it is the same party or not, wants to embark on its own new projects. Manifestos of aspirants are full of new projects that are not costed and sources of financing not identified. New ministers focus on what they can start and deliver within the four-year term of the administration.
- Poor conceptualization of projects and lack of adequate funding has led to significant cost and project overruns. It is not unusual for the revised cost of contracts brought to FEC for approval to be three times what the cost was at the time it was first approved, usually by a previous administration.
- Weak institutions, in particular weak economic institutions because of poor governance and weak and incompetent management, whose KPIs are measured by the number of contracts awarded to political associates and godfathers, which are in some cases not executed. It is called the dividend of democracy in most developing countries.
- Expensive governance structure and duplication of agencies. The presidential system of governance is effective for a large economy such as the US, but it has proven to be too expensive and less effective for a country with a small economy and high rate of poverty, such as Nigeria. State governments' recurrent expenditure has continued to increase exponentially over the years and about eight states are unable to meet their recurrent expenditure obligations.

Transparency: a system-wide solution to waste

Tackling waste is not simple, even in the most advanced of societies. According to the *Washington Post*, a recent watchdog review found that at least 6.5 million active social security numbers belong to people who are at least 112 years old and likely deceased.[3] Only 35 living individuals worldwide had reached that age as of October 2013. If this kind of vulnerability can occur in the US, it can occur anywhere.

In this chapter we will examine numerous measures that have been effective in reducing waste drastically and that, at the same time, increased efficiency. We will look at examples from Nigeria

[3] *Washington Post*, 28 December 2017.

as well as other countries that have implemented useful measures. These measures may differ in their execution, depending on whether federal, state or local government units are concerned. A general principle that works regardless of which tier of government is involved, however, is transparency. Adopting a transparent approach ensures that common problems such as duplicated functions, inflation of contracts, issues around nepotism, award of contracts to the least qualified and sometimes most expensive, other corrupt practices, etc., are reduced or eliminated altogether. Several credible NGOs, local and international, as well as government agencies have risen recently using information technology to facilitate transparency. BudgIT, the Nigeria Extractive Industries Transparency Initiative (NEITI), Transparency International and a handful of others have proven to be dynamic players in this regard but primary responsibility still resides with government ministers, permanent secretaries, directors and CEOs of parastatals.

Perhaps the most rapid result of a system-wide adoption of transparency that I witnessed while in government was achieved through working with the Comptroller-General of Customs at the time. We introduced the following measures to closely monitor revenue performance and block leakages:

- Automation of the customs clearance procedure, which facilitated faster, smoother clearance at the ports and was tied to e-payment to the banks directly.
- Periodic publication of revenue generated in national newspapers for the first time.
- Regular system audit to monitor duty payments in all the ports.
- Improved quality of customs workforce through training, provision of modern equipment and improved welfare packages.

The month the electronic payment system was installed, revenue increased significantly. I requested they double the revenue target and also start to publish the result. The Nigeria Customs Service met its 2011 revenue collection target (₦596 billion) set by the federal government. The service generated ₦602 billion into the Federation Account, whereas before 2011 the average monthly collection by the service was less than ₦30 billion, which progressively increased through the four quarters of 2011.

Customs have continued to publish revenue generated in National newspaper and revenue continues to rise every year, hitting ₦1.5

trillion in 2020. The Bureau of Public Procurement and the publication in national newspapers of revenues allocated from the Federation Account to federal, state and local governments were all introduced by the Obasanjo administration to improve transparency.

Leo Tolstoy's *How Much Land Does a Man Need?*

Another reason for the leakages is the insatiable appetite for wealth and misunderstanding of what the dividend of democracy is. I reiterate, it should be about good governance not opportunity to steal public funds.

Leo Tolstoy's offer of valuable lessons on the issue of greed are just as important today as they were centuries ago. One such lesson comes from the story of Pahom in *How Much Land Does a Man Need?* Pahom is of humble means but bemoans not owning enough land. He grows many crops and amasses a small fortune but it is still not enough. Eventually he hears about the Bashkirs, a simple people who own a huge amount of land deep in Central Asia. Pahom meets the Bashkirs on the vast steppe. He is prepared to negotiate a price for as much land as possible but, before he can do so, the Bashkirs make him the same offer that they make to anyone who wishes to buy land from them. For 1,000 roubles (a large sum in those days), Pahom can walk around an area as large as he wants. He must start at daybreak and mark his route with a shovel at key points along the way. If he returns to the starting point before sunset, the land that he has marked off will be his. If he fails to return on time, the money will be forfeited. Pahom is certain that he can cover a great distance and that he will have more land than he could have ever imagined.

The next day, with the Bashkirs watching from the starting point, Pahom sets off. At various points he begins to think that he should change direction and work his way back, but he is constantly tempted by the thought of adding just a bit more land. The day wears on and, as the sun begins to set, Pahom discovers that he is still far from the starting point. Realizing that he has been too greedy and taken too much land, he runs back as fast as he can to where the Bashkirs are waiting. He arrives at the starting point in the nick of time, just before the sun sets. However, as the Bashkirs cheer his good fortune, Pahom drops dead from exhaustion.

In the story, Tolstoy addresses the age-old question of how much wealth a person needs. How much is enough? Political leaders and public office holders who enrich themselves by corruption should answer this question honestly. Perhaps that would make some of them begin to rethink the futility of their corrupt practices and inordinate wealth accumulation. It is a reminder of the importance of rebuilding Nigeria's values system as soon as possible.

Getting our priorities right in life can be difficult unless we have answers to five fundamental questions: Who am I? Where have I come from? Why am I here on Earth? Where am I going when my time here on Earth ends? How do I get there? Not many people have answers to these questions in their lifetime, but when they do, they start having a purpose to life and a better understanding of the meaning of life itself.

A continental challenge

As things stand at present, Africa may not meet the sustainable development goals target of eliminating extreme poverty by 2030, if its natural resource wealth is not managed well. About 64.3% of Sub-Saharan Africa's population lives in multidimensional poverty. While other regions of the world are experiencing rapid poverty reduction, the Human Development Report of 2019 notes that the decline is much slower for Sub-Saharan Africa. COVID-19 has further stretched the resources available vis-à-vis what is needed to fund essential services such as education and health. The resulting increased continental debt burden and limited inflows of aid and foreign direct investment increase pressure more than ever to raise revenue locally and manage Africa's resources better.

There is an urgency for Africa to summon the political will needed to close the ducts that allow capital flight and illicit financial flows, which are mainly from Africa's extractive sector and have led to Africa remaining the poorest continent in the world. The Economic Development in Africa Report 2020 shows that the extractive sectors lose about $50 billion annually, which represents the largest source of illicit financial flow from Africa.

Oil, gas and minerals are non-renewable resources: the more you extract, the less is available and there is lost opportunity to develop on the proceeds. The multinational corporations in the extractive sector, unfortunately, do not pay their fair share of the cost, and Africa's development based on its natural resources remains a mirage. As such, the Africa Mining Vision and the report of the high-level panel on illicit financial flow recommended the optimization of domestic resource mobilization and leveraging the extractive sector to drive inclusive and sustainable growth. The Trade Justice Network Africa calls for African governments to improve the transparency and accountability of multinational corporations to end secretive jurisdiction and tax havens, and to promote the automatic exchange of information and citizen participation in extractive revenue management. Additionally, countries should review policies that allow overly generous tax incentives and publicly report the revenue forgone to subsidize the multinational corporations. Generally, there is need to reimagine public policy and deploy strategies that address Africa's vulnerabilities, which became more visible with COVID-19.

The paucity of development resources in Nigeria is an aberration, because the country is richly endowed, but poor allocation and utilization widens the resource gap.

We can manage our oil and gas better

Oil accounts for about 70% of Nigeria's national income and about 90% of its foreign earnings. The economy depends on the sector but over the years we appear to have missed the opportunity to maximize oil revenue and manage the resource better. I will give two examples:

1. Level of production: when I was Minister of Finance in 2010, Nigeria produced about 2 million barrels a day and it was projected to rise to 4 million within three or four years. In 2022 (12 years after) we could only account for about 1.4 million barrels a day and yet our budget and investment needs as a country have skyrocketed. This means that by now, Nigeria should be generating at least three times the revenue it is generating from crude oil today. The understanding is that export pipelines have been vandalized and that only a small percentage of oil produced reaches the terminals. In some pipelines close to 80% of the oil is stolen. It also took close to 20 years to finalize the Petroleum Industry Act, which was supposed to create a better environment for investment in the sector. Unfortunately, the effectiveness of the Act has been reduced significantly because

of the world's position on cleaner energy and, of course, the inability of the Nigerian government to prevent oil theft. Oil theft is an economic and financial crime but to date, no one has been charged and publicly prosecuted. NEITI reports have also identified several leakages including large discrepancies in the volume of crude oil claimed to be exported and the actual volume exported, but these are not followed up. The security forces should work with the EFCC to bring this threat to Nigeria's economy to an end.

2. Value addition: oil was first discovered in Nigeria in Oloibiri, Balyesa State, in 1956. It is hard to understand why a country that discovered oil about 66 years ago still exports crude oil and job opportunities and imports petroleum products and poverty in 2022. In between we had three functioning refineries but for many years now these have become another avenue for huge wastage and leakage. In fact, when I was Minister of Finance, the president directed that we must not fund any turnaround proposal again and we must reconsider the privatization of these refineries because the waste was unexplainable.

South Korea has no proven oil reserves and yet in 2020 it had a total refining capacity of around 3.57 million barrels a day. South Korea imports most of its crude oil from Saudi Arabia. I have already discussed how Saudi Arabia invested heavily in value addition and gas industrialization. Oil and gas have been used effectively to diversify the economy and revenue sources. That is the opportunity Nigeria has missed so far but there is time to address this if we act quickly.

The good news is that the private sector has come to the rescue. Hopefully, by 2023, the Dangote refinery and petrochemical complex in Lekki, Lagos State, will have been completed. It will be the second-largest refinery in the world, producing enough for local consumption and for the export market, generating foreign exchange and creating thousands of jobs. Already it has started exporting fertilizer.

Reforming the EFCC

The new boss of the EFCC, Abdulrasheed Bawa, has signalled his intentions and has demonstrated an informed or enlightened knowledge of the issues and how to deal with them. Chairman Bawa is young, passionate about his job, vibrant, analytical and full of the right ideas that will take the EFCC into the 21st century. He has the benefit of being an insider and an investigator, and he understands that the EFCC has to become a stronger institution if it is to deliver effectively on its mandate. The government must now support the institution to succeed by turning the EFCC into a stronger, more effective and enduring economic institution. Here are some proposals:

- Protect the EFCC from political interference by making it independent. The appointment and removal of the chairman should be approved by two-thirds of the senate. Something similar to what Nigeria has now for the CBN. The act of appointing an acting chairman for more than three months should be discouraged.
- Introduce a code of conduct for all EFCC operatives, monitor its implementation and discipline erring officers.
- Remuneration. Pay the staff well. You cannot pay them peanuts and expect them to fight corruption effectively. No. If you want results, pay them well, hire and retain the best.
- The agency must go beyond dealing only with individuals to fighting corruption systemically. This means:
  - Developing and implementing both preventative and detective controls.
  - Adopting a risk management approach by identifying high, medium and low-risk sectors, MDAs and introducing additional procedures for high-risk sectors. The banks need to do more.
  - Working closely with the international community, including Transparency International and the Financial Action Task Force.

Donor agencies and governments should adopt a comprehensive approach that includes the police and the Director of Public Prosecutions, rather than focusing on anti-corruption agencies alone.

Over the years, Nigeria has made good progress in tackling corruption, however, the 2021 report by Transparency International shows that Nigeria has not built on the earlier successes and that there is more work to be done. In the report, Nigeria ranked 154 out of 180 countries surveyed. This compares to a ranking of 149 out of 180 in 2020, and 136 in 2015.

Nigeria would definitely be on a path to winning the war against corruption if the above ideas were to be vigorously implemented and the EFCC gets the political support it requires.

Combatting a negative perception of Nigeria

As a nation we have made good progress on the issue of corruption since President Obasanjo's administration created the EFCC and other relevant institutions more than 15 years ago. The Special Control Unit Against Money Laundering reported to me as Minister of Industry, Trade and Investment, so I know some of the efforts it made. Still, the efforts Nigeria has made have not been given the recognition it deserves internationally. For example, most banks in the Western world still unjustly classify Nigeria as high risk. Bank accounts of Nigerians are closed arbitrarily, banks refuse to open accounts for some Nigerians and Nigerian institutions, transfers from Nigeria are returned, etc. This is partly due to their lack of appreciation of the progress the country has made, its strategy and poor communication of the progress made to date.

Discussions with investors and the foreign media suggest that the Nigerian media and the Nigerians active on social media inadvertently fuel this negative perception and image about the country. This includes how the media or social media report suspicions of corrupt practices even before court judgements and write negative and in some cases false stories about the country and individuals, forgetting that we live in a global village now and that news travels fast. This is extremely damaging to the sovereign goodwill of the country and Nigerians. Countries and international organizations, and foreign recruiters/employers now gather information about individuals from the internet and assume all the stories are true. Nigeria must manage its communication within and outside Nigeria better.

Lessons learned from NLNG

If there was one big lesson learned by the government from Eleme and the NLNG company in Bonny, it is that government has no business running businesses. While it may set up or invest in some strategic companies, its primary role is to set the rules of operation, act as umpires and to create the enabling environment for businesses to thrive, create jobs and pay taxes to the government. The same lesson was learned from Nigerian Airways, which was run down completely many years ago.

I have already discussed NLNG in detail in Chapter 4, so I will be brief here. The federal government had majority shares in NLNG and controlled the board before it was restructured. Today, NLNG is the most successful investment the government has made in a private sector majority-led venture. There are five reasons for this success:

- Integrated oil and gas companies' majority shareholding: this meant that they were able to run the company as a private company, with no political interference.
- As an incorporated company, NLNG is answerable to a board of directors. The independent board led to faster decision-making. For example, the Bonny airstrip was completed within two years.
- The CEO was outside political influence: the appointment was based on merit and also completely outside political influence.
- Self-funding ability from own revenue and international borrowing.
- Global corporate governance standards/shareholder committee. The shareholders had industry knowledge and over 100 years combined sector experience.

As far back as 2016, NLNG had successfully transferred technology (97% reliability), reduced gas flares from 65% to 20%, delivered strong financials ($90 billion revenue), while delivering 7% of the world's liquified natural gas. Today, the senior management team is 100% Nigerian, while the employees are 95% Nigerians. The Nigerian government had earned $33 billion by 2015 in dividends, taxes, etc.

NLNG has also built a vocational college and set up a utilities company in Bonny Island. It awards secondary, tertiary and post-graduate scholarships and has built and equipped laboratories in six Nigerian universities. NLNG supplies over 50% of cooking gas in Nigeria, sponsors Africa's biggest science and literature prizes with cash values of $100,000 and actively supports local manufacturers, including those who exported $10 million goods to Korea, etc.

This is a win–win model that plays to the strengths of the shareholders and the nation. It is a model that can be replicated in many areas, including the oil refineries. I reiterate that the government has no business running businesses. Its primary role is to provide an enabling business environment.

I was always delighted to receive then CEO, Babs Omotowa, when I was Minister of Finance, because NLNG generated the highest and most stable return for government. When I was in the MITI, the regular briefing continued because in my new role my job was to ensure that we created an environment that allowed companies to build on their successes and that all contracts were respected. In return, and the country received non-oil foreign income from the export of gas (trade), investments and jobs. I visited the company a few times in Bonny and was highly impressed with the standard of governance and management of the business. They even won a global award during this period.

Breaking leakages and waste of corruption

Corruption has in many ways become the defining issue of the 21st century, just as the 20th century was characterized by large ideological struggles between democracy, fascism and communism. It is a global issue and not limited to developing countries. Today a majority of the world's nations accept the legitimacy of democracy and at least pretend to hold competitive elections. What really distinguishes political systems from one another is the degree to which the ruling elites use power to serve a broad public interest or simply to enrich themselves, their friends and their families. They forget that we all benefit and raise our standard of living if we work towards building a strong, productive and good society for the benefit of all.

Corruption comprises a wide range of behaviours, the economic and political effects if which vary greatly. Economically, it diverts resources away from their most productive uses and becomes a kind of regressive tax that supports the lifestyles of the elite at the expense of everyone else. Politically, corruption undermines the legitimacy of political systems by giving elites alternative ways of holding on to power other than through genuine democratic choice. It hurts the prospects of democracy when people perceive authoritarian governments to be performing better than corrupt democratic ones and undermines the reality of democratic choice.

It is remarkable that, for all of the academic efforts in the study of corruption, there is still no broadly accepted vocabulary for distinguishing between its different forms. Before examining how corruption can be tackled, there is a need to gain some conceptual clarity about what it is and how it relates to the broader problem of good governance.

Ashraf Ghani, president of Afghanistan from September 2014 to August 2021, described Afghanistan as, by any measure, 'one of the most corrupt countries on earth'. In his essay on tackling corruption in Estonia, former Prime Minister Mart Laar argues that corruption was so ingrained that it had become a way of life, noting, 'We didn't even understand that it wasn't normal.' President Muhammadu Buhari of Nigeria uses that same language to describe corruption in Nigeria as a 'way of life' under 'supposedly accountable democratic governments' and points to evidence suggesting that between $300 billion and $400 billion of public funds has been lost to corruption since Nigeria's independence in 1960.

Without true values-based leadership, many of the rules, institutions and mechanisms designed to address corruption will never actually bite. When the root causes of corruption are addressed, waste and leakages can be eliminated, and available resources can be stretched to deliver most of the development objectives as well as attract private and foreign capital.

According to an OECD report, between 1999 (the year the OECD convention tackling transnational bribery came into force) and 2014, 361 individuals and 126 companies were sanctioned for foreign bribery in 17 countries, with at least $5.4 billion imposed in combined monetary sanctions and 95 people put behind bars.[4]

José Ugaz, a lawyer and former chairman of Transparency International (2014–17), describes some of the ways that new technologies have been employed to bring about real change. In Guatemala, a public campaign over a customs fraud scandal forced the resignation of the president and vice-president. In Brazil, 40 civil society organizations mobilized two million Brazilians to use online actions and events to successfully campaign for a new law that

[4] Council of the OECD. 2019 Foreign Bribery Report.

prevents candidates convicted of corruption from standing for public office for at least eight years! When El Salvador gave citizens the right to ask for information about public officials' assets, 6,000 citizen requests helped to uncover cases where the wealth of public officials had grown by 300% during their time in office. In Venezuela, a new smart phone app is allowing ordinary citizens to report instances of bribery and any irregularities during elections, with more than 400 complaints registered for follow-up during the most recent parliamentary elections.

Theft or misuse of taxpayers' money can be exposed by opening up budgets and procurement so that people can see exactly how their money is used and they can demand that those concerned be held to account when there is proven misappropriation. There should be sustained effort in areas that Paul Collier describes as the 'pockets of high corruption', including corruption-prone sectors such as the extractive and construction industries.

At the heart of all of this is international cooperation on transparency. In the UK there is adopted legislation that gives the public unrestricted access to beneficial ownership information on UK companies and properties through a public central registry, so that people can see who really owns and controls companies.

We must also tackle the causes of corruption

Why is the issue of corruption in Nigeria taking so long to be fully addressed? Yes, the country needs to strengthen and empower the relevant anti-corruption institutions, including EFCC and ICPC, but that alone will not solve the problem. There is a combination of reasons for what I refer to as the "causes" of corruption:

- The level of poverty and inequality in the country is so high and there is no effective safety-net programme that is deep and large enough. The current school-feeding programme is a right step in the right direction and should be applauded but it needs to be institutionalized and aggressively expanded.
- The civil service, which should be the backbone of any government, is more like a social security organization where they are paid just enough to push a pen and look for other sources of income.

- The serving civil servants and others have seen the fate of retired civil servants and pensioners. At the moment it is not unusual to serve the country for decades, make pension contributions, retire and then get almost nothing from the same government after your retirement as pension payments, despite your contributions under the pension scheme. The purchasing power of any amount received is so small because of inflation, and yet some governors receive houses, cars, large allowances and pension for life after serving for eight years only.
- The level of unemployment is so high and many are dependent on family and friends. At least 15 adults are financially dependent on the one member of the family that is deemed to be successful or in employment.
- There are no basic amenities such as housing, healthcare, electricity, water, good public education and mass transit. The cost of living for the average Nigerian is very high.
- Our elections are among the most expensive in the world. According to Transparency International, Nigeria's election spending ranks among the top two or three in the world. The majority of voters are uneducated and poor and therefore more likely to sell their votes. Political parties are openly funded by those in public office with government resources.
- Greed, greed and greed, the culture of recognizing wealthy people in the society regardless of where or how they acquired their wealth.

The implication of this is that many have to fight for survival first, struggle to meet their responsibilities and therefore compromise themselves. The solution goes beyond a strong EFCC and ICPC. A holistic approach that addresses these causes must be adopted.

There are, of course, many other unintended consequences, such as the issue of democracy itself. A lack of understanding among citizens of public policy and voting power means that most developing countries end up having a government of the political class, by the political class and for the political class, rather than a government for the people. Democracy can only be efficient if based on the premise of educated voters, competitive elections, strong political institutions and relatively low political transaction costs.

Disconnect of governance network

The historical pattern in the Nigerian government system is for every new administration to introduce new projects and abandon what others have done well or started. The current approach of the Buhari administration to continue the rail projects started by the Jonathan administration is commendable and should be sustained. The civil service, and in particular the Ministry of Finance and the budget office, must insist on continuity and completing ongoing projects first. A five-year rolling budget that ensures commitment of resources to existing projects would help. Annual allocations must be enough to move the projects forward until completion. Projects must also be in line with the national plan.

There is inadequate supervision and accountability by revenue-generating and large programme agencies. Some appear to operate a pattern of rising operating cost with revenue. The proposal in the federal government budget of limiting their cost/revenue ratio to 50%, although commendable, still leaves room for cost inefficiency. It needs to be further interrogated.

High cost of governance

You cannot have a small state revenue and big state spending. It will only lead to bankruptcy. Nigeria needs to restructure the governance system and boldly address the high cost of the size of government, which partly explains the persistent rise in recurrent expenditure and the waste of resources that ought to be deployed to development initiatives. Successive governments have identified this as major constraint to financing development but it has been difficult to address, partly because those who are empowered to make the change are the beneficiaries of the system. For instance, it is unlikely that legislators will vote for 'part-time' to replace the current system of 'full-time' legislators or any proposal to significantly reduce their pay or allowance. The presidential system of governance is not a bad system but it is too expensive for the size of the Nigerian economy.

Nigeria can learn some lessons about cutting down the cost of governance drastically from other countries. Ghana, for example, has undertaken the following:

- Cut down discretionary spending by up to 30%.
- Cut down by 50% the value of fuel coupons given to public officials.
- Suspended the purchase of imported vehicles for government officials in 2022, especially four-wheel drives.
- Placed a ban on foreign travels for government officials except in critical cases.
- Weeded out ghost workers from the payroll.
- Reviewed electricity suppliers' capacity charges.
- Prioritized ongoing projects over new projects.
- Reduced expenditure on meetings and conferences by 50%.
- Reviewed interest payable on public loans to bring down loan servicing costs.
- Liaised with organized labour to review salary inequalities.
- Reduced ministers' salaries by 30%.

Sweden has frugal measures for its legislators, which Nigeria can also learn from. A Swedish legislator occupies the office as a public servant and cannot use any facilities provided towards the functionality of the office for personal gain. Sweden expects a legislator to use public transport for meetings and travel within the country. Not only that, but Swedes expect their legislators to use the cheapest available form of public transport, otherwise the legislators are liable to refund the difference to the state.

Reigniting a good-values system

Singapore is singled out for consideration because it is a multiracial nation like Nigeria, smaller in population but has gone through some of the challenges Nigeria is going through now. Singapore began its development strides with national value internalization, which rests on national unity and common purpose, supremacy and legitimacy of civic rights, justice irrespective of class or race, along with community-wide mobilization of resources for communal uplift. Communities are treated as partners, while government facilitates.

Entrenched in Singapore's national values, which it borrowed from Confucius, are respect for properly constituted authority, society before self, family as foundation of the society, respect for education and knowledge, hard work as a virtue, frugality and judicious management of resources, sense of shame, delayed gratification, fidelity among friends, etc. Of course, most of these did not happen without challenges. In order to ensure continuous adherence, Singapore includes all these in its educational curriculum.

For developing countries, including Nigeria, it is important to realize the role the educational institutions must play in cracking down on corruption, better managing our assets and diversification, and embedding our values system in society. Every visible value system is sustained through early life education, promoting a community sense of identity and internalized beyond lip service. It is time for Nigeria to use its education policy and institutions to entrench the core values such as integrity, contentment, protecting the assets of the nation and creating and sustaining a good society.

Cost of elections in Nigeria

The cost of Nigeria's elections has increased dramatically from just over ₦1 billion in 1999 to over ₦100 billion in 2015, making them among the most expensive in the world. The huge cost of elections has surpassed that of the world's largest democracy, India, with a population six times larger than Nigeria's!

According to the National Institute for Legislative Studies, with 67 million registered voters, Nigeria spent over $625 million on the 2015 elections, or $9.33 per voter.[5] The $625 million Nigeria spent on funding went towards infrastructure and systems for information technology, the creation of maps and voter lists, the training of returning officers, and personnel for field work and special events. Other parties, including security services that took part in the polls, faced additional costs that were not included in this enormous spending. Additionally, money was spent on campaigns, commercials and other campaign-related expenses by the candidates, political parties and support organizations.

As many officers from the Nigerian police and other security agencies are employed to prevent rigging and other irregularities, security costs in Nigeria are extremely high (e.g. the request for security

[5] National Institute for Legislative Studies. Nigeria's 2015 General Elections Expenditure Report.

for the Anambra governorship election of 2017 was initially ₦1 billion but later reduced to ₦300 million).

In most cases around the world the trend is that countries that do not have or enforce laws regulating election funding/financing effectively are often those that have very high cost per voter. Nigeria has limits on campaign financing but the candidates and their political parties disregard these limits and there has not been any occasion that they were held to account. All these contribute to the leakages in the system.

There is light at the end of the tunnel

Over the years, different governments have embarked on various reform programmes, coordinated by the Bureau of Public Service Reforms (BPSR), and some of these have been very successful. For example, the introduction of IPPIS has reduced the federal civil service personnel to 720,000. IPPIS led to the weeding out of about 70,000 ghost workers from the service and a saving of ₦220 billion by the federal government. According to the BPSR, "the TSA has also led to savings of ₦10 trillion over the years. Government, especially at the top, is always able to see what has come into our TSA today and what has gone out of it. So, planning has been simplified". Budgeting has been simplified. Prior to the introduction of the TSA, MDAs operated different accounts with commercial banks, interests on deposits were not always accounted for and MDAs were not aware of some bank accounts opened by their predecessors, which had large balances.

A new system, the Government Integrated Financial Management Information System (GIFMIS), which now allows the office of the Accountant-General of the Federation and the Ministry of Finance to see what is happening in all MDAs of government, has now introduced transparency and accountability into the system. According to the BPSR, 'Every activity you are doing under GIFMIS somebody is watching you and is monitoring that activity.' International rating agencies have more confidence in Nigeria now because they have access to information and data that they were not able to get before. As part of the reforms in the service, GIFMIS has almost made government business paperless and reduced person-to-person contact and processing, payments in MDAs to a minimum.

This is a great achievement for the government, and all the administrations from presidents Obasanjo through to Yar'Adua, to Jonathan and to Buhari must be commended for the success. But there is still much to be done.

Chapter 7

Our biggest and most important asset: our people

'The most authentic thing about us is our capacity to create, to overcome, to endure, to transform, to love and to be greater than our suffering.'

Ben Okri on Nigerians

There are four things no one can take away from Nigerians:

- Our kindness towards one another.
- Our sense of humour even when faced with severe adversity.
- Our entrepreneurial and can-do spirit.
- Our confidence and ability to excel anywhere in the world.

We are curious, dynamic, solid and creative. Whether in the vibrant and colourful textile markets of Kano City or the sprawling waterfront shops of Onitsha, whether inside the bustling scenes of urban Lagos or across cosmopolitan cities of the world, the Nigerian spirit stands out and we tend to win against all odds!

Given wings, Nigerians fly in every profession. When three colleagues and I accompanied President Goodluck Jonathan to meet with President Barak Obama at the White House in 2010, he was very complimentary of Nigerians in the US. In particular, he told us that there were more than 20,000 Nigerian doctors and consultants in the US. Today, that figure is at least 30,000, including highly accomplished, world-renowned and credible medical professionals. Nigerian medical professionals supporting the UK's National Health Service (NHS) numbered 10,494 as of 31 March 2021. If second-generation Nigerians and Nigerians having dual citizenship are included in the numbers in the UK, the figures are likely to come up to 20,000. Nigeria ranks sixth out of 212 nationalities represented in the NHS. At the last count, more than 5,000 Nigerian medical professionals were working in various South African hospitals. Nigerian doctors, lawyers, accountants, investment bankers, nurses, asset managers and other professionals are also very successful in Europe. Indeed, reputable universities have successful, bright and acclaimed Nigerian scholars. The US space programme and laboratories at Stanford and Oxford have Nigerians working in them.

Nigerians are fecund. We are, for example, the ones most likely to birth twins of any nation in the world. Our fecundity is not just physical. The Nigerian imagination brought the first Nobel Prize in Literature to the African continent. Ten Nigerians have won Grammy Awards in different categories for music. Nigerian artists sell out the largest music arenas in Europe and America *in minutes*!

Without intensive training, public investments or extensive inputs, the ingenuity of young Nigerians in fintech particularly has caught the attention of venture capital firms around the world, with 60% of funding for new investments in Nigeria going to fintech alone in 2021.

So, why has this nation remained underdeveloped, and how do we break the chains holding us back? This chapter answers this question regarding our most important asset – our people.

Why are people our most important asset?

People drive the institutions that determine whether nations fail or succeed. The more qualitative these individuals are, the more qualitative society tends to be. It is also not resources such as oil, gas, solid minerals, etc. that make countries rich, it is about what the people do with these resources.

In the case of Nigeria, we have a quantity advantage, and our demographic is the envy of the rest of the world. The average age in Nigeria is about 18.6 years. This compares to about 42.5 years in Europe and 38.4 in China. We have enough population to be our primary market. Tooled up and trained correctly, this vast human potential can make Nigeria the hub of productivity in Africa and a catalyst for the size of the economy we deserve. Indeed, it is now time for Nigeria and Africa to turn this favourable demography and quantity advantage into an economic benefit. This means prioritizing and investing in the people to acquire the right skills – knowledge relevant to the economy and developing a values-based society where hard work, competence, integrity, enterprise and learning are adequately rewarded and where there is equal opportunity.

Unfortunately, over many decades we have not recognized and invested enough in our most important asset. This has led to high levels of illiteracy, poverty, unemployment and underemployment (particularly among the youth), insecurity, underdevelopment and a relatively small economy, to mention just a few things. But we can correct this and make the necessary transformation quicker than some would believe, if we prioritize and address the following areas.

Build a values-based society

History has shown that the world's most successful companies and countries are built on core values as the foundation. We cannot achieve sustainable economic growth and development unless we build on a solid foundation and develop community-spirited Nigerians who live these values. Evidence shows that the difference between a rich and a developing nation is not the size of the population, the demography or the age of the nation; it is not the natural resources it has, but it is about the *people* – their values, their attitudes and ability to convert their resources to prosperity. Unfortunately, our values system has broken down and we need to rebuild it urgently. Values such as integrity, compassion, patriotism, hard work, industry, honesty and selfless service that underpin good societies throughout the world have all been thrown out of the window and replaced with greed, lust for power, wealth and position, avarice, materialism, rent seeking and taking, selfishness, etc.

That said, Nigeria still has that opportunity to be great and leapfrog many developed countries to become one of the world's most prosperous and influential nations. Building a values-based community and, in the process, producing leaders who are driven by these values is not new to us. In the days of my father, grandfather and our founding fathers, our families and communities were based on solid values. The Yorubas have the concept of *Omoluwabi* (also written as *Omoluabi*), a Yoruba philosophical and cultural concept to describe a person of good character. An *Omoluwabi* is a person of honour who believes in hard work, respects the rights of others and gives to the community in deeds and action. Above all, an *Omoluwabi* is a person of integrity. The *Omoluwabi* concept is an adjectival Yoruba phrase with the words 'Omo

+ ti + Olu-iwa + bi' as its components. These values are reflected in the level of the consciousness of the nation, in the quality of leadership, teachers and teaching, and the critical role played by our religious organizations in our societies, schools/educational system, etc. Those were the days when communities, families and individuals were only recognized based on their values and contributions to the community and not on their wealth; the days when your wealth meant nothing unless the community knew the source and considered it credible.

The only unfortunate thing is that anyone under 45 years of age may not have experienced this era. And if we consider that the average age of Nigerians is about 18.6 years, it is evident that most Nigerians today did not experience this era. The clear message is that we live very close to a time bomb, and drastic action is required immediately. However, I still believe that, because we have been there before, it should not be too difficult to rebuild our values system as long as the *will* to change or transform our country truly is there. It is an opportunity we must not miss.

So, what do we need to do?

- We need a practical national values reorientation programme, institutionalized at least for some years. Joint or shared values unite people, unite communities, unite a nation. We must seek unity based on our common or shared values. We must define or redefine our values as a nation and let that be the foundation on which we build our country. We must institutionalize the implementation of these values across society – the educational system, political parties and the INEC, civil service, judiciary, National Assembly and the private sector. Programmes must be practical, embedded in the system and backed by law and policies. If well implemented, we will create a new society of Nigerians who are ready to serve and put the country first (not personal interest), prepared to help their fellow Nigerians selflessly and with compassion, regardless of tribe or sect, and ready to fight corruption.
- The National Assembly should review the relevant sections in the Constitution where national values are addressed and enact appropriate amendments after extensive consultation. This will not only identify the values our institutions should be built upon but ensure that they are embedded in the Nigerian educational system.

- The national honours, awards and conferment should be linked to our national values system, especially with values such as hard work, merit, professionalism, integrity, compassion, patriotism, honesty, contentment, commitment to country, and other core values as important criteria for determining awardees. All institutions, including religious organizations and traditional leaders, must be encouraged to only recognize and reward Nigerians who demonstrate these values amongst other considerations.
- One of Nigeria's foremost programmes for integration, youth training, reinforcement of patriotism and getting young people ready for employability – the National Youth Service Corps (NYSC) – should be re-engineered to promote values-based leadership principles and encourage Youth Corpers to live these values.
- Civic education should be reintroduced into our national school curriculum at primary and secondary schools to entrench time-tested values of patriotism, integrity, honesty, compassion, hard work, the quest for the common good, communality, selflessness, etc.
- A penalty and reward system, as well as consequences for any wrongdoing, should be clearly defined, codified, institutionalized and implemented without let or favour.
- The judiciary should be provided with requisite financial, material and human resources to enable it to execute its mandate as the last line of defence against discrimination, impunity, lack/poverty and criminality; and as the source of resolution of civil dispute, dispenser of justice, equity and fairness, and a leveller for everyone, regardless of means, status or social standing.
- The government may consider the establishment of a national leadership training institute or revamp the National Institute for Policy and Strategic Studies in Kuru to deliver this.
- Practitioners in certain parts of the entertainment and media industry, including film-making ('Nollywood'), traditional print and electronic media, social media, music, etc., should consistently educate and encourage people regarding their duty of care and the need to project positive values when deploying their influential platforms. The government and community stakeholders will support this effort.

The ICPC has taken the first important step. It has developed a national ethics and integrity policy. All efforts should now be made to raise awareness of the policy and the values contained in the document. The quality of implementation at *all* levels will be crucial to its success.

Develop a law-and-order society

It is possible to argue that a law-and-order society and a values-based society are two sides of the same coin, which is why it is essential to address both in this chapter. Law and order are critical to creating a good society, the right environment for citizens and our most vital asset to thrive and excel in this case. No wonder former President Yar'Adua included law and order in his seven-point agenda.

To avoid ambiguities, I have chosen to use the United Nations' definition to explain what I mean by law and order:

> 'A principle of governance in which all persons, institutions and entities, public and private, including the state itself, are accountable to publicly promulgated, equally enforced and independently adjudicated laws, and which are consistent with international human rights norms and standards. It requires, as well, measures to ensure adherence to the principles of supremacy of law, equality before the law, accountability to the law, fairness in the application of the law, separation of powers, participation in decision-making, legal certainty, avoidance of arbitrariness and procedural and legal transparency.'[6]

Generally, Nigeria has appropriate laws in place, albeit some may be dated. The areas of weakness are equal enforcement and respect for the rule of law, the deficiency of which has led to impunity and a lack of confidence in the system.

Why is law and order important?

Law and order are essential because they provide guidelines on what society accepts. Law and order encourage people to do the right thing

---

[6] The United Nations defines the rule of law and order in its Charter, which was adopted and signed in San Francisco on 26 June 1945.

for the common good and also help to protect lives and property. This creates an environment for its people to thrive and is one of the essential prerequisites for patient capital to be invested in the country and to gain respect from other countries. The characteristics of a law-and-order society and some of the benefits include:

- Peaceful coexistence: the peaceful coexistence among ethnic groups and religious institutions, which thrives on law and order. This is so important for a diverse country like Nigeria, with more than 250 ethnic groups and various cultures, where some parts of the country have been divided along ethnic and religious lines for decades.
- Peaceful elections: electioneering activities such as campaigns, voting, transmission and announcement of results are orderly, peaceful and according to the law or guidelines. The relationships between the different tiers of government are harmonious.
- Obeying traffic regulations: voluntarily obeying traffic regulations for the benefit of all road users and to better manage the resources deployed by the police to keep the roads safe.
- Queuing culture and decorum: citizens join the queue(s) in an orderly manner in public places, such as bus stops, petrol stations, airports, banks, etc., to access public utilities. Polite behaviour and respect for others in interpersonal, intergroup and inter-communal relations are standard features of societies where law and order are exhibited.
- General respect for the country and its people: when there is law and order in a society, the society respect the comity of nations and other organizations.

As a country, we need a panel of eminent, credible and knowledgeable Nigerians to review the entire system and all the relevant institutions, develop and implement a national plan to strengthen the law-and-order society in the country. This panel should of course include eminent lawyers, the civil society, the judiciary, women, police, distinguished academics and the youth. These people should mostly come from the younger generation. They have lived in societies where there is law and order, they are creative and will bring in fresh ideas, including how technology can be used to address some of the issues.

Focus on enablers: education, health and welfare

To turn Nigeria's quantity advantage to productive advantage requires investments in education (academic and technical), health and welfare. That is the only way a country gets maximum return on its assets. The expected returns include good governance and values-based leaders to run the country for the benefit of all Nigerians, a substantial and diversified economy, a robust and highly educated workforce, an increase in national income through taxes, employment, provision of advanced services, patriotic Nigerians with a nation-first mentality, peace and security, etc. Education health and welfare are critical areas and will be discussed separately.

Education

An educated population with a high literacy rate and skills relevant to the economy is a tremendous asset to any nation. The focus on education should be to transform the country by redesigning the curriculum to provide relevant, well-rounded education and skills training, and to significantly increase the government's investment in human capital to raise productivity. Technical colleges should be given a lot more attention to give 'life' to the concept of the 6-3-3-4 education system that Nigeria adopted in 1983. This provides for a child to spend six years in primary school, three years in junior secondary school from where they either go for technical/vocational training or proceed to senior secondary school for another three years, and then spend another four years in university, depending on the course of study.

The idea is to satisfy the educational '3Hs' of the head, heart and hands. Most graduates of junior secondary schools move to senior secondary even when they lack the capacity, academically, for higher studies. The technical gap created by this implementation deficit has led Nigeria to depend on neighbouring West African countries for artisans (plumbers, electricians, etc.) and low-level skills critical for inclusive economic growth. Most of our graduates today are unemployable and have not acquired the education or skills that are relevant to the economy.

Nigeria also needs to refocus its educational system to deliver academic excellence, character formation (values) and spiritual insight. The system should allow a person to attain quality education that emphasizes what is being taught and *how* it is being taught, such that the student can contribute to the economy and development of the nation and thus become relevant to the community and economy. Quality education should be free, compulsory and accessible up to secondary school.

When I joined the government, I recall that in one of our meetings there were discussions around setting up more state universities. I challenged it because, for me, the focus should be the quality of education and not just the number or presence of institutions in the various states, as argued by some other members. Some of my colleagues chuckled, and some smiled at my seeming incomprehension of the politics of schools and schooling in Nigeria. The priority was to have at least one university in every state, regardless of whether or not the country had adequate resources and workforce to run these universities effectively. Most ended up like glorified secondary schools! But we cannot have our cake and eat it. We cannot sacrifice quality on the altar of quantity and remain qualitative.

As Nelson Mandela once said, 'Education is the great engine of personal development. Through education, the daughter of a peasant can become a doctor, a mineworker's son can become the mine's head, and a child of farm workers can become the president of a great nation. What we make out of what we have, not what we are given, separates one person from another.' We had seen evidence of this in some parts of Nigeria when Chief Obafemi Awolowo made education free and compulsory in the Western Region. Many children of farmers who saw farming in their villages as the only option for survival had to go to school. Today many of them are renowned international professors, doctors, engineers, etc. That is why the name Awolowo remains indelible in the hearts and minds of so many Nigerians.

Yet the number of professors and professionally trained lecturers has increased only marginally over the same period. The perennial strikes of teachers or lecturers also means that a three-year course is elongated to a four-year course or more. This has had a significant effect on the quality of education. The result is an educational system that produces unemployable graduates and indirectly contributes to the high youth unemployment and underemployment.

Education reform programmes must prioritize:

- Free and compulsory education up to secondary school and a strategy to stop the high level of children dropping out of secondary (estimated at 52% for male students and 48% for female students in the middle school in 2018). Children must be kept in school long enough for them to be able to contribute to the economy of the country and have a descent life.

- Special programmes for particular states. One cap does not fit all. For example, the north-east and north-west need an educational system that recognizes the regions' culture and peculiarities.
- Robust training and retraining programmes for teachers. The teaching profession must be made very attractive. In most countries that are ranked highly in education, such as the Scandinavian countries, teachers are some of the highest-paid workers, enabling them to attract and retain the best talent in the teaching profession.
- Prioritize quality over quantity. Develop a regulatory programme that includes school inspectors for schools and universities to ensure standards are set and maintained. There should be stiff penalties when institutions and the quality of teaching fall below average.
- The school curriculum should be developed to deliver academic excellence, character formation and spiritual insight, technical skills, leadership and entrepreneurship training.
- Inculcate national core values, civic education and education to eradicate all forms of corruption and its effect on national development.

Scandinavian countries have done very well in education, and Estonia has recently been identified as one of the best in Europe, particularly in mathematics and science. In Estonia's case, the rebuilding of its educational system involved developing a new national curriculum, upgrading vocational education training, reorientating teacher training and focusing on more innovative teaching practices and student-centred approaches. The rebuilding was successful because of a combination of factors: heavy investment in education, equal opportunities for all, focus on the national core curriculum and school content, and they were able to attract academically qualified teachers at all levels of education.

It is not by accident that India produces the most highly regarded graduates in engineering in the world today and also has a very highly developed technology industry. It is because a visionary leader, Nehru, who was the first prime minister of India, decided to establish the Indian Institute of Technology (IIT) more than 50 years ago to produce world-class chemical, electrical and computer engineers who would play a transformative role in India. Today, that dream has been realized, the IIT is regarded above the Ivy League universities and its graduates are the hottest commodity in the world, leading many of the Fortune 500 companies. The IIT has become the source of the biggest talent export to the world, including the US. Nigeria can do the same.

Nigeria once had one of the best educational systems. Nigerians also value education, and there are Nigerian lecturers and professors in all the best universities in the world, so I have no doubt that if the nation decides to prioritize education, it can quickly become one of the best again. I very much look forward to that time.

Health

We must develop a cost-effective national health service scheme that works for all. Productivity is higher when you have a healthy nation, and national patriotism is almost guaranteed when the people's basic health needs are met. The COVID-19 pandemic has reminded us of the need for a robust national healthcare system.

The UK was once like Nigeria and was worse in some areas. It was around 1948 that the change to its NHS began under Clement Attlee, the leader of the Labour Party and the UK's prime minister from 1945 to 1951. Under him, the government established the NHS based on the idea that good healthcare should be available to *all*, regardless of wealth. There were reforms in the social security system to make life better for all and address the aftermath of the First World War – high unemployment and poverty. Today, the NHS is considered with great pride in the UK and at a time, the most valued institution in the UK.

It is about time we provided a comprehensive, qualitative healthcare system for our people. If the UK did it after the Second World War, with a high rate of poverty and high debt, we can do the same, but it will require creativity and learning from those who have already embarked on that journey to manage our costs.

Nations and leaders in the developing world can learn from Mahathir Mohamad, Malaysia's longest-serving prime minister. He served as the fourth and seventh prime minister of Malaysia. He held office for 24 years, from July 1981 to October 2003 and later from May 2018 to March 2020. He was primarily responsible for the transformation of Malaysia. One of the legacies he left behind was the National Heart Institute (Institut Jantung Negara)'. In 1989, at the age of 64, he had his first heart attack and the team of surgeons that performed the procedure on him was led by Dr Yahya Awang, a Malaysian, even though the team included some American surgeons. Mahathir had two more heart attacks in 2006 and underwent quadruple bypass surgery a year later. He was offered treatment abroad but refused. He insisted that it was an opportunity to develop a heart specialist hospital that would meet international standards in Malaysia and serve all Malaysians. And this he did. All his heart treatments and subsequent chest infections have been treated at the National Heart Institute in Malaysia. Today, the Institute has a highly competent team of cardiologists, paediatric cardiologists, cardiothoracic surgeons, cardiac anaesthesiologists, and support staff to handle emergencies, even the most complicated cases. It provides the highest-quality service to local and international patients. The National Heart Institute has served more than 3.7 million patients.

Welfare, security of life, assets and pensions

There is no organized and institutionalized welfare scheme that meets the needs of the majority of the poor, or those who are not able to afford basic necessities in Nigeria, even though the country started some social investment schemes recently. Let me use the UK to explain what I mean by a reasonably comprehensive institutionalized organized welfare scheme. In certain circumstances, legal residents in the UK are entitled to several social benefits. These include income support for people with low income, job seekers' allowance, child benefits, housing benefits, disability living allowance, invalid care allowance, state pension, unemployment benefits, childcare costs support, an NHS for everyone free of charge, free schools up to secondary level, subsidized university education, free bus pass and medication for over 60s and more. Yes, it is ambitious and expensive to provide these benefits, but if we manage our economy and resources better, as discussed in an earlier chapter in the book, and with some creativity, we can at least start and gradually work towards attaining a national goal. Monies recovered from waste and corrupt practices can be used to finance this welfare system.

For effective implementation, it might be necessary to establish a Ministry or agency of Values, Pensions and Welfare to develop and implement the recommendations on values, pensions and the welfare system. The performance and coordination of sustainable development goals should be part of the responsibilities of this new ministry or agency. We must develop and implement policies, programmes and strategies around the following priority areas:

- Job creation: a comprehensive strategy to include accelerated development of housing, infrastructure and other sectors and projects with the capacity to create thousands of jobs.
- Wealth creation: this is about baking the cake, making it much more significant and improving the quality and sources. This calls for a paradigm shift that puts more emphasis on baking rather than sharing the national cake. It needs to be comprehensive and may require an amendment to the Constitution, which currently only talks about sharing of revenue.

Making the governance, economy and structure work for the people

The leadership and governance system must be effective and efficient to get the best out of the people. This means that there must be equal opportunities for all to participate in governance and the economy, that the cost of governance is affordable, and the structure of the country and its operation devolves power and financial autonomy to the state government. The government should be able to provide security, quality education, healthcare, potable water, safe and well-maintained roads, electricity, housing, adequate care for the poor and marginalized, and so on.

Instead, some government actions and inactions appear to cause enterprises to fail. Companies spend most of their time trying to avoid or circumvent these actions and the net effect is that fewer people can contribute to the development of the economy or create jobs. There is also no patriotism; the loyalty is to friends and families who have made it possible for you to send your children to school, pay your hospital bills and contribute to your welfare.

It is essential for successive governments to address these issues and pay more attention to people-focused policies. The restructuring will bring governance closer to the people. My guidance to my staff when I was in government was always to ask themselves two critical questions when working on an initiative, policy or taking any action: What does this mean to the people? What would they get, see and feel as a result of our efforts, initiatives or policy?

Tooling the people up: perspectives from Brazil

There is no need to reinvent the wheel. Regarding population size, natural resources and climate alone, Brazil most closely compares with Nigeria. Brazil has put in place systems and institutions that are dedicated to developing the youth and turning them into a highly skilled labour force for the economy. While serving as minister, I wrote a report on my observations of how the system worked in Brazil, based on interactions with the students in Autopark and discussions with the relevant ministers and heads of the agencies during my visits to the country.

Brazil has five relevant institutions, some similar to those we have in Nigeria, through which various interventions are made. For example, the Brazilian national service for industrial training (SENAI) is the equivalent of Nigeria's ITF. The only significant differences between the two are the number and quality of training equipment and programs, the demand-driven approach to training, which almost guarantees that about 80% to 90% of those trained secure employment within three months of completing the training, and the significant number of Brazilians trained every year. SENAI has industrial training parks across the country. I remember visiting one of the automotive industrial training parks and meeting a very young boy of about 15 who had already gone to school in the morning and was reporting for automotive skills training in the afternoon. His father went through the same programme, and I think President Lula also went through a similar programme. In one of the parks they had the engines, accessories and equipment for different cars all donated to the training centre by the OEMs. This example inspired Nigeria's Auto Parks Production Training Centre, which was going to be located in Badagry, Kaduna and Nnewi, according to the automotive policy that the FEC approved, the planned Badagry centre had two objectives: training Nigerians in the automotive sector with international accreditation and producing the car components and accessories.

The training programme in SENAI is based on a national skills gap survey undertaken annually or biannually. The survey identifies the job opportunities and skills required to fill those vacancies based on existing and pipeline investments and specific training to fill the gaps, identified. For example, we knew Dangote was investing in one of the world's largest refineries and petrochemical plants in 2013. There were plans by several foreign and local investors, such as Jim Ovia and Indorama, to invest in petrochemical plants. Such a survey would have captured their labour requirements and skills required to fill the vacancies. These would then be made available to the training institutions and universities to develop a program to fill those positions when the project was completed. Again, as a result of the sugar cane to sugar policy, we knew that BUA, Flour Mills and Dangote were investing in five northern states and had the potential to create thousands of jobs. This survey would have captured their requirements, when they would be required, what they were likely to be paid and would have started training Nigerians to fill these positions. The survey results could be used by the Ministry of Industry and the government agencies responsible for training, the Ministry of Education and the private sector technical skills training institutions, etc.

The experience in SENAI led to the ITF Train-To-Work programme and the First National Skills Gap Survey, which I asked UNIDO to undertake, working with the ITF and the NBS in 2014. Unfortunately, it was not completed before I left government in May 2015 and the ITF director-general, who worked closely with me and led the effort, also left before it was completed. Brazil also has SEBRAE, SENAR and SENAC which has 24,000 teachers and has trained 55 million people since inception.

Pakistan and a few other countries rely on such surveys for developing schools' curricula and training programmes. Singapore also has something similar, but most countries learned from Germany and adapted this to their local needs. I also arranged for a team led by the director-general of the ITF to visit and study the German approach. Our goal was to revamp the whole system based on the successful models we have seen around the world.

I have only outlined an example from Brazil. There are compelling lessons from Malaysia, South Korea, China and India on rapid skills acquisition for the population. None of these rely on agriculture alone, as Nigeria does. Nigeria's growth path must include modern industries in three sectors: oil and gas, steel and solid minerals, and agriculture-related value-added industries and services.

Developing sustainable plans for empowering the youth and middle class

The middle class in Nigeria is large and one of the fastest-growing in Africa and the world. That allows Nigeria to build consumer and aggregate demand, which are critical to economic growth and tax revenue. This is a compelling reason to decisively deal with unemployment, poverty and insecurity through focused job creation, as China, Malaysia and Brazil have done. Sometimes we get it right, as in the case of Nigeria's film industry, popularly referred to as 'Nollywood', which is gradually becoming a goldmine as the second-largest film industry in the world. Providing economic activities for more than a million people, making it the country's second-largest employer, Nollywood generates an impressive estimated $590 million annually and it is believed that, if the industry is managed correctly, a million more jobs could be created in the sector.

The Nigerian music industry is also gaining global recognition, with several artists winning global awards. The international community's growing interest shows the great potential of talent in Nigerians that the world needs. Today, there is hardly any club in the UK that does not play the music of these highly talented artists.

The youth and the middle class will be the major drivers of the creator economy and the fintech sector. The creator economy encapsulates the industry of people who create online content and make money from it, independent of a third-party brand. Funding to venture capital-backed creator economy companies in 2021 was estimated to be $939 million and as of July 2020 was $637 million. The government only needs to provide an enabling environment and support these sectors directly or through the SWF. I have no doubt that the fintech sector and the creator economy will produce at least eight unicorns in the next five to eight years if well supported.

The graphic representation of the shape of our demography is by itself a picture, in equal measure, of opportunities and challenges. The youth bulge is the most concrete manifestation of this dual reality. The shape of the Nigerian population is such that the curve is near perfect into the 21st century if the people, especially the youth, are knowledgeably empowered.

We need to create a level playing field with equal opportunity so the youth can get the right jobs they need. We need to create avenues for them to start and run their businesses. We need to involve them in governance; they can go into relevant agencies to build their capacities. They also need to be encouraged to set up credible NGOs that will hold governments accountable or provide regular credible information to Nigerians. BudgIT, set up by some creative and cerebral young Nigerians to monitor the budget, cash backing and performance, is an excellent example of such a NGO. Developing and empowering new consumer groups, particularly the growing middle class and those near the bottom of the pyramid, must be the priority of any government, particularly in Africa. Brazil achieved some success in this area. According to *The Economist* in 2010, 'Since 2003 some 20m Brazilians have emerged from poverty and joined the market economy. These new consumers buy everything from cars to cookers and fridges to flights.' They implemented a programme that moved the poorest to the lower-middle class and the middle-middle class.

Build on and leverage our strengths

Diversity is one of Nigeria's strengths; it is not a weakness. Most successful institutions today embrace and celebrate diversity because it has been identified as a prerequisite for success, more so now than previously.

In today's world, both the public and private sectors in the developed economies promote inclusiveness, proactively seek, celebrate and leverage on diversity, but in Africa it is still a tool for oppression and division to gain unfair advantage. President Barack Obama of the US, UK Prime Minister Rishi Sunak, Nigerian-American Wale Adeyemo, the US Deputy Secretary of the Treasury, and Nigerian-British Kemi Badenoch, the UK Secretary of State for International Trade are just some examples of what is possible when a country understands the power and importance of embracing and leveraging diversity. It requires enacting the enabling laws and developing and rigorously implementing the policies that promote inclusiveness.

The government must promote and make it easier for Nigerians to see themselves first as Nigerians by creating an equitable society where there is fairness to manage diversity. Singapore, albeit a much smaller country than Nigeria, recognized the importance of diversity in national development and chose to manage it better by:

- Putting in place policies that will ensure that no one ethnic group dominates others.
- Ensuring that national fusion is reinforced in their Constitution. Article 42 of the Nigerian Constitution speaks of this by prohibiting discrimination based on race, descent or place of birth.

The younger generation, especially those living abroad, do not see or know the difference between the Yoruba, Igbo or Hausa. They speak a common language (English), albeit ideally this should have been a Nigerian language, and they are active on social media. They are married to spouses outside their tribe, were born outside their father's place of origin and birth, have not been to their father's state of origin and do not speak the language. By default, the Nigerian Constitution, which does not recognize the state of residence, is inadvertently locking out such Nigerians from participating fully in governance, social and economic opportunities in their own country.

I will give you another example. Let us look at the case of some like Musa Chukwuemeka, who was born in Kano to Igbo parents. He grew up in Kano, went to school in Kano and all his friends are from Kano. He speaks Hausa fluently but he has never been to the eastern part of Nigeria where his parents come from. Why can Musa and people like him not have equal opportunities in Kano State like his other friends from Kano? Why can he not claim and represent his new state of residence in his own country? That is pure discrimination in your country and limits Kano State's talent to develop Kano. The NYSC is a brilliant idea for national integration and has served many other purposes, including providing skills and a workforce to the different states. It has also led to many inter-tribal marriages.

A constitution or policy that protects the interests of native-born or established inhabitants against those of resident immigrants who have thoroughly imbibed the culture, values and language of their state of residence, which some will describe as a 'deep vein of xenophobia and nativism', can only lead to division, sustained agitation for separation, unrest, lack of development and loyalty to the nation, and poor management of diversity. One of the political parties included this in its manifesto to amend the constitution but did not have the will to carry it through when it got into government.

Singapore, for example, in its early days as a new nation, was beset by ethnic tensions and race riots. Its diverse population consists of Chinese (74.2%), Malay (13.3%), Indians (9.2%) and others (3.3%). It is also one of the most religiously diverse nations in the world. The country made a deliberate effort to address these issues and bring an end to the incessant riots and tensions in several ways:

- Identifying multiculturalism as one of the values the country is built on. The five shared values that were eventually adopted on 15 January 1991 were:
  - Nation before community and society above self
  - Family as the basic unit of society

  - Community support and respect for the individual
  - Consensus, not conflict
  - Racial and religious harmony
- Treatment of every race, language and religion as equal. It made an asset of its ethnic and religious diversity, and the result is relative racial harmony. In Singapore, 85% live in very decent, mostly owner-occupied public housing, and racial quotas mean every block, precinct and enclave fall in line with the national ethnic population percentages. Forcing different peoples to live together as neighbours broke up the ethnic ghettoes and the all-Chinese, all-Malay or all-Indian blocks that could be found at the country's founding in 1965. According to Deputy Prime Minister Tharman, the housing policy was 'authoritarian, intrusive and it turns out to be our greatest strength. The units are heavily subsidized for young couples buying a starter home in one of the world's most expensive cities. The houses were clustered near commercial centres, offices, etc., which meant that people did not have travel far to work and it supported the integration policy.
- The same thinking that went into Singapore's forced integrated housing went into its schools. People of different ethnic and racial groups not only live together, they learn and grow up together. Everyone gets a fair shot at going to a good school, which in turn (and in conjunction with housing policy) leads to a meritocracy in which people of different ethnic and religious minorities are well integrated socially.
- Singaporean law makes wounding the religious or racial feelings of another person a punishable crime.
- Singapore's religious and community leaders also worked hard to make sure that their faiths are practised in a way that fits Singapore's multiracial and multi-religious context.

The National Assembly missed an opportunity to make the necessary amendments during the last review of the Constitution in 2022, but I am hopeful that this will be revisited. Nigeria needs a bold, courageous, visionary government, and a National Assembly that understands the strength of the country's diversity to make the necessary changes to the country's Constitution. The benefits are immeasurable and include peace, security and unity. It will go a long way in addressing the concerns of the agitators or advocates for a break in the country, support meritocracy and promote one nation mentality and patriotism.

The National Assembly should review the relevant sections in our Constitution where citizenship is addressed and enact appropriate laws after extensive consultation. It will also provide a permanent solution to the issue of ethnicity, which many have taken advantage of to create division (divide and rule) for their own selfish personal interests. They should clearly define what qualifies a Nigerian to be a citizen of a state regardless of the state of origin of the parents.

Our silver bullet: a highly credible and accomplished diaspora

According to an African proverb, 'No bird, however magnificent or mighty, flies with one wing.' The Nigerian nation must learn to utilize our hugely gifted and accomplished diaspora. The Nigerian coat of arms features the symbolic representation of the people, a rampant eagle. Given the extraordinary number of highly successful Nigerians in the diaspora, one could be forgiven if the two wings of the eagles are interpreted to represent Nigerians within the country and the Nigerians in the diaspora. These two must work together if Nigeria is to reach the heights of its destiny. That was why the NLI seminars bring the highly accomplished and credible Nigerians in the diaspora and from within Nigeria into a class of 24 maximum. You should hear the quality of discussions in the room – it is simply electric, regardless of whether it is the senior fellows, fellows or the associate class – you come out of the seminars enriched, determined to play a role in transforming your country and humbled at sitting in a class with such superstars, who have distinguished themselves internationally and locally. For some it was life-changing.

Brain drain?

The African Capacity Building Foundation investigated the twin problems of productive capacities of the education systems and the local absorptive capacity of the products of those institutions. Specifically, the Foundation posited that:

> '... migration need not be a zero-sum game as source countries can benefit from brain circulation and brain gain if conditions

are implemented. This suggests that countries need the capacity to track and monitor their diaspora – identifying who they are, where they live, what they do, and what they might be interested in doing if they return to the homeland.'[7]

I would amend the last line to read 'homeland or how they can support the development of their country of origin from the new place of residence'. They do not have to return to the homeland to make valuable contributions; this can be done in many ways. For example, I have proposed the establishment of a Presidential Honorary Diaspora Council (PHDC) made up of highly accomplished credible Nigerians in the diaspora and Nigerians in certain critical sections such as economy, health, education, finance, technology and innovation, science, trade and investment, etc. The selection criteria, which should be based on merit, accomplishment, etc., should be transparent and adhered to strictly. It would be an honour and privilege for any Nigerian to serve on this council because they ideally should represent some of the best, if not the best in their fields and would be well connected locally and internationally. The PHDC would be hosted by the president, who would be expected to attend meetings twice a year to discuss the state of the nation, the plan, status of implementation, challenges for each sector and support or assistance required. The different sector representatives could be assigned to research specific sectoral challenges and report back to the president/PHDC. This, for example, could be the platform for looking into the feasibility, researching and development of a plan for the Nigerian national health service for all Nigerians, leveraging the knowledge and expertise of the thousands of Nigerian doctors in the diaspora and those working in the NHS in the UK. My experience with the NLI tells me that this could be a game changer if well implemented and not politicized.

On remittances, the Bloomberg Economics Hernandez and Orlik (2021) study indicated the potential for Nigerian migrant worker remittances to boost its GDP by 0.4 percentage points or more.[8]

---

[7] African Capacity Building Foundation. Strengthening the Capacity of Africa's Higher Education Institutions to Produce and Absorb Relevant Skills (2018).

[8] Bloomberg Economics. Migrants to the Rescue: How Increased Remittances May lift Nigerian's GDP (2021).

Available statistics indicate that there are over 20 million Nigerians in the diaspora and, in the last one year, money remitted into Nigeria was in excess of $20 billion. Efforts must be made to access this capital in an organized way and channel it to areas where it can be most effective and impact the FX in Nigeria as additional supply that should moderate the exchange value of the domestic currency. It could also be a source of investment into economically viable strategic projects. India and Ethiopia have done this very well.

Religious organizations

Religious organizations played a significant and positive role in education and health in Africa in the 1960s and 1970s. Religion is a key part of the life of an average African, and it plays a critical role in human development and society. We recognize this fact but, unfortunately, have used it more as a tool for division rather than as a tool for spiritual, human and national development. One of the universal functions of religion is to help promote a good society by giving meaning to life, reinforcing social unity and stability, promoting physical and psychological well-being and motivating people to work for positive social change. In many nations, including the US, religious organizations provide substantial social capital through civic and social networks. Religious organizations in Nigeria need to become more relevant to nation-building and society, like they were in the 1960s and 1970s. They are recognized as the nation's conscience, the voice and defender of the people, including the oppressed, marginalized and poor, and the custodians of the nation's moral compass/values.

Our revered and highly respected religious leaders must come together to develop and implement a comprehensive programme that would raise the spiritual awareness and consciousness of Nigerians based on the 'love of neighbour as self and God above all'. This must be a way of life – how we live and interact with our fellow Nigerians daily. They should also live and teach the love of neighbour and God above all through providing affordable (cheap) quality education and healthcare facilities in the country.

Almost one in four primary schools in the UK is funded or partly funded and influenced by the Church of England. Hindu-inspired schools are now springing up as Avanti schools in the UK. The vision of the Avanti schools is to provide the very best in values-led education to the young people of those schools, focusing on three things:

educational excellence, character formation and spiritual insight – and they are delivering. According to the regulators' (Ofsted) report on one of the Avanti schools,

> 'The ethos and practice of respectfulness is a unique feature of the school's work. The provision of pupils' spiritual, moral, social and cultural development is exceptional. Behaviour and attitudes shown by pupils and adults are exemplary because everyone believes in the school's core values, most pupils achieve highly in many subjects, and the curriculum is linked intrinsically to the school's vision.'

The schools are fully inclusive and welcome pupils of all faiths, religious beliefs and those with different abilities and needs. I have met the founder and I was inspired by his vision and meticulous approach to delivery.

Our religious organizations (Anglican, Methodist, Catholic, Baptist, Ansar-Ud-Deen, Ahmadiyya, Islamiyah, etc.) did this many years ago, and most of our leaders today were beneficiaries of such benevolence from these organizations. It can be argued that our religious organizations and leaders are in a better and stronger position to transform the country than anyone, including the government, because of the type and size of their followership.

Religious organizations and their leaders must not miss this golden opportunity. For example, one of the goals of one of our most respected religious organizations in Nigeria is to have a church within a five-minute drive or ten-minute walk. I must say that they have been exceptionally successful in planting churches all over the world (not just in Nigeria). What a remarkable success! Now imagine if churches within a particular area add a school, like the Avanti schools, to provide the very best in values-led education to young people, and a hospital or health centre! This would significantly affect the development of our nation's most important and prized asset – our people.

I know that the particular church I referred to and some religious organizations have established top-quality schools, universities, health centres, etc. We must commend them for this, but I must emphasize two things: they can do much more to become even more relevant to national development, and this is not just about setting up a school but about establishing schools with a particular focus on character formation, educational excellence and spiritual insight (values-led education). It will require the development of a model that works from the centre and using that model as the template for all religious groups. On finance, show that it works, then arrange for government match-funding. This can become a perfect private–public partnership model for investing and supporting the development of critical soft infrastructure – human capacity/people. This has been done in other countries and can be done in Nigeria effectively.

Large population and an enviable demography

Not surprisingly, many nations with rapid population growth rates have low living standards. Suppose that, as current trends suggest, we add roughly six million people to our population yearly. This is a recipe for crisis if we fail to grow a bigger economy and turn our quantity advantage to productive advantage as China did. The six million added to our population yearly is about the size of countries such as Congo, Namibia, Liberia, Mauritania and the Gambia. I have already mentioned how Nigeria's population is growing in comparison to that of the UK. Our population is growing faster than the economy, which only means one thing – poverty. More poverty and crises coupled with social unrest as a possible result. We can do something about it now. Turning our quantity to productive advantage will require skills training to ensure that the youth have the skills relevant to the economy, full implementation of the NEDEP and the NIRP, and developing policies that would create jobs. When Nigeria successfully skills up and empowers the youth, it will create another new group of consumers who contribute to the national income through taxes, as discussed in Chapter 4.

We the people

Ultimately the buck stops with the people. They elect the leaders to serve them and are therefore responsible for holding them accountable. The Berlin Wall in Germany fell mainly because the people took responsibility and said enough was enough. The law that eventually allowed women to vote in the US was passed into law because the people took control. More recently, the UK left the EU because the people wanted to take back control. Nigerians must take back control, and they can. The 2023 elections have shown what is possible when there is a strong will and determination. The youth and educated Nigerians must be ready to continue to take the lead and make the necessary sacrifices as enlightened stakeholders to create an excellent and well-governed society for the benefit of all Nigerians. There are many strategies to achieve this, including encouraging Nigerians to vote, educating them in local languages on the power of their votes, not allowing politicians to buy their votes, and highlighting the consequences of making the wrong choices. Some may decide to go into politics at different levels, proactively, or perhaps support a candidate or party that can be trusted to create the good and prosperous country we all want.

Recent efforts to revive our country have focused on combatting corruption, which some have called the most incredible machine for manufacturing poverty. Those in charge of fighting crime in our country, against impossible odds and at significant risk to life and limb, have shown the world what Nigerians can do when they set their hearts on it. We have seen more room than ever before created for intelligent, progressive Nigerians, who are not necessarily professional politicians, to participate in the task of reviving the nation.

The greatest danger we face right now – our nation's soft underbelly – is not necessarily the politician trying to buy their way into the presidency, governorship or the Senate. Our greatest weakness is the Nigerian citizen who needs to be reminded what it means to be a citizen all over again. In the age of the Nigerian citizen, perhaps up until the 1970s, it was routine to find the most dedicated schoolteachers in every school in the country. We had dedicated doctors, nurses, dispensers, civil servants and permanent secretaries who eschewed the pursuit of wealth for its own sake but instead derived honour from service. We had a postmaster, who rode a bicycle up and down our streets, diligently delivering mail, a simple act that was, in fact, crucial to the functioning of society. We had neighbours who kept watch over others' children as attentively as their own. These community leaders kept everything in balance.

We now need the old Nigerian citizen who is ambitious and believes Nigeria can scale any height attainable by citizens in any other country. We now need a new Nigerian citizen who is truly committed to a good society and is ready to work for it regardless of the challenges. In short, we need a new Nigerian that looks a lot like the Nigerian of old – community-spirited, virtuous, courageous, proud, unintimidated by the challenge of national reconstruction.

Conclusion

A century ago, Nigeria had about 16 million people. Today the story is drastically different, with an estimated 216.7 million people. We need to invest in our people, starting with the rebuilding of our values system and the development of a law-and-order society. We must reform the health and educational system to make our education more relevant to the economy and national development. We need schools focusing on character formation, technical skills acquisition, educational excellence and spiritual insight. It is time for a robust welfare system and a dependable security architecture we can rely on. Governments exist to make the governance structure and the society work for the citizens, and in Nigeria that includes a sustainable plan for empowering the youth and middle class.

Nigeria is a blessed nation and has a lot going for it. To fully reclaim its pride of place as the jewel, Nigeria must leverage its strengths, which include the ample, highly accomplished and credible Nigerians in the diaspora, regard diversity as one of its strengths and leverage it, turn religion into a tool for development rather than division, and turn its large population and enviable demography into a productive advantage and a strong consumer group. That is the society, the country, we need to build. A government that cares for its citizens and will go the extra mile to provide and maintain the basic facilities for its citizens and meet its obligations. In return, the citizens will care for and love the nation. Our shared values should define us; they should explain what it is to be a Nigerian, not our tribe.

In the final analysis, it is axiomatic to acknowledge that government reforms are not unusual, even in developed countries that work well. African leaders must embrace and embark upon significant government reforms, as most governments have remained vulnerable to 'major malfunctions', very high cost of governance, weak political, economic and social institutions, weak economies, high levels of poverty, unemployment, insecurity, waste, predictable failures, flaws in the governance structure, and so on. The reforms must be system based and not reliant on individuals to be sustained. This is the only way leaders can begin to untie the chains that have caused so many breakdowns and failures in the past and that have continued to frustrate the efforts to achieve Africa's great potential and make the progress that the continent deserves as it confronts new social, economic and political threats.

Chapter 8

The triple threat: poverty, unemployment and insecurity

'As far as I can understand, the aggressors against peace and stability in Nigeria are abject poverty, hunger, disease, squalor and ignorance. They are the enemies which must now be crushed and crushed ruthlessly.'

Chief Obafemi Awolowo,
Vice-Chairman of the FEC, 16 May 1970

In contemporary Nigeria it is common for commentators to use the convenient catchphrase 'corruption' as an easy way out of rigorous thinking about what really troubles the country. In this chapter we will go beyond the mantras and nostrums to examine what the data reveals about the phenomena and what to do about it.

Our situation in Nigeria today is vastly different than in the 1980s, when China's GDP per capita was only $193, lower than Malawi, Nigeria and Burundi. The oil boom as well as the fiat economy of the times has yielded to a diversifying economic arrangement. My time as both Minister for Finance and as Minister for Industry, Trade and Investment, and the development since 2015 to date, has helped me in no small measure to isolate what may be described as the economic and national triple threats: poverty, unemployment and insecurity. If China, Indonesia, Malaysia, India and South Korea could overcome their economic challenges, moving these countries out of pervasive poverty and destitution, there is no reason why Nigeria cannot do the same.

Poverty

Overcoming poverty is a primary function of government. It is the protection of a fundamental human right, the right to dignity and a decent life.

Poverty is a frontline global challenge that has been identified as the key problem affecting the socio-economic well-being of people. This has necessitated global leaders to prioritize eradicating it as the number-one goal of sustainable development. According to the World Bank's definition of poverty 'a person is considered poor if their income level falls below a minimum level necessary to meet basic needs,' such as food, water, shelter, health and clothing.

As Banerjee and Duflo (2011) explained in *Poor Economics,* the poor often lack understanding and critical pieces of information, they usually do not know what their politicians do when in office, and therefore do not know whether they have performed well or badly in office.[9] When the percentage of the poor is high in a country, it completely weakens democracy, because people are more likely to vote for someone of their ethnic group or sell their votes at the cost of good governance. The poor bear responsibility for too many aspects of their lives, whereas the richer you are the more you get from government and the more the right decisions are made for you. The poor have no pipe-borne water, so they do not benefit from the chlorine that the government puts into the water supply. The poor do not benefit from a government's contribution to a retirement benefit plan or contributions to social security, and they therefore have no savings or income to support them when they are old. In most cases, the poor cannot afford fortified food and therefore are left without nutrients.

Poverty is a global issue. Today, Nigeria ranks highly in the world in the number of the absolutely poor and has one of the highest levels of inequality.

An overview of poverty in Nigeria

- Out of a population of over 210 million people, almost half are extremely poor.
- The number of poor had risen from a little over 75 million in 2016 to 87 million in 2018 and it was projected to be at 95 million by 2022 if nothing was done.
- The number of Nigerians in extreme poverty increases by six people every minute. The poverty world clock claims that the

---

[9] A. V. Banerjee & E. Duflo, *Poor Economics: A Radical Rethinking of the Way to Fight Global Poverty* (2011).

number of the absolute poor in Nigeria is closer to 102 million, the highest in the world.

- There are limited basic amenities such as housing, healthcare, electricity, water, good education and mass transit for Nigeria's increasing population.
- Oxfam ranks Nigeria top in the list of countries in which the gap between the rich and the poor has worsened. Nigeria was ranked 157th out of the 189 countries covered by Oxfam's inequality index 2019.[10] And in the 2021 Commitment to Reducing Inequality Index, the Nigerian government was ranked 157 out of 158 countries on commitment to reducing inequality in areas of education, health, social protection, taxation and workers' rights.[11]
- The 2021 Multidimensional Poverty report issued by the NBS in November 2022 puts the level of poverty at 133 million, about 63% of the country's population; 67.5 % of children within the ages of 0–17 are in this group, and 51% of all poor people are children; 65% live in the north and 35% in the south of the country.[12]

Figure 8.1: Nigerian population by household income 2017

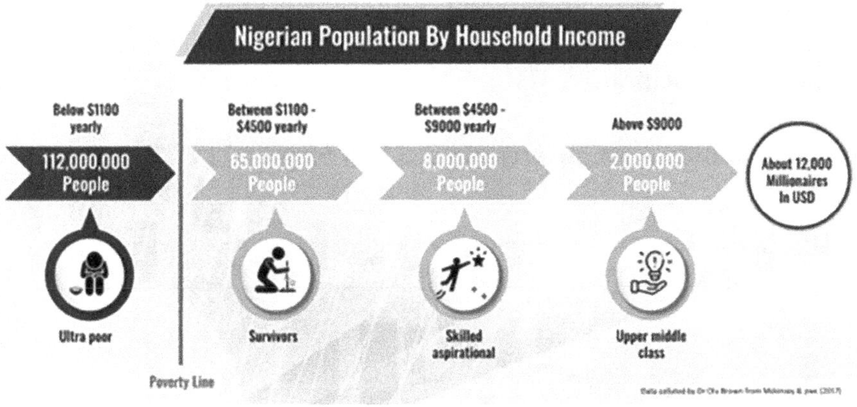

[10] Oxfam. The Commitment to Reducing Inequality Index 2019.
[11] Oxfam. The Commitment to Reducing Inequality Index 2021.
[12] National Bureau of Statistics. 2021 Multidimensional Poverty Index Report.

The data appears daunting but, in fact, many countries have faced these same challenges at various times in history and they have emerged victorious. Some determination and discipline is involved but it is eminently doable. The UK in the aftermath of the Second World War is a good case in point.

Measuring poverty

Nigeria recently joined the league of countries that adopted the multidimensional approach to measuring poverty. This is designed to achieve poverty eradication, zero hunger, quality education, climate action and inclusion. This action is expected to elicit robust discussion among the key stakeholders, such as government agencies, NGOs, civil societies, development partners, private investors, among others. This is imperative to enhance governments' accountability and help to design intervention programmes that will tackle poverty.

From the global perspective, poverty gap and poverty headcount are two of the most common metrics for measuring the extent of poverty. Figures 8.2 to 8.7 show the poverty gap index (a measure of the intensity of poverty or average shortfall of the total population from the poverty line) in Nigeria in comparison with two selected countries that have been successful with poverty reduction (China and Indonesia), the latter having similar economic endowment to Nigeria in terms of natural deposits such as crude oil and agricultural endowment, as well as a large population.

Figure 8.2: Indonesia poverty gap at $1.90/day (2011 PPP)

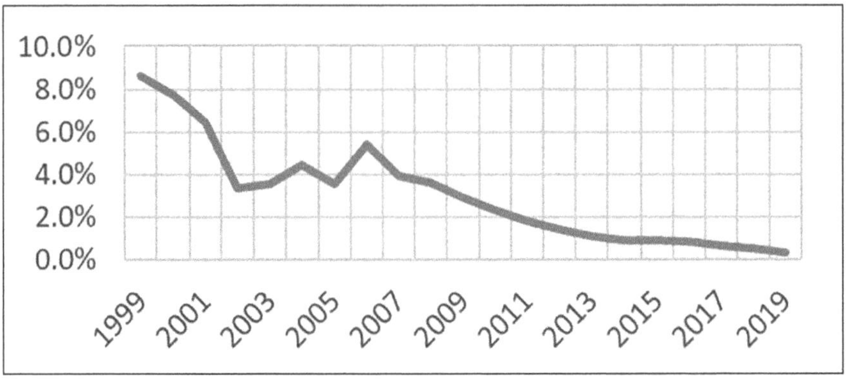

Figure 8.3: China poverty gap at $1.90/day (2011 PPP)

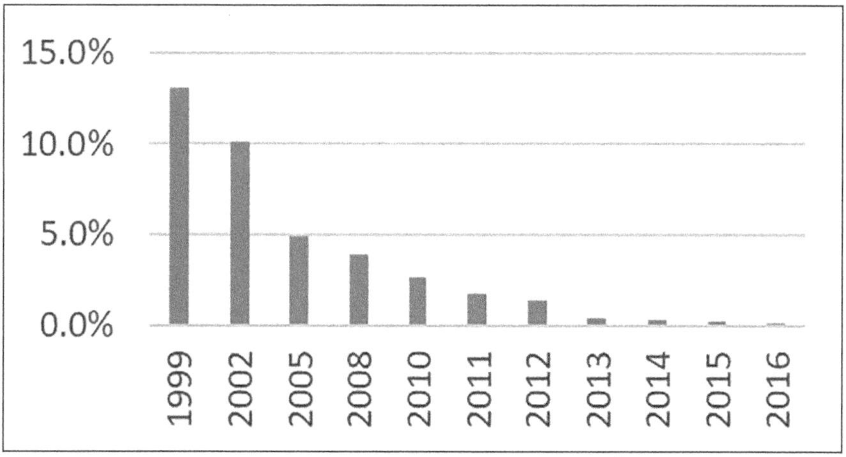

Figure 8.4: Indonesia poverty headcount ratio at $1.90/day (2011 PPP, % of population)

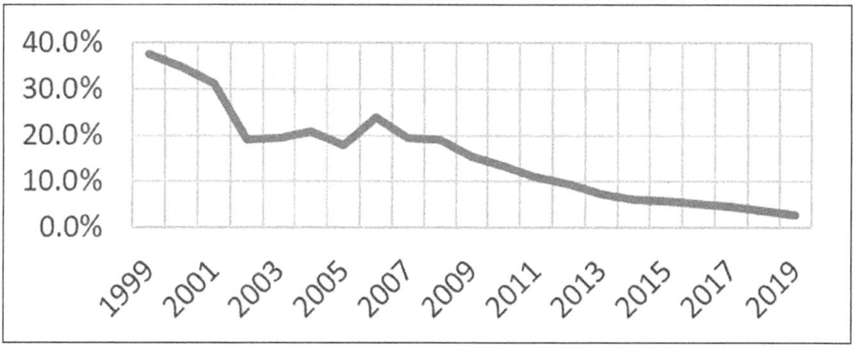

Figure 8.5: China headcount ratio at $1.90/day (2011 PPP, % of population)

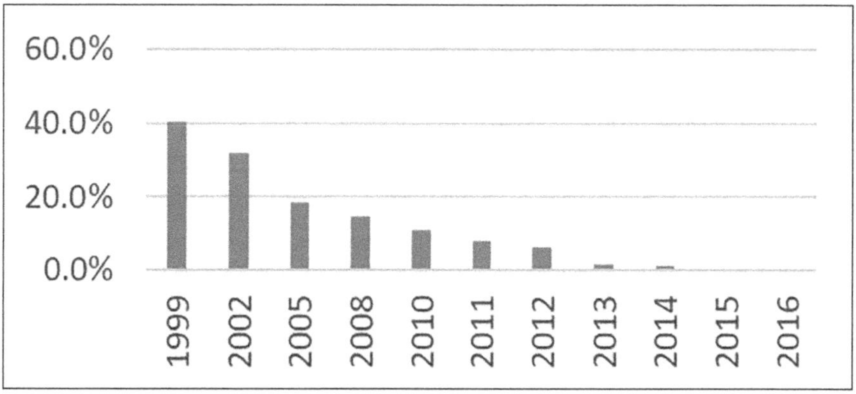

Figure 8.6: Indonesia poverty gap at $5.50/day (2011 PPP, % of population)

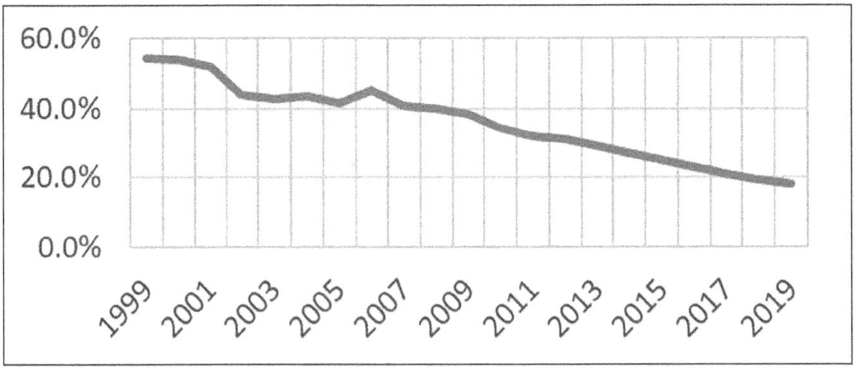

Figure 8.7: China poverty headcount ratio at $5.50/day (2011 PPP, % of population)

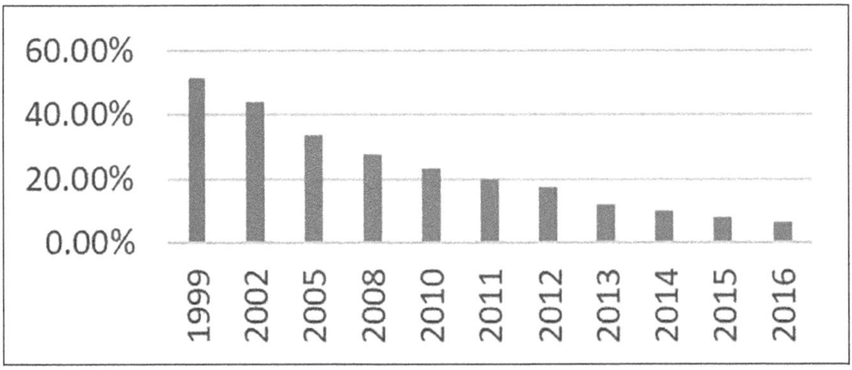

Source: World Bank

The key inference is that China and Indonesia's development plans have specific strategies designed to tackle poverty through friendly industrialization policies that attract local and foreign investments, production and export drive policies. These policies have a ripple effect in alleviating the degree of poverty in these countries.

Over 20 years, the number of people in China with income below $1.90 per day fell by 500 million. China's approach to poverty reduction has been based on two pillars: the economic transformation, which delivered double-digit, inclusive growth persistently for decades, raised average income and the targeted support provided to individual households, and the focus on areas disadvantaged by geography.

It is important to note that Indonesia, just like Nigeria, is rich in oil and gas. However, the country diversified into non-oil sectors to drive the sustainable inclusive economic growth that has had significant impact in improving the standard of living of its people. A similar chart for Nigeria shows that its economic growth is not inclusive by nature, mono-product driven and the focus on MSMEs is unsustained. This is why the economic growth has had no impact on alleviating poverty.

Lessons from Indonesia's Poverty Reduction Strategy

Indonesia had a national medium-term development plan that had several social protection programmes, including Smart Indonesia, which works through education and training, social welfare and health to build the citizens' character, values for patriotism and promotion of diversity for peaceful coexistence. These programmes have been implemented consistently over a *long* period, with procedures in place to monitor quality of implementation and measure success. The specifics of some of the strategies deployed are as follows:

- The government created employment opportunities through expansion of the manufacturing sector; development of a simple regulatory framework, which triggered a friendly investment climate; and the development of a comprehensive social protection system through social security programmes that targeted the vulnerable and informal workers, just like the UK does now, as explained in the previous chapter.
- An exit strategy and complementary framework for the poor aided by the social security benefits.
- Promotion of viable livelihoods to expand accessibility to capital and microfinance, skill development for entrepreneurship. Development of programmes such as microenterprise group to enhance their productive capacity.
- Provided access to basic services through expansion of infrastructural facilities. This was followed through with a system for monitoring and evaluation of the delivery of the basic services.
- Development of entrepreneurship programmes for the vulnerable and facilitation of access to finance and patronage through government ministries and agencies.

- Deployed a verified integrated data system that supports the development of family economic productive activities and training and skills acquisition programmes.
- Enhancing consumption among the vulnerable, such as subsidized rice delivery to the poor and the promotion of a savings culture among the vulnerable.
- Designed social rehabilitation centres for people living with disabilities, while centre-based, community-based and direct aids are targeted at the older citizens to cater for their welfare. This covered many poor people to guarantee their future productivity. Indonesia's conditional cash transfer is also tied to compulsory schooling for the beneficiary children and maternal care for pregnant women.

The important message here is that it is not only about reducing the poverty rate, but also about keeping poverty levels consistently down. This requires governments to sustain economic and poverty alleviation programmes that have worked and to develop new ones to address current or new drivers of poverty, as Nigeria and other countries that have seen their poverty levels rise again have found out. This will require consistent and adequate allocation of resources from the annual budget and periodic reviews of the programmes and their effectiveness.

Brazil, under President Lula between 2003 and 2010, lifted over 20 million citizens from abject poverty and turned them into new consumer groups by implementing similar strategies.

Lessons for Nigeria

As part of the efforts to eradicate poverty, the Obasanjo administration created the National Poverty Eradication Programme. The Jonathan administration tried to consolidate the different programmes, including the programme under the Millennium Development Goals to eradicate extreme poverty and hunger, while the Buhari administration has deepened the social investment programme and made some progress in developing a register for the extremely poor. It is, therefore, fair to say that all the immediate past three administrations have made some efforts to eradicate poverty but the number of the absolute poor, particularly since 2017, suggests a review of the actions taken so far is urgently needed. Clearly there has been lack of continuity, and there is a need for improvement in the quality of implementation and scope of the programmes, and an urgent need for a more comprehensive strategy, which should involve SMEDAN, to be implemented and well-funded over the next ten years.

The registration of qualified Nigerians provides some database that we can act on. This was started by President Buhari's administration. However, Nigeria needs a comprehensive strategy. An agency with presence in each state should be established to implement this policy, working with the local governments, ministries of Industry, Trade and Investment, Agriculture and Rural Development and Solid Minerals, and reporting to the appropriate ministry and not the presidency, to ensure accountability. NEC should ensure that the programs are well designed and coordination from the Local governments to the State and Federal governments.

Going by the Nigerian government's policy direction and investment in agriculture, it is important to shift from subsistence agriculture to mechanized, commercial and modern agriculture for it to be perceived as a go-to job and to significantly increase yield income for the farmers.

It is worth noting that Nigeria has or had some of the programmes implemented by other countries. But the problem has always been the lack of continuity, the size of programmes, the lack of funding, the quality of appointments made and the lack of any monitoring and reporting mechanism to ensure accountability. If the Nigerian government can adopt some of these initiatives in tandem with policies that will bring about macroeconomic stability, as noted in the previous chapters, and address the issues raised above, there should be significant reduction in the level of poverty seen today.

Unemployment

The NBS defines unemployment as the proportion of people between the ages of 15 and 60 who are currently available for work, actively seeking work but could not find work during the reference period. The level of unemployment in Nigeria is also relatively high at over 33.4%, and many are dependent on family and friends. The unemployment situation has worsened as a result of the COVID-19 pandemic. A breakdown of the aggregate level of unemployment shows that it is highest between the age bracket 18 to 40.

Global perspective of unemployment

High unemployment is prevalent in developing economies. The global unemployment rate steadily increased from 4.8% to 6.4% between 1991 and 2020, although the trend is uneven across regions. Lower-middle income countries, where Nigeria is categorized, were projected to experience an increase in unemployment by 5.9% in 2021 and 5.5% in 2022, while the labour force participation rate was projected at 53.9% and 54.3% in 2021 and 2022, respectively.

Figure 8.8: Unemployment rate in selected countries

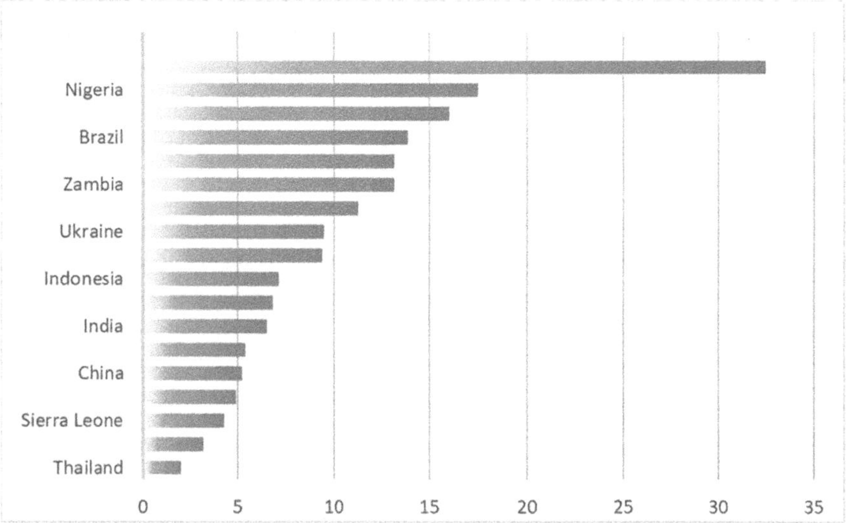

Source: Nigeria Bureau of Statistics

Nigeria's untamed unemployment rate

Nigeria's unemployment rate is growing at a geometrical rate. Along with inequality, this remains a major threat to the government's drive to tackle poverty.

A myriad of factors are responsible for the over 23 million people out of 70 million people that are unemployed in Nigeria, including:

- The precarious state of the economy, which has dwindled the capacity to create jobs and forced many industries to close shop.
- High import dependency, which renders our industries sub-optimal in fulfilling their goals. Some of the imported products

are cheaper than the locally produced goods because of the high cost of production, distribution and doing business.

- Growing labour force without corresponding jobs. At least two million students graduate from university every year. Employment strategies and policies are not properly designed to mop up the growing labour.
- Mismatch of relevant skills to the current market needs. The curriculum and courses taught in schools and universities are outdated, hence the large number of graduates whose skills do not fit the 21st-century market realities and are not relevant to the economy.

The federal, state and local governments are tackling unemployment through different social intervention programmes. For instance, Lagos State government designed a graduate internship placement programme to engage 4,000 unemployed graduates and pay a monthly sum of ₦40,000 for six months to each one of them. This programme is designed to upskill the graduates and expose them to corporate organizations where they also learn soft skills. The internship programme should enhance the capacity of the interns and trigger networking, thus providing a pool of human resources for MSMEs at no cost to these entities. This is a laudable initiative, which should be expanded and replicated across the different states of the federation to partly address unemployment.

Figure 8.9: Nigeria: unemployment rate by states, Q4 2020

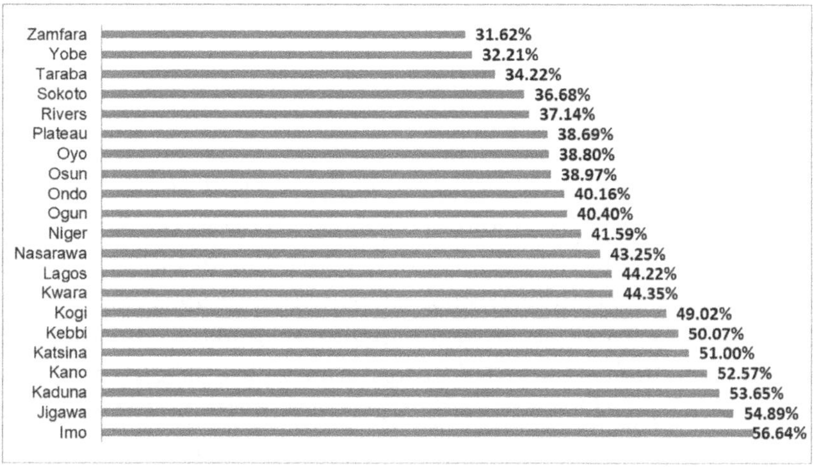

Source: National Bureau of Statistics, Q4 2020

Nexus between poverty and unemployment

As unemployment continues to grow, poverty is expected to rise, resulting in illegal and criminal activities that threaten the socio-economic peace and stability of Nigeria. There are diverse views on the appropriate strategy for measuring poverty, whether to adopt a consumption- or income-based approach. However, the latest data available on poverty analysis in Nigeria adopted the consumption-based approach because it also serves to determine the welfare state of individuals. Also, household income is difficult to access in developing countries like Nigeria, since there are different sources of income, including support provided by family members, which most people are not ready to disclose officially.

Figure 8.10: Poverty headcount rate by household head's education and gender

	Nigeria (%)	Urban (%)	Rural (%)
No education/less than primary school – male	66.17	43.14	70.82
No education/less than primary school – female	34.72	24.66	39.17
Primary education – male	41.25	19.16	50.33
Primary education – female	26.93	19.35	32.74
Secondary education – male	25.00	12.97	35.87
Secondary education – female	14.08	11.20	18.96
Post-secondary education – male	18.13	8.86	31.20
Post-secondary education – female	5.66	3.42	10.15

Source: National Bureau of Statistics

In line with a priori expectations, both men and women with post-secondary education are at lower poverty levels. However, the disparity between men that have post-secondary education and those that have only secondary education is small. This may indicate that, although individuals take extra steps to attain post-secondary education, the effect it has on their standard of living is miniscule owing to insufficient job opportunities. The poverty headcount is more prevalent among individuals (male) with no access to education in both the urban

(43.14%) and rural (70.82%) Nigeria. If something drastic is not done to curtail this growing unemployment rate, the aftermath will be heightened insecurities, compared to what the country is experiencing now.

As such, the government needs to develop empowerment programmes, such as vocational skills acquisition programmes, that will enhance productive capacity, support trading out of poverty programmes, encourage mechanized agriculture, revive the textile industry and for those in Urban Nigeria, expand the digital economy, including the creator economy, to harness the talents of the young Nigerians.

Figure 8.11: Post-secondary school unemployment in Nigeria as at Q4 2020

	Total unemployed	Unemployment rates (%)			Underemployment rate
		Old Nigeria	New Nigeria	International	
BA/BSc/ HND	2,382,052	52.6	40.1	28.8	12.5
Tech/Prof	52,835	55.8	28.2	14.8	27.6
Masters	97,196	45.7	27.8	11.6	17.9
Doctorate	12,483	37.6	16.9	0.0	20.7

Source: National Bureau of Statistics, Q4 2020

Figure 8.10 shows the effect of human capital development policies on women in addressing poverty in Nigeria. Women seem to require more than primary education to make a difference in their poverty situation, as the difference between women that have no education and women that have primary education is quite small. In comparison, secondary school education makes a much bigger impact on the poverty situation of women. When comparing male and female poverty headcount rates, men tend to have a higher poverty headcount than women at every educational level. The poverty headcount disparity between rural and urban areas at every educational level is concerning, although it seems to be bigger for men.

Figure 8.12: Poverty headcount by income-generating activity and gender of household head (%)

	Nigeria	Urban	Rural
Agriculture only – male	58.76	30.11	63.20
Agriculture only – female	37.75	27.96	39.02
Non-farm enterprise only – male	25.45	15.22	41.68
Non-farm enterprise only – female	19.45	18.12	22.48
Wage work only – male	17.52	11.87	28.72
Wage work only – female	13.99	11.38	21.14
Diversified – male	46.90	23.92	53.25
Diversified – female	31.54	24.99	33.79
Apprenticeship/not working – male	34.24	18.60	47.14
Apprenticeship/not working – female	24.13	11.00	34.81

Source: Nigeria Bureau of Statistics 2019

As shown in Figure 8.12, those that generate income by agriculture only or diversified activities have a higher poverty headcount than from any other source of income, showing that subsistence farming does not create wealth for the farmers and cannot be considered a source for national income diversification, even though it is a relatively sizeable part of the country's economy. Wage work seems to generate a significantly lower poverty headcount than any other income-generating activity. Unlike with education, the poverty headcount disparity between men and women is smaller at each income-generating activity. Men that live in urban areas and generate income through agriculture perhaps only fare better than those in rural areas due to mechanization and advanced farming methods. Also, men in urban areas fare much better in terms of non-farming enterprise only, diversified and even apprenticeship as well. This shows that men in urban areas generally have significantly lower poverty headcount levels than men in rural areas. Although women in rural areas have significant differing poverty levels with their counterparts in urban areas, it is not as significant as those of the male population.

Figure 8.13: Gini coefficient of Nigeria: urban and rural regions

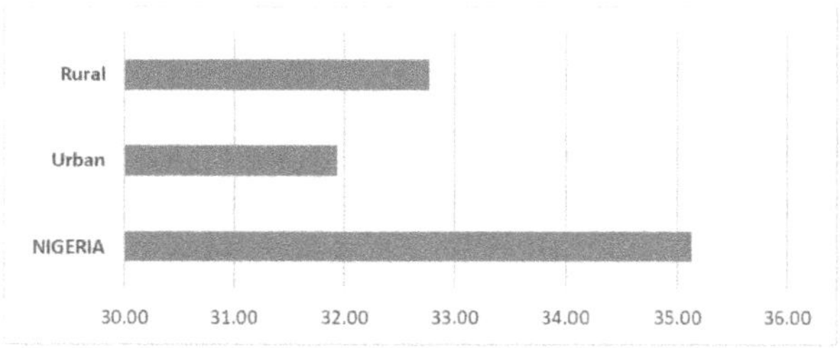

Source: National Bureau of Statistics, 2019

There is relatively higher inequality in rural areas than urban areas. This can largely be attributed to the fact that the rural settlers are exposed to similar challenges that limit their capacity to engage in productive activities that will mitigate the inequality level. However, those that maximize the opportunities tend to earn more than the average village dwellers.

Figure 8.14: Gini coefficient of states in Nigeria

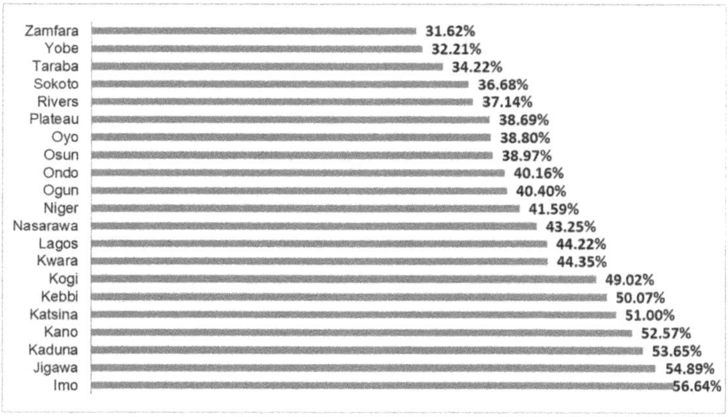

Source: National Bureau of Statistics and BAA Consult

States in the middle belt area of Nigeria, or its immediate surroundings, have the highest inequality based on the Gini coefficient statistics. Drawing inferences by using the yardstick of southern and northern states, 17 southern states have Gini coefficient figures of less than 30%, while 13 northern states are within this class. One southern state and two northern states, including the FCT, have a Gini coefficient above 30%. Insecurity constitutes one of the key challenges widening inequality across the states.

Insecurity

Insecurity has plagued Nigeria and hindered economic growth, industrialization and sustainable development. The country is faced with all manner of insecurity, from Boko Haram insurgency, Islamic State West Africa Province territory incursions, kidnapping, armed banditry, militancy in the Niger Delta region, child abduction/trafficking, political/religious crisis, among others. These have resulted in the daily loss of lives, properties, businesses, internally displaced persons, settlement displacement, capital flight, while people continue to live in fear and abject poverty as a result of low productivity, further heightening unemployment.

Due to a long absence of constructive government presence in large swathes in many areas currently experiencing insurgency, the insurgents have turned to taxing areas under their influence in exchange for providing utilities to the people. This means that the insurgents are already engaged in the battle for the hearts and minds of the people. If these elements are seen as providers of amenities, then winning the war against insurgency is going to be much more difficult than it is today.

Dr Abubakar Siddique Mohammed, director of the Centre for Democratic Development Research and Training in Zango Shanu, Zaria, and whose centre carried out research on banditry, kidnapping and killings in Zamfara and Katsina States, identified three crucial components to the looming anarchy in the north-west of Nigeria:

- Under-policing.
- Large ungoverned spaces presently reliant on local, ill-equipped and ill-trained vigilantes.
- An absence of widespread legitimate economic activities.

Perhaps the one form of insecurity that has most negatively affected economic activity and productivity is kidnapping for ransom. While data is still being gathered for a more holistic picture, the available information is disturbing enough.

Figure 8.15: Number of kidnapping across the regions

	Jan–Feb 2021	Jan–Feb 2020
South West	36	8
South South	73	45
South East	2	5
North West	571	103
North East	56	80
North Central	443	226

Source: Reuters

The insecurity within the Niger Delta region is triggered by the environmental degradation caused by oil exploration. Over the years, employees of the oil firms have been kidnapped, while the activities of this group have paralyzed oil production for years. However, the Amnesty programme of late President Umaru Musa Yar'Adua restored peace within the region and this consequently improved the activities of oil firms in the region.

According to the ACLED (Armed Conflict Location and Event Data) dataset, extrapolated in Figure 8.16, in 2020 there were 2,404 security incidents recorded in Nigeria: 844 were coded as battles, 220 as explosions/remote violence, 297 as riots and 1,043 as violence against civilians.

Figure 8.16: Nexus of poverty, insecurity and unemployment among states with high risks and extreme security metrics

	State	Poverty head counts	Security report	Unemployment rate (%)	IGR (₦ billion)
1	Adamawa	75.41	Extreme	54.89	8.33
2	Bayelsa	22.61	High risk	50.07	12.18
3	Benue	32.90	High risk	49.02	10.46
4	Borno	N/A	Extreme	44.35	11.58
5	Delta	6.02	High risk	43.25	59.73

6	Ebonyi	79.76	High risk	41.59	13.89
7	Enugu	58.13	High risk	38.97	23.65
8	Gombe	62.31	High risk	38.69	8.54
9	Imo	28.86	High risk	37.14	17.08
10	Jigawa	87.02	High risk	36.68	8.67
11	Kaduna	43.48	High risk	34.22	50.77
12	Katsina	56.42	High risk	31.62	11.40
13	Plateau	55.05	High risk	16.55	19.12
14	Sokoto	87.73	High risk	14.48	11.80
15	Taraba	87.72	High risk	12.99	8.11
16	Yobe	72.34	Extreme	11.98	7.78
17	Zamfara	73.98	High risk	11.65	18.50

Source: NBS 2020 Q4 report on unemployment and 2019 poverty report / PR24 Nigeria May 2021 and NBS Report on IGR 2020

Figure 8.16 shows the data from the selected states that have high security threats based on the reports from PR24Nigeria (a private security outfit) on security. Comparatively, matching this report with the unemployment and poverty rate within these states, 11 out of 17 have poverty level above 50%, while 12 have unemployment rate above 30%.

Figure 8.17: Nexus of poverty, security and unemployment

	State	Poverty head counts	Security report	Unemployment rate	IGR (₦ billion)
1	Abia	30.67	Medium	56.64	14.38
2	Akwa Ibom	26.82	Medium	53.65	30.70
3	Anambra	14.78	Medium	52.57	28.01
4	Bauchi	61.53	Medium	51.00	12.50
5	Cross River	36.29	Medium	44.22	16.18
6	Edo	11.99	Medium	40.40	27.18
7	Ekiti	28.04	Medium	40.16	8.71
8	FCT Abuja	38.66	Medium	38.80	92.06
9	Kano	55.08	Medium	32.21	31.82
10	Kebbi	50.17	Medium	31.55	13.78
11	Kogi	28.51	Medium	31.26	17.36

12	Kwara	20.35	Medium	31.14	19.60
13	Lagos	4.50	Elevated	29.83	418.99
14	Nasarawa	57.30	Medium	26.59	12.48
15	Niger	66.11	Medium	25.36	10.52
16	Ogun	9.32	Medium	25.28	50.75
17	Ondo	12.52	Medium	17.99	24.85
18	Osun	8.52	Medium	17.25	19.67
19	Oyo	9.83	Medium	17.09	38.04
20	Rivers	23.91	Medium	16.36	117.19

Source: NBS 2020 Q4 Report on Unemployment and 2019 Poverty Report/ PR 24Nigeria May 2021, NBS Report on IGR 2020

Implications and recommendations

- There must be an agency responsible for alleviating poverty and addressing issues of employment. This agency should have presence in all 36 states and the FCT and should be the secretariat for the Presidential Jobs Board at the federal state level.
- SMEDAN should be supported to develop the MSME sector. There were 41.5 million MSMEs as of December 2017, and if half of them create one job each, that is about 29.8 million jobs created. Rigorous implementation of the One local government one product (OLOP), which is part of NEDEP will help.
- Develop specific economic plans for economically disadvantaged regions/states with low levels of IGR, high unemployment and poverty, and a high level of insecurity.
- Develop programmes that target the poor at the local government areas, using the ward-based model. This will help to create a comprehensive database to address poverty from the grassroots level.
- For policy development and monitoring, organize an annual policy dialogue/colloquium that brings together world-acclaimed experts in the areas to assist federal and state government in policy formulation.
- Action against hunger/poverty designed mainly for children, the elderly and women, working with local and international experts and NGOs.

- Business solutions to end poverty will include skills acquisition and setting up of social enterprises. Helping the unemployed to acquire new skills and trade out of poverty.
- Effective private sector solutions and resources must be deployed to support government initiatives.
- Create an educational structure that aligns with industry needs to tackle these tripod challenges.
- Develop a framework for MSMEs' entrance and growth and their accessibility to finance and information.

Steps to restore security

The first step is to restore and maintain law and order, and both the government and the police have a major role to play.

The purpose of the Nigerian police is to uphold the law fairly and firmly; to prevent crime; to pursue and bring to justice those who break the law; to protect, help and reassure the community; and to be seen to do this with integrity, common sense and sound judgement. To do this effectively, Nigeria must undertake a holistic review of the police force and commence a police reform programme that will address the following areas:

- Size: the number in the police force in Nigeria of about 371,800 officers is grossly inadequate for a country of about 216 million people.
- Structure: I would argue that the benefits of having state police far outweigh the concerns, particularly if the law is designed to address the areas of concern. Most crimes are local, and local intelligence is critical to addressing the issue of insecurity. The presence of the police must be felt at the local government level.
- Compensation package: ensuring the police force is well equipped with modern equipment, well paid and properly trained with welfare packages.
- Recruitment and training: a rigorous recruitment process and regular training in the use of modern equipment, intelligence gathering, psychology, etc. The net effect is to have a highly professional, community friendly and a highly respected police force.
- Funding: budgetary allocation needs to be increased significantly. There will be a need to identify alternative sources

of funding which will involve the private sector to support budgetary allocation. We all benefit when we have a safe and peaceful environment to run our businesses.
- Criminal justice: the reform of the whole criminal justice apparatus to ensure fair hearing and to reduce the time it takes to get judgement.
- Community service and crime recording: introduce community service and suspended sentences as some of the punishment for non-criminal offences.

Private security

The formal introduction of a well-regulated private security industry to support the police would be critical to the success of police reform. The firms offering private security should be licensed if they meet certain criteria, such as vetting the selection or recruitment criteria, determining that they are fit and proper, competence of the staff, the training provided, etc.

Some examples of economic interventions required – agricultural sector

Nigeria is a top-five producer of at least eight agricultural commodities in the world. These are not only food items but are raw materials for several products that can also be exported. Take the case of sorghum, where Nigeria is the third-largest producer in the world after the US and India. Sorghum is the number-one food of the majority of people in the northern part of Nigeria. It is also used in the production of biscuits, syrup, etc. and it engages the largest number of farmers in the northern part of Nigeria. The Nigerian Breweries Plc has committed resources to increase farmers yield per hectare.

Government should support initiatives like these to scale up production and replicate the programme for rice and maize. This, together with setting up agricultural processing parks in strategic areas, will go a very long way to addressing the issues of jobs, hunger and poverty and it will reduce insurgency.

Another major intervention required is the commodities exchange. I saw the impact it had on jobs, the quality of commodities produced and wealth creation for farmers. In the MITI, we identified the six commodities we wanted to start with but the lack of resources and the change of administration prevented us from fully launching the Nigerian commodities exchange before we left government. We have laid the foundation and started building on it. This is a low-hanging fruit for any government that wants to address the issues of poverty, unemployment and insecurity in the agricultural sector.

Conclusion

Overcoming the triple threats of poverty, unemployment and insecurity is massive but not insurmountable. Their existence simply means that government needs a coordinated strategy for creating employment, alleviating and eradicating poverty as well as both kinetic and non-kinetic security measures.

The huge youth population is a challenge. Finding creative and productive outlets for this energetic segment of the population is an imperative.

Nigeria is on the move. Africa is on the move. The success of the African industrial journey will determine the quality of lives of hundreds of millions of our citizens over the coming decades. First and foremost, industry means jobs for youths, wealth for our families and revenue for our governments. The industrial sector will position our continent on the world map as a strong economic centre. This is not just a journey we should undertake, but a path we must follow.

We must industrialize. But we can not industrialize or grow our economy without dealing with the treble threats. It is impossible. When Africa industrializes, it will send a strong message to the developed nations that, while the past decades belonged to the West and the present time belongs to Asia, the future indeed belongs to Africa.

Chapter 9

Leading and working with multilateral organizations

'Aid is not always the solution. Investment in institution building and sectors of inclusive economic growth is always the solution. It is a win/win strategy.'

Olusegun Aganga

In this chapter, I discuss my roles and thoughts on important multilateral institutions of the modern world. In addition to bilateral relations, there exist multilateral institutions facilitating international development through trade and finance. My thoughts and experience will focus on the WTO, established in 1995, and the two Bretton Woods institutions: the World Bank and the IMF, established in 1944 as part of the post-Second World War global economic reform and reconstruction agenda. The WTO traces its roots back to GAATS which was established about the same time as the two Bretton Woods Institutions.

As at 31 December 2022, the World Bank had 189 member countries, also referred to as shareholders. Each is represented by its finance or development minister to form the board of governors, which is the ultimate policymaker, although it delegates certain specific duties to the 25 executive directors, appointed or elected by the governors. They, in turn, select the president, who is the chair of the board. The executive directors are responsible for the day-to-day management of the bank.

The governors convene annually at meetings of the board of governors of the World Bank Group and the IMF, where policies are considered and approved and there are discussions on issues of global concern, including the world economic outlook, poverty eradication, economic development and aid effectiveness.

The WTO, unlike the world bank, is a member-driven organization with 164 members. Accordingly, power is not delegated to a board of directors or the head of the organization. It seeks a level playing field for trade, sets up and interprets trade agreements and facilitates dispute settlement. WTO rules are enforced by the members themselves under agreed procedures that members negotiate.

In 2010, as the representative of Nigeria, I assumed the role of chairman of the board of governors of the World Bank and IMF. The world was just recovering from a major financial and economic crisis, and many countries were instituting far-reaching reforms in their financial sectors. Also, while serving as Nigeria's Minister of Industry, Trade and Investment, I chaired the Eighth WTO Ministerial Conference (MC8) in Geneva. This is the topmost decision-making body of the WTO, working on a two-year process that ends with the ministerial conference.

The MC8 took place at a very difficult time for the WTO, especially in view of the prevailing stalemate in the Doha round negotiations and significant differences within the membership. Indeed, after MC6, held in Hong Kong in 2005, members were unable to come together until the MC7 in Geneva in 2009. This background informed the efforts to ensure that MC8 provided a veritable pathway forward.

Experiences of the World Bank and the WTO

Since gaining independence in 1960, Nigeria has carried the responsibility in Africa as one of the largest economies and the most populous country on the continent. It certainly mattered what we did as a country and even more how we did it. When it comes to multilateral organizations and development finance institutions, Nigeria has a fairly interesting history. Committed to the World Bank, the WTO and the multilateral trading system, Nigeria has the necessary skilled technocrats to navigate these modern institutions in order to gain maximum advantage.

I worked very closely with different groups in these multilateral organizations – the African Group, the African Caribbean and Pacific Group of States, the least developed countries and the EU. My experiences with these institutions and their decision-making processes can be outlined in the following broad areas:

- Leading three main multilateral institutions.
- The leadership approach adopted in these multilateral institutions led to the breakthrough in Bali in 2013, which I discuss later.
- Relevant reforms required to make these multilateral organizations more effective in delivering their mandates.
- An evaluation of whether these institutions are working for Africa and what needs to be done to get the best from them.

Leading: World Bank, IMF and WTO

I was the first and only African to chair *both* the World Bank and IMF in 2010 and WTO in 2011. As Minister for Finance and Minister for Industry, Trade and Investment at different times, I interacted at the leadership level with these bodies to form concrete views about what Nigeria (and Africa) needs to do in order to make a meaningful impact.

I assumed office as chairman of the board of governors when the world was just recovering from the recession caused by the global financial crisis of 2008. This crisis had a severe impact across the globe, heightening existing problems and creating new challenges. The World Bank proffered creative solutions to the problems. There are, of course, interactions with the president of the World Bank and IMF. We discussed wide-ranging reform ideas to modernize the annual meetings. Most of our meetings were about the preparation for the annual meetings and what could be done differently and better.

That year was significant for the world and for Africa in particular. The World Bank added a third African chair and agreed to grant voting power to developing and transitioning economies, giving them a 47% share of the vote. The ongoing general quota review at the fund also aimed to build on the 2008 quota and voice reforms by shifting 5% of the quota to dynamic emerging markets and developing economies.

Chairing the WTO was far more hands on because it is a members driven organisation. In the two years leading to the conference, it required extensive consultations with the trade ambassadors, meetings with Ministers of Trade to identify common grounds and areas of disagreements and regular consultations with the General Council and the Director General. To succeed, members need to trust and respect the Chairperson and in turn he or she must be a good listener, pay attention to details, respect and regard the views of all members, seek common grounds and be able to negotiate.

Laying the foundation for the success in Bali

The foundation for the success that was achieved at MC9 in Bali was laid during MC8, where, as chair, I played multiple roles of chairing the opening session, plenary meetings, meetings with members and the closing session, working with three vice-chairs.

A lot of the work had been done over the two years preceding the conference by the Governing Council led by Ambassador Agah, who worked closely with other permanent representatives/ambassadors to the WTO, and its director-general, Pascal Lamy. The team and I had several consultations with different stakeholder groups of the WTO, thus enabling the Governing Council, the secretariat and the office of the chairman to listen to all members, identify their priorities and concerns, find common ground and areas for agreement. These pre-conference meetings and consultations directed more energy to areas of disagreement, found negotiation points and consulted regularly with all member states in an open and transparent way.

The outcome document for MC8 comprised two parts: the agreement and the chairman's summary of the discussions. The agreement contained the political guidance across the three elements of the WTO and multilateral trading system, development and the regular work of the organization. The commitment generated from MC8 galvanized the successes at MC9 in Bali on the TFA, tariff-rate quotas and issues relating to least developed countries, and carried further to MC10 in Nairobi on the export competition pillar in agriculture. Another important success of MC8 was the accessions of the Russian Federation, Samoa and Montenegro.

The successful outcome of MC8 was significant because of the difficult times. In particular, debt to GDP ratios were high, economic growth reversed and there was inertia and inability to reach major agreement. Bilateral and regional trade agreements were becoming common and protectionism was beginning to revive.

Meetings with ministers and different groups of ambassadors on the status and nature of negotiation of the Doha Development Agreement (DDA) suggested strong doubts that the negotiations could be completed simultaneously in the near future. The ministers agreed to a provisional consensus on protectionism and, for the first time, that the DDA could be done on a piecemeal basis, rather than as a single undertaking. This was the masterstroke that laid the foundation for Bali! Between 2011 and 2013, all the efforts were geared for success in Bali after the Governing Council had approval from the ministerial conference to work towards the agreement, reversing the inability of the WTO to reach any agreement since it was established. I remember the kind and generous message that the US Trade Secretary sent, congratulating the team for the quality leadership and the diplomacy that led to a very successful conference and how Nigeria was congratulated for making Africa proud.

Breakthrough in Bali – the WTO story

The Minister of Trade for Indonesia (Gita Wirjuawan) chaired and hosted MC9 in Bali in 2013. He had three vice-chairs, and, working with Roberto Azevêdo, the new WTO director-general, they were determined to achieve success in Bali.

Based on my experience in MC8 and the success that was achieved, I was invited to work with Minister Gita and his team, who was determined that we would not leave Bali without an agreement. We worked very closely with several groups, including the African Group, African Caribbean and Pacific Group, low-income developing countries and the EU. I had an informal meeting with all the ministers from West Africa and was invited to dinner by Anand Sharma, the Minister of Commerce and Industry of India, with other ministers from Asia and India to elicit their views. I also worked closely with Mounir Abdelnour, the Minister of Industry, Trade and Investment of Egypt, and we became the bridge between the chairman, director-general and many other members who still had concerns. The last day of the conference was the most difficult and nerve-racking. At about 8pm on the day the meeting was supposed to have ended there was no agreement on some thorny issues and the closing section had to be postponed. At midnight we were nowhere near and about at 2am we had made some progress but not enough to believe that we would leave Bali with an agreement. It was not until about 3.30am that we started seeing some glimpses of light at the end of the tunnel and at about 4am an agreement was reached. History was made!

The closing ceremony of MC9 was as much a milestone as it was emotional. There were tears of joy for some but the best was reserved for the chairman, his team and the WTO's director-general, when all the ministers rose to give them a standing ovation for a job well done. The director-general and everyone involved were overwhelmed by the successful trade agreement, which was the first of its type in the organization's history. It was a memorable day because of the implications of the agreement for the global economy and, in particular, the economies of developing countries and the jobs that would be created when the agreement is properly implemented by all the members.

However, one important takeaway from the various consultations and negotiations that were undertaken at both MC8 and MC9 is the guiding principles for the processes – sensitive handling of the meetings, in concentric circles, underscored by the principles of transparency and inclusiveness, smaller group meetings convened that reported to the full membership through meetings of the heads of delegations.

Breakthrough in Bali

> 'Coming together is a beginning, staying together is progress, and working together is success.'
>
> Henry Ford, founder of Ford Motor Company

The rationale for the phrase 'Breakthrough in Bali' was the unanimous agreement reached in the country, for the first time in WTO history, and the culmination of the Doha development round that started in 2001. Post-Bali, the members had to get their governments to ratify and endorse the agreement before implementation. One major reason for implementation delay was the need to clarify the political link between the Decision on Public Stockholding for Food Security Purposes and the TFA.

The members came together at the end of November 2014 in a Special General Council meeting and took three very important decisions:

- Clarified the Bali Decision on Public Stockholding for Food Security Purposes. The peace clause will remain in force until a permanent solution is found – this was a key issue for India.
- Work on the WTO's post-Bali agenda will resume with respect to the Bali ministerial decisions on agriculture and cotton, the monitoring mechanism, and the least developed countries' decisions on duty-free-quota-free access, the services waiver and rules of origin. This meant agreeing the work programme on the remaining DDA issues, with a new target date of July 2015, when agriculture, services and industrial goods would presumably be back on the table.
- The Protocol of Amendment, which formally inserted the TFA into the WTO rulebook, was adopted and ready for implementation.

It is estimated that the implementation of the TFA could reduce trade costs by up to 15% in developing countries. This is important for Africa, where the cost of customs procedures is estimated to be 30% higher than the global average, according to the United Nations Economic Commission for Africa.

The TFA holds the promise that specific support will be provided to developing countries to build the capacity to implement the necessary domestic reforms. For countries with weak customs infrastructures, this agreement meant new and additional technical assistance and funding, which would be channelled through a new initiative, the Trade Facilitation Agreement Facility. This should provide support to least developed countries and developing countries to create projects and access the required funds to improve their border procedures. This will help African governments in prioritizing trade facilitation issues and to address these challenges as part of their national development plans as well as their regional trade and integration agendas. Indeed, trade facilitation/governance and related services issues, not tariff negotiations, are Africa's most pressing challenges in regional integration and trade promotion. For Africa, the adoption of the WTO TFA comes at an opportune time. It offers the opportunity to focus more sharply on the related governance challenges and to mainstream trade facilitation into local integration agendas. The first opportunities will come when the African Continental FTA is fully in place and the Tripartite FTA built-in agenda is completed.

Implications of the deal for Africa and the rest of the world

The agreement in Bali has a key bearing on trade facilitation, agriculture and special and differential treatment for developing countries. One of these is the tariff-rate quota administration that deals with how the quota system is implemented and managed. There are certain categories of government programmes under general services and stockpiling for food security and export subsidies.

The deal has the potential to create $1 trillion global output and 21 million new jobs, as well as lowering the cost of doing international trade by 10% to 15%. A report from the Peterson Institute for International Economics used three metrics to quantify potential benefits of the agreement to include export gains, jobs supported and GDP gains (or losses averted).

Figure 9.1 shows that the aggregation of the potential long-term pay-offs across the seven core areas of deliberation was projected to result in over $2 trillion exports, 34 million jobs and $2 trillion in global GDP gains (or losses averted). This shows the estimated gains to merchandize exports from trade facilitation improvements. Developing countries are also projected to have greater benefits from trade facilitation improvements, with Sub-Saharan Africa projected to have a 27% share of the merchandize, while Latin America and the Caribbean countries will have a 29.5% share.

Figure 9.1: Potential long-term pay-offs from the world trade agenda

S/ No.	Agenda topic	Export gains ($ billion)	Export jobs supported	GDP increase
1.	Trade facilitation	1,043	20.6	960
2.	International services	1,129	8.6	1,039
3.	International digital economy	178	3.7	147
4.	DFQF market access	8	0.7	7
5.	Agricultural subsidies	5	0.1	5
6.	Food export controls	n/a	n/a	45
7.	Environmental goods and services	10	0.3	9
	Total	**2,374**	**34.1**	**2,212**

Source: Peterson Institute for International Economics

There is no doubt that a combination of factors, such as the delay in implementation, COVID-19, the economic downturn, the Ukraine–Russia war, would have had a significant impact on some of these projections. There is a need to revisit and reassess the impact of the full implementation of TFA.

Implication of the deal for Sub-Saharan Africa

The TFA creates opportunities for developing countries to increase their trading in manufactured goods for export, helping to reduce export of primary goods, which constitute a larger share of their exports and have the tendency to increase imported inputs to produce finished goods for export, and thus increase participation of developing countries in global export value chains. The TFA specifically includes freedom of transit, inter-agency collaboration and customs cooperation.

The critics of the Bali deal argue that it is not beneficial to African countries as it mainly encourages imports without significant export impact, thus adversely affecting African trade balance. Others argue that it supports and encourages both and is more about how the different countries implement it and accelerate their value addition programmes to produce and export products that meet with international standards.

The WTO remains important in the global post-COVID world in opening and keeping open the international market. It remains relevant as a champion to fight against protectionism, and to stimulate economic growth, employment and development, foster global cooperation and support its members, settle disputes and assist in integrating developing countries into the multilateral trading system, improve trade support institutions and policies on export, address business environment and market access. It also works with other development institutions to provide assistance to its members.

Reforms required to make WTO more effective

With these roles come several challenges and criticism of the WTO. The WTO has not faced the kind of crisis it has experienced over the last six years, due to the priorities of the US administration in that period. One of the greatest challenges is having 164 countries reach a consensus and come to a decision where there are still issues relating to:

- Multilateral convergence, while maintaining transparency and inclusiveness. A smaller executive body should accelerate and make faster decisions.
- Several existing regional, bilateral, multilateral and continental trade agreements, which could undermine the WTO multilateral system.
- Need to strengthen and make the rules-based multilateral trading system more responsive to the needs of members, especially in the challenging post-COVID environment. This should stimulate employment, economic growth and development.
- Climate change, COVID-19 pandemic, the expanding digital economy, the Sino-American trade wars, the Ukraine–Russia war, unilateral tariffs imposition and increasing use of security as justification for exploiting the loopholes in the law.

All these have tested the WTO system, demonstrating that the functions and activities could be disrupted and underscoring the need for reform. The question is: how will the WTO be reformed and by who?

The above-mentioned recent developments and a new director-general, Dr Ngozi Okonjo-Iweala, a reformist and former colleague in the cabinet, have provided an opportunity to carry out reforms that should consider the following:

- The dispute settlement system that will guarantee security and predictability of the multilateral trading system.
- Update of the rule book in compliance with 21st-century realities such as e-commerce and the digital economy.
- Working procedures of various WTO bodies to enhance members' participation and acceptance.
- Global carbon pricing mechanism to assuage the fears of 'green protectionism'.
- Controlling the COVID-19 pandemic through the nexus of trade and public health.

Is the WTO working for Africa?

Trade is a critical tool for economic development, wealth and job creation. Therefore, having an organization that deals with the rules of trade between countries can only strengthen the established strong link between trade and development. While the rules-based multilateral trading system has been helpful to Africa, perhaps the greatest impact on trade in Africa would be the full implementation of the TFA that:

- Boosts global, regional and domestic trade by reducing the delay to and cost of trade.
- Makes it easier for big and small businesses in Africa to participate in trade to support job creation.
- Reduces the barrier in trade as well as the total trade cost by 10% in advanced economies, and by 13% to 15% in developing countries.
- Increases export of developing countries such as Nigeria by at least $57 billion, particularly if value-added products are exported.
- Creates an estimated 18 to 21 million jobs in developing countries, with Nigeria potentially accounting for a large proportion of this because of the size of its economy and potential to export manufactured goods that meet international standards.
- Boosts intra-African trade and supports the AfCFTA zone.
- Increases Africa's share of global trade from 2% to 3%.

The WTO has now had two Africans chair the ministerial conference, and two others chair the Governing Council. The WTO has also had an African deputy director-general and now the first female director-general. So, Africa has been well represented at the governance level, but some would argue that the issues that affect African and developing countries, mostly agriculture subsidy, development and agriculture, are not prioritized and take too long to be addressed.

Strategies for improving agreement between the WTO and African countries

To derive the full benefits of the agreement, Nigeria and the other African countries must take responsibility for developing and implementing a plan, while the WTO provides technical and financial support in collaboration with other development financed institutions such as the AfDB and Afreximbank.

However, there must be political will and support from government. The former president of Kenya, Uhuru Kenyatta, and the current president of Rwanda, Paul Kagame, provide good examples. Both have been the leading factor in the remarkable progress East Africa has made in trade facilitation. The Common Market for Eastern and Southern Africa is far ahead of the other African regions on trade facilitation.

Africans believe more can be done in trade support for development and agriculture, and that the agriculture subsidy provided by the Western world to farmers must also be addressed to provide a level playing field. There is clamour for a deal on food stockholding, whereby some advanced countries buy food, store and distribute to the poor, thereby distorting the market, as the goods could be resold in the local market.

The African trade ambassadors in Geneva have done a terrific job to ensure that the voice of Africa is heard at the WTO. But they and Africa can achieve much more if they have the regular active support of their trade ministers. They must come together more often, not only before a ministerial conference, but also to discuss and agree on trade-related issues and strategies to secure support and understanding from other members.

Mounir Abdelnour and I decided to commence an initiative that would bring the African ministers together more regularly to get the WTO to work better for Africa. Three other ministers from South Africa, Kenya and Senegal were invited to join us at an inaugural meeting in Cairo, in 2014. We could not hold the follow-up meeting in 2015 because I left the government in early 2015 and I think Mounir also left shortly after that. But I would encourage the current ministers to revisit the initiative and give more regular support to the ambassadors in Geneva. It is for Africans to make the WTO work better for them.

The World Bank and its poverty reduction mandate

The World Bank plays a critical role in economic growth and development by providing financial and technical assistance to developing countries to reduce poverty and support development. It has played major roles in supporting African countries, and Nigeria in particular.

One of the easiest ways to measure the bank's performance is to consider the impact that its interventions have had on the level and causes of poverty. The poverty level in Nigeria has continued to increase at an alarming rate and has worsened with COVID-19. The World Bank indicated that, if nothing significant is done to reduce poverty, by 2030 nine out of ten extremely poor people in the world will live in Nigeria and other Sub-Saharan African countries. Similarly, the Bill & Melinda Gates Foundation assessed that, by 2050, if nothing is done, more than 40% of the extremely poor people in the world will live in the Democratic Republic of Congo and Nigeria.

Comparing the mandate of the World Bank and the situation in Africa makes clear that the bank's intervention is not working in Nigeria and Africa. Richer countries and development and multilateral institutions such as the World Bank have always tried to intervene by providing aid to address hunger, poverty, insecurity, etc. Despite this, poverty, hunger, corruption and insecurity have increased significantly in many countries as the attention has been on the symptoms and not the root causes. A change of approach and investing in the root causes should start with building strong and effective political, economic and social institutions. This should involve incentivizing and rewarding countries that demonstrate full commitment to building and strengthening their institutions by tying loans and investments to strong economic institutions established through annual surveys on the quality of institutions.

Required reforms to make the World Bank more effective

The following are recommended strategies for tackling poverty through the World Bank:

- An emergency action by all parties to invest more in the main causes of poverty.
- The World Bank should review its approach to addressing poverty and the causes of poverty, especially in Africa where the number is rising.
- Engage the African Union through the country representatives to develop country-specific programmes to address poverty in a

holistic and strategic manner. Development finance institutions also spread their resources too thinly across many areas and therefore make little or no impact, despite their effort.

- Create a viable link between aids and level of poverty reduction. Aid, forgiveness of debt or renegotiation of loans should be tied to the commitment to poverty reduction and the building of strong institutions by various countries. The World Bank and countries should partner on desired outcomes and monitor progress.
- Establish a council of eminent individuals with requisite knowledge and experience, who are not in government to advise the bank regularly.
- Collaborate with some NGOs, such as TechnoServe, that have a strong track record in breaking the cycle of poverty.

Can a better implementation approach be developed?

The mode of operation of some multilateral institutions sometimes does not lead to the best outcome for Africa. As a result of the peculiarities of African countries, an approach that focuses on the goal or desired outcome should be deployed, measuring the outcome of their initiatives rather than the current emphasis on the process. The result in many cases does not justify the efforts and resources deployed.

In terms of human capital deployed for their projects, most of the consultants are not from Africa or, if they are, they are not the most competent to deliver on the project. While local consultants may not have the capacity and competencies to execute some of the projects, such instances offer opportunities for developing capacity in Africa by having foreign consultants partnering with local consultants. Over time, it reduces the cost of implementation, while technology and technical knowledge are transferred and the quality of implementation is better because of the peculiar local knowledge and expertise brought in.

The process for the appointment or selection of local consultants should be more rigorous and extensive to find the best team to deliver. There are many capable development consultants in the private sector who are not in the network of Multilateral institutions.

Chapter 10

The road to reclamation: Africa yesterday, today and tomorrow

Oh God of creation,
Direct our noble cause
Guide our leaders right
Help our youth the truth to know
In love and honesty to grow
And living just and true
Great lofty heights attain
To build a nation where peace and justice shall reign.

Stanza II of the Nigerian national anthem

How Nigerians react to the situation and the choices before us reminds me of the story in *The Ones Who Walk Away from Omelas*, a profound 1973 work of short philosophical fiction by American writer Ursula K. Le Guin. It is one of the readings at the NLI seminars.

Le Guin describes Omelas as a tranquil city of copious delight and happiness, but with a cost. The peace and splendour require that a single child be kept in perpetual filth, darkness and misery. Once citizens are of age, they learn the truth – some are initially shocked and disgusted, but they ultimately acquiesce to this one perfidy. Some citizens walk away from the city after seeing the child. They separately make their way out of Omelas, and no one knows where they go, but they do not come back. Le Guin's story ends with: 'The place they go towards is a place even less imaginable to most of us than the city of happiness. I cannot describe it at all. It is possible it does not exist. But they seem to know where they are going, the ones who walk away from Omelas.'

Many interpretations have been given to this story about morality. So, let us imagine that the child is Nigeria, the citizens of Omelas are Nigerians benefitting from holding Nigeria down and those who walk away disgusted are some of those who complain about the situation but do nothing to change it. There are moral questions for all of us. Is it justifiable to continue to derive your joy, happiness and wealth at the expense of the country and millions locked up enduring penury and poverty? Do we realize the injustice, get annoyed, feel disgusted but give up and walk away from Nigeria or do we accept the interpretation that Le Guin suggests – that the only way to create a better society is for one to stay and 'fix' their society, 'especially when there's nowhere to walk away to'. The choice is ours, but we advocate the last choice. We must never be the citizens who walked away when Nigeria cried for help and asked to be freed.

An enduring potential

On 24 July 2022, the world did notice Nigeria. In Oregon, the whole sporting world took notice of a Nigerian champion hurdler who did the unprecedented. Tobi Amusan broke the world record for the 100m hurdles race, not once but *twice* on the same day. It was the first time a Nigerian athlete had set a new track and field world record. This is a fitting metaphor for what Nigerians and Nigeria are capable of achieving. This is our innate capacity. This is the kind of performance we need to reclaim our position in Africa and the world. The rousing words of our national anthem, particularly in the second stanza, makes it plain that there is a part for every Nigerian to play, whether a leader or a youth.

In this final chapter we will go over the terrain already mapped in previous chapters. I will be sharing my thoughts on this immense African potential and the blind spots African leaders must avoid in these uncertain times globally. On the positive plane, this chapter will serve as a reminder of critical milestones on our reclamation journey.

Flashback to independence

There was a time when China was relatively poorer than Nigeria, when Nigeria's economic ratings were much higher than Malaysia's and its GDP per capita was higher than Singapore's. There was a time when our civil service was the envy of other nations, when our educational system was one of the best in the world and our universities had students from the US, the UK, South Africa and some other African countries. It was the exception to go abroad for university education. The generation of Nigerians who witnessed and lived these realities is still with us.

There was a time when the naira was stronger than the British pound sterling. There was a time when we were united and our tribe or religion did not matter. There was a time when all adults in the community helped in bringing up the children in that community regardless of their tribe or religion, when one was ostracized from the community if the source of one's wealth was not known. There was a time when you could travel anywhere in Nigeria at any hour of the day without fear. There was a time when we led the fight against apartheid in South Africa, sent and led peace missions across Africa to ensure that Africa and Africans realized their dreams. Yes, there was a time. Now is the time to reclaim the jewel. Some will say it is ambitious. I agree. Others will say it is impossible. I disagree. But we must start now.

Today, the reality is that China, Singapore, Indonesia, Brazil, Korea and Malaysia have all advanced economically and are well ahead of Nigeria. In the preceding chapters we have seen some of the changes that these countries have had to make in order to take positive strides forward since the 1960s. The example of Singapore is of particular interest and importance because it is a country that became independent at about the same time as Nigeria, even though it is relatively small compared to Nigeria. Also, Lee Kuan Yew, the prime minister under whose stewardship Singapore made the leap from third to first world, has shared his thoughts with other world leaders, particularly Malaysian and African leaders. Yew suggested some priority areas that leaders in developing countries generally should focus on to achieve development and bring to realization the development aspirations for their countries. They must, he recommends:

- Set a clear vision and sense of purpose, followed with determination to execute.
- Make appointments and choices based on meritocracy and multiracialism. Use incentives to attract the best hands.
- Encourage innovation and development of new products that generate economic value.
- Invest in human capital and impart a strong work ethic.
- Build institutional competence.
- Focus on entrepreneurship, including incessant efforts to identify market opportunities and translate them into economic benefits.

- Ensure managerial discipline and open new markets.
- Enhance creativity of the leadership, its willingness to learn from experience elsewhere, to implement good ideas quickly and decisively through an efficient public service.
- Maintain social order.
- Maintain peace with neighbours.
- Gain the confidence of investors by upholding the rule of law.
- Keep the size of government small, the economy open and regulation decidedly 'simple, transparent and effective'.

African leaders must embrace and embark upon major government reforms, as most governments have remained vulnerable to 'major malfunctions', very high cost of governance, weak political, economic and social institutions, weak economies, high levels of poverty, unemployment, insecurity, waste, predictable failures, flaws in the governance structure, and so on. The areas already covered and the recommendations in this book should be an aid for such major reforms. It requires and calls for authentic, values-based leadership. It requires courage, vision and commitment to improve the well-being of the people we serve. The reforms have to be system based and not reliant on individuals to be sustained. This is the only way leaders can begin to untie the chains that have caused so many breakdowns and failures in the past and that have continued to frustrate the efforts to achieve Africa's great potential and make the progress the continent deserves as it confronts new social, economic and political threats.

An Africa-wide call to action

African countries have had an inconsistent development story, from advances that raised hope and high expectations, to disappointments arising from poor policy design, sequencing and implementation. Occasionally there have been sparks of reform across the continent, but somehow the impact has not been durable.

Looking at Africa from the different perspectives of economy, human development, population dynamics, democracy and social capital, a picture emerges of a continent where there is dire need for quality leadership and enduring change that will create the desired future from the potential that has been in discourse for decades now.

Value addition as goal for African economies

If Africa is to progress, focus must shift from dependence on commodities, including crude oil, condensate and associated gas for the oil-producing countries, crude mineral and ores for some others, and unprocessed agricultural produce. They must shift their emphasis to value addition, producing high-quality goods and providing services that are competitive. That is where and how the wealth is created. Many African countries have unfortunately focused on aid, grants and loans geared more towards consumption and white elephant projects. Subsidies have been directed more at consumption rather than production, resulting in massive waste of resources that are critical to development.

Strengthening the African Union

The African Union has a real opportunity to change the African development story. In 2019 the African Union heads of state declared 7 July of every year as Africa Integration Day, since then making it a tradition to commemorate milestones throughout the week leading up to the day, instituting the African Integration Week.

The 21st century was billed to be 'Africa's century'. There is a need for strong regional platforms for Africa to work and to be recognized globally. The African Union has a higher number of members (55) than the EU, which has 27 members, but ten members of the EU have a strong economy, while there is no strong economy within Africa. Regional economic integration would be ideal, where some of the economies are strong and can provide the stability and resilience in times of global economic turmoil.

The place of Nigeria in Africa

Nigeria is a great country with all the assets it requires to be one of the most successful countries in the world. But we lack great managers to manage those assets and generate consistent superior risk-adjusted returns to the shareholders – Nigerians. One day that green passport will be our greatest asset.

For several obvious reasons – situation, endowments and antecedents, among others – Nigeria is well favoured to take the leadership in

Africa. It has the history of a pivotal leadership role in eradicating racism in South Africa, peace missions in several African countries at war and even the expansion of Nigerian businesses into the rest of Africa, while welcoming businesses from other African countries and allowing them to thrive without hindrance.

As already espoused in this book, there are lessons to learn from several countries that got some things right, and such lessons can be applied in a pragmatic manner. Earlier in the book we saw how South Africa, Saudi Arabia, Malaysia, Indonesia, Botswana, the UK, Brazil and Scandinavian countries, among others, leveraged on their tangible and intangible assets to transform those countries. We do not need to reinvent the wheel in Nigeria. We do need, however, to leverage our greatest assets and to build the capacities necessary to transform our economy.

Some prescriptions for reclaiming the jewel

There are general imperatives that cut across all strata of government, such as the urgent need to implement automation and institute controls to eliminate waste. At federal, state and local government levels, for instance, the principle and practice should be to complete the execution of a given project before embarking on new projects. This was done to a degree while I was in government, when in preparing the 2010/11 budget, funds were only allocated to ongoing projects and the guideline to all MDAs was to complete those projects in the national plan first, before embarking on new projects. Beyond the general and broad approach, however, the following specific tasks should be taken seriously in Nigeria and all Africa:

1. Get the political governance structure right. Organize political institutions in such a way that bad and incompetent rulers are prevented from doing too much damage. Make politics unattractive to those who see politics as a route to wealth. Democracy only works when it is adapted to suit local circumstances such as the economy, quality of democratic institutions, level of literacy and poverty, diversity, etc. An expensive system of governance, where the electorate is not able to hold the politicians accountable or punish a government by not electing it back due to poor performance,

is not a government for the people and by the people. Proportional representation may help deepen democracy in developing countries. The presidential system as practised now is not ideal for the country and it is too expensive. Reform political institutions and systems to ensure that elections are less expensive, promote accountability, provide transparency in election financing, transmission and collation of results and that vote buying and taking is an economic and financial crime. Legislators and civil/public servants must comply with a new code of conduct, which must be strictly adhered to and rigorously enforced.

2. Unless Africa and other developing countries address the issues of education and poverty the democracy practised by these countries will never produce a government by the people, of the people and for the people. Most of the poor and uneducated do not know what to expect from their leaders because they do not understand what they do or know what a well-governed country looks like. They do not know the consequences of their vote and therefore are more likely to vote on tribal linings or for vote buyers at the cost of good governance and increased corruption. Developing countries either develop a home-grown system with the principles of democracy or address these twin issues aggressively. We all suffer and destroy our country every time we fail to elect competent leaders. Diaspora voting helps to alleviate some of these deficiencies, but unfortunately the politicians who benefit from these deficiencies are naturally unwilling to support diaspora voting.
3. Set up a reform council backed by law to develop and supervise the implementation of a national reform blueprint/agenda over a fixed period of ten years at least. This includes supervising the drafting of a new constitution or amending existing ones, working with the National Assembly. It should be protected from politics and made up of credible, experienced and knowledgeable Nigerians with a proven track record, selected only on merit. This is to ensure continuity and quality of implementation.
4. Build and sustain a professional, neutral, well-paid, meritocratic civil service to consistently deliver good governance. Reform the FEC to focus more on policies and national issues and less on

awarding contracts. Restructure and change the composition of the NEC to deliver on its mandate.

5. Build and sustain strong political, economic and social institutions. The quality of institutions largely determines whether nations fail or succeed. The social institutions must deliver citizens who are ready, and have the competence and character to drive the political and economic institutions.
6. The economy is number one. You can not have a small state revenue and big state spending relying on borrowing to fund recurrent expenditure. It will only lead to one thing, bankruptcy. Shift emphasis to value addition, producing high quality goods, providing services that are competitive and developing a strong MSME sector. History has shown that no country has ever become rich by exporting raw materials without also having an industrial sector and in modern terms an advanced services sector. The more a country specializes in the production of raw materials only, the poorer it becomes. Industry multiplies national wealth! Relying on the interest rate mainly as a tool to moderate inflation in developing countries where there are structural issues driving inflation does not work. Focus on what works to protect the welfare of the people.
7. Ensure we have a strong and predictable macroeconomic environment, an investor-friendly foreign exchange regime, a business environment that attracts and retains investors. Simplify regulation, remove bureaucracy and inefficiency and invest adequately in industrial and trade-related infrastructure, such as electricity, rail and quality infrastructure for exports.
8. Manage resources better, blocking leakages and waste and addressing corruption decisively.
9. Focus on our most important asset, our people. That means developing people-oriented policies, quality education for all and a healthcare system that works and is affordable. No one must be left behind. Turn quantity advantage to productive advantage. Proactively engage the diaspora community and have a system that turns brain drain to brain gain. Our educational system must be reformed to ensure adequate financing and be structured to deliver academic excellence, spiritual insight, character formation and skills and knowledge that are relevant to our economy. Remove and diminish the

relevance of divisive tools such as ethnicity and religion and let our shared values define us.

10. Build a nation that is united, based on common values. History has shown that the most successful companies and countries in the world are built on a set of core values. These become the foundation on which the nation is built. We cannot achieve sustainable economic growth and the development we seek unless we build on a solid foundation and develop community-spirited Nigerians who live these values. It is an investment worth making in our greatest and most important asset – our people. A united nation where there is peace and security, leveraging our diversity, starts with creating a values-based society where there is law and order, justice, equity and fairness. Recognize and reward hard work, celebrate merit and values/culture carriers. Enhance the social security systems, including pensions and health insurance.
11. Always keep an eye on the triple threat: poverty, unemployment and insecurity. If any of them is untamed, they spread like wildfire and fuel the other threats, then they become uncontrollable and have a major effect on the economy and society.
12. Put a system in place that helps direct resources from multilaterals to where they are needed most. For example, what if for the next three years all the multinational institutions pool their resources together to work with African countries on solving electricity/energy poverty in Africa? Achieving this alone solves many other problems, including poverty.
13. Nigeria must take its leadership role in ECOWAS and Africa more seriously. This is one situation where leading from the back is ineffective. Appointment to major roles in ECOWAS and AU must be done on merit. For too long political considerations have played a major role in these appointments and for far too long ECOWAS and AU have suffered from these decisions. COMESA is far ahead of other African regions because of the quality of leadership and the institutions. Nigeria must work closely with Multilaterals (World Bank, IMF, WTO) and implement agreements like the Trade Facilitation Agreement to get the best from these institutions. Particularly now that the ACFTA is now in place.
14. Create a comprehensive funding model and strategy for the country. This is an urgent need, both at the national and

subnational levels. Over the years, the lack of required funding has had devastating effects on all sectors. It is one major limiting factor that cuts across all the areas: education, security, health, infrastructure development, social benefits and welfare programmes for the poor, etc. Various governments have reacted to the limiting factor differently and in most cases have come up with responses that cannot be sustained or have not been well thought through. Such a strategy will start by reviewing current sources and uses of funds, what an accountant would refer to as 'sources and application of funds'. It will develop strategies to improve on the quality, size and sources of funds, determine how and where they should be applied going forward, based on the different sources of funds and the nation's priorities.

There will be targets set for the relevant MDAs for revenues, in particular foreign income from oil and gas, and solid minerals and value-added non-oil exports. The approach to each sector will be different. For example, the size and sources of funds for security are not the same for economically viable infrastructure projects such as roads or for financing our universities and the lecturers. The application process will include both 'detect' and 'prevent' controls, penalty for misapplication of funds, the blocking of most of the waste and leakages in the system, including the better management and control of the cost of governance. If well done, it will help the country develop and adopt a governance structure that it can afford. It should be reviewed periodically as newer sources of funding are developed or identified and the needs of the country are reprioritized. Again, Nigeria needs its best, drawn from the relevant sectors, to build the model, and to develop and implement the strategy. At a minimum, it should include accountants, investment bankers, economists, tax experts, development experts, etc. with practical experience and track record. Experience, creativity and ability to think out of the box will be essential. And for the private sector a comprehensive review of the financing ecosystem including the value chain is overdue.

Endnote

There is no nation without challenges. The only difference is that the successful ones address their challenges as they arise, learn from them and ensure that they never happen again, and if they do, that there are mitigants or solutions already in place. Africa and indeed Nigeria tends to find a way around most challenges rather than addressing them and sometimes wishes that these problems would go away by divine intervention, forgetting that God will work with you, not for you. The effect of this is that the challenge becomes bigger and bigger and, in most cases, they are overwhelmed by the problems. To make matters worse there are no consequences for not addressing these issues. Otherwise, how do you explain a government winning an election that has not paid salaries for at least six months or under whose watch the levels of poverty, unemployment and insecurity have risen? We must change this paradigm to succeed.

Finally, the ultimate aim of all this is to make Nigeria a great nation again. To reclaim the Jewel of Africa that it was for many decades. As former President Olusegun Obasanjo said, 'The task of nation-building spans several lifetimes; in fact, it is a never-ending endeavour, and each generation makes its own contribution to it. To be effective in the task, people must constantly refresh their vision of the kind of nation that they wish to build and adopt strategies and disciplines that will lead them to their desired destination.' This implies, among other things, that each generation must demonstrate and activate its leadership capacity; if it fails to do so, it may find that it has wasted its opportunity to claim a respectable place in history.

In the end, every Nigerian must have an instinctive confidence that he or she will be treated with justice and equity in any part of the country, regardless of the language they speak or how they worship God. This is the great task that trumps all. Unless we are able to achieve this, all other claims to progress, no matter how defined, will remain unsustainable. The challenge before all nations of the world today is unique and, therefore, fundamental assumptions about each nation must be revisited. For us in Nigeria, this is the time to set aside all distractions that have hindered our coming into our full potential. I know we can do it. I also know that this is the time to do it, for our sakes and the sake of Africa as a continent.

Major reforms of the government are not unusual, even in developed countries that are deemed to be working well. The US, for example, held a 2022 election campaign season with an increase in the percentage of the American public demanding a major reform of government despite decades of grand reforms dating back to Truman's post-Second World War reorganizations. So, it is not unusual to call for and expect Nigeria to embrace and immediately embark on a major reform programme, as recommended in this book, if it is to reclaim that jewel back.

In the last few decades I have engaged with Nigerians in Nigeria and in the diaspora. The NLI brought me into contact with so many credible and highly accomplished Nigerians in the country and in the diaspora (Europe, Asia, North America and South Africa), while my trips promoting trade and soliciting for investment as Minister for Industry, Trade and Investments took me to more than 68 countries. On each occasion, we met with the Nigerian community in those countries. In Nigeria, my job as Minister of Industry, Trade and Investment also took me to different parts of the country – from north to south and from east to west – where I interacted with many Nigerians across the social ladder, whether rich or poor, educated or uneducated, old or young. Everywhere I went, everyone I spoke to wanted one thing: a better and prosperous Nigeria where things work. I was inspired because I saw the can-do spirit and the intellect of the average Nigerian in action. I realized that Nigerians excel anywhere and everywhere in the world and that if we create the same right conditions at home, we have the intellectual robustness, energy, innovation/creativity, confidence, excellence in the average Nigerian that will see us through and create a new and prosperous Nigeria.

During the endsars protest led by young, well-educated and exposed Nigerians, the world saw a new and different way of protesting. The protest was not motivated by self-interest but the interests of all Nigerians. They wanted a better Nigeria, a police force that is well equipped, better paid and disciplined, an improvement in the governance of the country, etc. It was more spontaneous than pre-planned and they had no leader or leaders. It was peaceful, yet full of activities to engage the protesters. They had limited resources but were able to provide food, medical care, etc. for protesters and those sent to dislodge and infiltrate them. Everyone was looked after, regardless of whether they were in support or against the protesters – it did not matter as long as they were fellow Nigerians. They protested until late at night, but what caught the eyes of the world was that before dawn on every day that they protested, they came back to tidy up the streets before resuming their protests. The level of discipline, organization, thoughtfulness and creativity was just unprecedented. They did Nigerians and their parents proud and clearly demonstrated their readiness and capacity to play leadership roles in the governance of the country. These were some of the factors that confirm that Nigerians are now ready and able to reclaim the jewel.

From the outside, before I left Goldman Sachs in London to serve in government, I *felt*, like everyone else, that Nigeria and Africa had great potential. When I got in and served first as Minister of Finance and later as Minister of Industry, Trade and Investment, I *saw* that Nigeria did in fact have all it takes to be a great nation and that there is a bright light at the end of the tunnel. Six years after leaving government, I have moved from feeling and seeing to *knowing* that the future of Nigeria is indeed very bright, despite the current challenges, and I do not take these challenges lightly. The younger generation gives me hope and inspiration that when, not if, the matters in this book are fully addressed, there will be no stopping Nigeria and Africa! Patrice Lumumba must have seen this when he said, 'The day Nigeria wakes up, Africa will never be the same again.'

The future is brighter than many people think or know. I end with Nelson Mandela's (Madiba) quote: 'The black people of the world need Nigeria to be great as a source of pride and confidence.' I agree.

God bless Africa. God bless Nigeria. Nigeria will rise again.

Index